ROUTLEDGE LIBRARY EDITIONS: THE NINETEENTH-CENTURY NOVEL

Volume 36

RELIGIOUS FEELING AND RELIGIOUS COMMITMENT IN FAULKNER, DOSTOYEVSKY, WERFEL AND BERNANOS

RELIGIOUS FEELING AND RELIGIOUS COMMITMENT IN FAULKNER, DOSTOYEVSKY, WERFEL AND BERNANOS

JEREMY SMITH

LONDON AND NEW YORK

First published in 1988 by Garland Publishing Inc.

This edition first published in 2016
by Routledge
2 Park Square, Milton Park, Abingdon, Oxon OX14 4RN

and by Routledge
711 Third Avenue, New York, NY 10017

Routledge is an imprint of the Taylor & Francis Group, an informa business

© 1988 Jeremy Smith

All rights reserved. No part of this book may be reprinted or reproduced or utilised in any form or by any electronic, mechanical, or other means, now known or hereafter invented, including photocopying and recording, or in any information storage or retrieval system, without permission in writing from the publishers.

Trademark notice: Product or corporate names may be trademarks or registered trademarks, and are used only for identification and explanation without intent to infringe.

British Library Cataloguing in Publication Data
A catalogue record for this book is available from the British Library

ISBN: 978-1-138-67777-7 (Set)
ISBN: 978-1-315-55928-5 (Set) (ebk)
ISBN: 978-1-138-67005-1 (Volume 36) (hbk)
ISBN: 978-1-138-67007-5 (Volume 36) (pbk)
ISBN: 978-1-315-61781-7 (Volume 36) (ebk)

Publisher's Note
The publisher has gone to great lengths to ensure the quality of this reprint but points out that some imperfections in the original copies may be apparent.

Disclaimer
The publisher has made every effort to trace copyright holders and would welcome correspondence from those they have been unable to trace.

JEREMY SMITH

RELIGIOUS FEELING AND RELIGIOUS COMMITMENT IN FAULKNER, DOSTOYEVSKY, WERFEL AND BERNANOS

GARLAND PUBLISHING, INC.
NEW YORK & LONDON
1988

© 1988 by Jeremy Smith
All Rights Reserved

Library of Congress Cataloging-in-Publication Data

Smith, Jeremy, 1954–
Religious feeling and religious commitment in Faulkner,
Dostoyevsky, Werfel, and Bernanos.

(Garland publications in comparative literature)
Bibliography: p.
1. Religion in literature. 2. Faulkner, William, 1897–1962—
Religion. 3. Dostoyevsky, Fyodor, 1821–1881—Religion. 4.
Werfel, Franz, 1890–1945—Religion. 5. Bernanos, Georges,
1888–1948—Religion. I. Title. II Series.
PN49.S56 1988   809'.93382   88-21223
ISBN 0-8240-7495-5

The volumes in this series are printed on
acid-free, 250-year-life paper.

Printed in the United States of America

ACKNOWLEDGEMENTS

First of all I would like to thank my parents, who are important in a way that is beyond the power of words to express. My chairman, Merritt Lawlis, has merely been the best of chairmen. I would like to thank him, as well as James Hart, James Justus, Breon Mitchell, and David Smith, for their astute intellectual guidance, their critical attention, and their fairness. I would finally like to express my gratitude to the late Newton Stallknecht, whose philosophical spirit remains an inspiration and a reason for hope.

TABLE OF CONTENTS

        Introduction. 1

PART ONE

I. Empathy and Characterization in
   Light in August 21

II. Light in August and
    the Question of Universality 53

III. Light in August and
     the Mystery of the Human Condition 85

PART TWO

IV. From Faulkner to Dostoyevsky: Two Kinds
    of Religious Experience in the Novel 119

V. Characterization and the Experience
   of Conviction in The Idiot 133

VI. Religious Unease and
    The Structure of The Idiot 164

PART THREE

VII. Evocation of Feeling and Avowal of Commitment
     as Artistic Aims: From Faulkner and
     Dostoyevsky to Werfel and Bernanos 205

VIII. Confusion of Aim and the Lack of Fictional Form
      in Werfel's Embezzled Heaven 222

IX. The Conflict between Rhetorical
    Aim and Fictional Form in Bernanos'
    The Diary of a Country Priest 245

        Conclusion 283

        Works Cited 286

INTRODUCTION

The aim of the present study is to define the role of religious meaning in the modern novel. My treatment of this problem rests upon a certain understanding of literary meaning and religious experience in general. The crucial distinction within religious experience is that between religious feeling and religious commitment. Religious feeling involves a sense of the world as a mystery, and raises the question of the meaning of human life in a world that may seem to equally justify hope and despair. Religious commitment, which can arise as a response to this feeling, is reliance upon and loyalty to a cause through which life is made, or is made to appear, meaningful. The thrust of my study is that a novel can successfully express a religious feeling, but not a religious commitment. I shall support this claim through a comparison of two novels that aim to communicate a religious feeling--Faulkner's <u>Light in August</u> and Dostoyevsky's <u>The Idiot</u>--with two novels that aim to communicate a single definite commitment--Werfel's <u>Embezzled Heaven</u> and Bernanos' <u>The Dairy of a Country Priest</u>. Through an analysis of novelistic techniques, I shall attempt to explain how the overall meaning of an aesthetically successful novel may be religious; how characters' religious commitments may be convincingly presented as an integral part of the whole; and why novels whose overall meaning seems to be a single definite commitment tend to be implausible and aesthetically ununified.

A treatment of these problems obviously requires an account of such notions as 'literary meaning,' 'the overall meaning of a novel,' and 'religious faith.' I join many others in rejecting the notion that religious and literary language are meaningless because the only criterion of meaning is scientific or mathematical verifiability. But I go further than some in insisting that religion and literature are not only meaningful, but that each possesses its own distinct kind of truth. I hold that the nature of, and relationship between, literary meaning and religious faith, must be understood in terms of the different kinds of truth they represent, and of the different ways in which that truth is verified. Either to conflate the two, or to locate all truth in one, denying it all meaningful relation to the other, is to misunderstand and underestimate them both.

Scientific truth is a species of propositional truth, to which everyday judgments of fact also belong. The crux of my argument is that truth does not have to do with propositions alone, but must also belong to perceptions, and to religious commitments. A true propositional judgment depends on the sensitivity and accuracy of a prior perception. And we do not perceive merely sense data, but also the underlying depths of reality. Those depths include other minds, and universals such as 'love,' 'personhood,' 'the world,' and 'the meaning of the world.' The reality of these depths is always indefinably more than we can grasp in any proposition. A true perception of reality involves one's awakening to these depths. It involves letting the concrete reality of the world appear in its original depth, significance, and mystery. Were it not for the meaning that appears through perception, both on the surface and in the depths, the abstractions from perception in terms of which judgments are framed, such as 'red' or 'love,' could not themselves have any meaning. Perception is prior to all deliberate, specific acts of judgment and position taking.

The function of literature is to make it possible for readers to relive a concrete perception of reality through which the depths of reality appear. The theologian Paul Tillich speaks as if the dimension of depth in works of art and literature somehow contains the implicit commitments of their creators. Tillich conceives of the "ultimate concern" in the depth of all great cultural creations not only as a questioning of the meaning of human existence, but as the answer to that question. Tillich says that "every style points to a self-interpretation of man, thus answering the question of the ultimate meaning of life."[1] In my view, the central aim of a literary artwork can be to pose the question of the meaning of life, but the meaning of a novel, such as any of the novels I shall study, cannot be the answer to that question.

A great work of art can evoke the concrete experience of an essential mystery in reality. While this mystery is necessarily vague, and eludes objective awareness, it is yet at the heart of the question we always face of the meaning of the world and of our own personal existence. To face this question is to face the situation we are in that encompasses and underlies all other situations. Awakening to the reality of this situation is a matter of perception in the deepest sense of the word. A perception through which this reality appears as it is, is a true one. I am willing to call such a perception a religious feeling.

The crux of my argument, in opposition to Tillich's view, is that a perception including the sense of the depth of reality is prior to <u>all</u> position taking. It is true that the meaning of a religious commitment, like the meaning of a literary artwork, exceeds all attempts at objective specification. But a religious commitment is nonetheless definitely the taking of a position. I hold, with H. Richard Niebuhr, that a person answers the question of the meaning of life through a commitment to a cause, be it the cause of one's society, one's family, truth, beauty, life, or God.[2] Only by actually making a commitment does one consciously live a meaningful life, and such living is in fact the verification of the truth of the commitment. The truth of an answer to the problem of meaning cannot appear through the depths of a literary artwork because the truth of an artwork is only the truth of a perception. The truth of a perception, I hold, can be relived. But it is nonsense to speak of reliving the truth of a commitment, since such truth can only appear through one's own actual taking of a position, through one's own actual living out of the commitment. In other words, the truth of a commitment cannot be verified aesthetically.

The example of Dostoyevsky shows that a novel can contain answers to the question of the meaning of life, appearing as alternative possibilities. Each answer appears both as possibly true and as possibly false. The Idiot, as a whole, does not "answer the question of the ultimate meaning of life." Experiencing the overall meaning of the novel, one experiences alternative answers, but one does not verify that any one answer is true. The perception in which the novel consists essentially involves all sorts of tendencies to go beyond perception and make judgments and commitments--but the novel is successful because it holds these tendencies suspended.

The aesthetic theory I have outlined is based on a distinction between three different kinds of truth--propositional truth, the truth of perception (which I also call, with Whitehead, the truth of feeling[3]), and the truth of commitment. Each of these kinds of truth is verified in its own independent way, and yet, each is essentially related to the others. Objective statements can legitimately interpret feelings and commitments, and yet must always be inadequate to what they interpret. Feelings contain tendencies toward objective judgment and religious commitment, but cannot themselves constitute the verification of a judgment or a commitment. The aim of a work of literary art is to communicate a true perception. Literary art makes the truth of certain concrete perceptions universally available by suspending direct reference to particular actualities. Through the evocation of an imagined world, many individuals can share a concrete perception that otherwise would have depended on their direct acquaintance with a particular, actual situation. The suspension of direct reference to actuality--both in terms of particular facts, and of religious and moral position taking in response to the depths of reality--allows the perception to emerge as a self-verifying experience. But the suspension of direct reference to reality does not utterly isolate the imagined world from reality. Rather, the verification of the truth of our perception of the imagined world involves the recognition of an indefinable sameness the depths of that world share with the depths of the actual world. The world of a successful literary work of art is thus both self-contained and referential. Our perception of that world is also a true perception of the actual world, even though our aesthetic perception involves the suspension of judgment, belief, and commitment.

In my treatment of religious meaning in modern fiction, I attempt to draw attention to the kinds of evidence that pose a challenge to certain alternative views. I hold that literary meaning is essentially the truth of a perception, and that perception does not involve any kind of implicit position taking. In this I oppose on the one hand those religious critics who hold that literary meaning involves implicit commitments, and on the other, the deconstructionists, who are unwilling to assert that truth or meaning are real in any context.

One of the achievements of the Romantic movement was its insight into the importance of concrete perception and of the dimension of depth implicit in perception. In my study, I attempt to philosophically define and to illustrate through literary criticism, both the validity and the limitations of the notions of concrete perception, feeling, and depth. In general, I argue that the tradition beginning with Wordsworth, Coleridge, Novalis, Schleiermacher, and Schelling, and developed further by William James, Whitehead, and Tillich tends to carry these notions too far. These thinkers all tend to assert that concrete feeling not only represents a unique kind of truth, but also that it offers a more or less direct revelation of the eternal and ultimate. Their discussions of the depth of feeling tend to evade the question of commitment. Are the 'imagination' of Wordsworth and Coleridge, 'the feeling of absolute dependence' of Schleiermacher, the 'more' of James, and the 'ultimate concern' of Tillich supposed to present the ultimate to the human mind as a mere possibility, or are they somehow identical to belief? And does human feeling in fact unambiguously reveal, in reality's depths, something ultimately good and worthy of worship? It seems to me that these thinkers do not clearly consider the distinction between feeling and commitment, and that they also tend to overvalue concrete feeling as a basis for ultimate commitment. Theologians such as Kierkegaard, Karl Barth, and H. Richard Niebuhr offer a corrective to the Romantic lack of attention to commitment, but then they tend to undervalue feeling. In very broad terms, what I am attempting to offer is a synthesis of these two kinds of viewpoints.

The work of Paul Tillich has served as the basis for much religious criticism of the arts that finds implicit in great works of literature an ultimate commitment. Tillich believes that the ultimate is implicit in the depths of all human experience. Even the despairing sense of an ultimate problem, which pervades much of modern art and literature, points to an ultimate solution. Nathan Scott has applied Tillich's viewpoint extensively to modern literature. Scott's assumption, like Tillich's, is that literary artworks, when appreciated in all their depth and ambiguity, still reveal the author's guiding commitment. That commitment emerges from the form of the artwork itself, and is not an abstraction forced upon the artwork from the outside. The heart of the form is a commitment. According to Scott, "The task of criticism . . . is, at bottom, that of deciphering the given work at hand in such a way as to reveal the ultimate concern it implies." [4]

The kind of theological criticism Roy Battenhouse represents also essentially aims to uncover a work's implicit religious commitments, but on a very different basis from Tillich's. For Battenhouse, 'dogma' is something distinct from literature, and yet fundamentally related to it.[5] He would not accept Tillich's view of religious belief as an ultimate concern emerging out of the depths of all human experience. Religious belief exists independently of aesthetic experience, and the ultimate is more than the deepest aspect of the world as we experience it. But it is nevertheless possible for belief to control and shape works of art. Belief is involved in art through a kind of intimate synthesis rather than through artificial imposition. Battenhouse does not seem to view the artwork itself as a revelation of the ultimate, as Tillich does. Rather, he claims that certain works which are shaped by a Christian commitment start the reader moving in the direction of supernatural revelation. My response to his view is that the world itself may indeed be a partial and inadequate revelation of God, and an artwork may awaken our minds to the world's revelatory aspects. But I will argue that, in the case of the novel at least, a commitment cannot be the fundamental guiding principle of artistic creation. The fact that a commitment may have influenced creation, or that a work may influence a reader to make a commitment, does not mean that the meaning of the work is a commitment.[6] The guiding principle of the aesthetic experience in which a novel consists is the truth of a perception. Aesthetic unity does point beyond itself to judgment and commitment, but this kind of pointing must be distinguished from the relation, which is the essence of a novel's truth, between the imagined perception the artwork communicates and our actual perception of reality.

I hold that while perception is not a revelation of the ultimate, it is nevertheless a kind of origin and presence. Propositions derive their truth from the truth of perceptions, and no conceptual interpretation can be adequate to a perception. According to Jacques Derrida, while we cannot avoid such talk of authority, presence, and origin, when these notions are explicated, they inevitably undermine themselves.[7] For Derrida, the model for all meaning is writing, which is to say, the relation between every 'signifier' and 'signified' is as arbitrary as that between strings of letters and what they are supposed to signify. Whenever we attempt to find a sameness underlying a difference, a sameness uniting signifier and signified, we will discover a difference underlying that sameness. Discontinuity underlies all apparent continuity. To be a signifier is to be 'infected' with otherness, and there is no signified that is not also a signifier. Derrida calls the infection of the signifier by the signified 'the trace' or 'differance.' Meaning is a kind of track or footprint on the sign that 'differs' completely from the sign and 'defers' away from the sign toward an endless play of signification. All talk of origin, authority, or presence is an attempt to hide from the endless and inevitable play of differance. Derrida claims that he has overcome the 'forgetting' that allows us to see the signified as an origin and a presence.

My response to Derrida is first to agree that in explicating meaning, we may well be led to inescapable contradictions, and that the process of explication is indeed endless. But my essential claim is that we are not doomed to follow only the 'trace,' and not trapped in the play of 'differance.' The play of differance is the explication of meaning--and our minds can do more than explicate meaning. The 'trace' is not the only path the mind can follow. The truth of perception itself emerges only when we suspend our active attempt to make explicit the implicit. Derrida is right that no amount of explication will ever arrive at the origin. But he calls presence 'the forgetting of differance' only because he cannot get beyond objectivistic thinking. By attempting to define the origin, we may find ourselves involved in contradictions. But when we define the origin, or the background, what we now have explicitly before our minds is no longer the background. The truth of perception emerges only through our letting the background appear as background, through the suspension--or 'forgetting' as Derrida has it--of objective explication. This letting appear occurs before we have described it, or explicitly defined it. And this letting appear is by no means automatic or primitive. Our ability to perceive is a capacity that needs to be developed, and it is developed precisely _through_ perceiving. Explicit reflection certainly plays a role in that development, but explicit reflection does not rule or provide the foundation for that development.

That reflection and perception cannot be brought into perfect accord is itself a paradox arising from the inherent limitation of the human mind. Derrida constantly, and unaccountably, jumps from the fact of limitation and paradox inseparable from all efforts to reach the truth, to a rigid doctrine of the <u>impossiblity</u> of truth. In contrast, I hold that experience does reveal an origin that is available, but at the same time beyond our grasp. This paradox, that the truth is open to us, but at the same time beyond our reach, is inescapable. It is the situation we are always already in, and precludes taking refuge either in absolute dogmatism or absolute scepticism. We can only live within this situation, accepting our involvement in something greater than ourselves, accepting our inability to clearly account for what we know we already accept.

Consider the moment when, for example, we realize that we have an obligation to another person. That moment does not arise through explication, through the 'following of traces.' It arises precisely through the suspension of that following. No definition of the obligation will be adequate, yet the moment presents itself as something we must be true to, as something that both requires and governs our thoughtful and active response. Our increasing sensitivity to the moral requirements of particular situations is not fundamentally a development of abstract knowledge, but of acuity and depth of perception. The truth of perception is prior to explication: explication can neither create it nor absolutely justify it. Our experience of truth is not something we can uncover and grasp, rather, it emerges insistently through a background we cannot meddle with. Explication may indeed be self-contradictory and self-defeating—but the truth we attempt to explicate is exactly what is never contained by our explications. But that explication has its basis in a prior perception means that explication has both a justification and a responsiblity--that it need not wander aimlessly, and that all explications are not equally valid.

The position of the New Critics generally falls somewhere between the position that the essence of a literary artwork is a religious commitment, and the position of Deconstructionism, which does not accept the notions of 'essence' or 'meaning.' The New Critics concentrate on establishing the independence of literary meaning from other kinds of meaning. The meaning of a literary artwork cannot be identified with a philosophical proposition, a religious belief, or an interpretive paraphrase. And literary artworks do have meaning, positivistic efforts to limit meaning to the realm of science and mathematics notwithstanding. But the attempt to establish the independence of literary meaning may lead to the apparent denial that literary meaning has any essential relation to extra-literary reality at all. Northrop Frye distinguishes works--such as philosophical, religious, or historical works--whose final direction of meaning is "outward" from literary works, whose final direction of meaning is "inward." According to Frye, "in literature, questions of fact or truth are subordinated to the primary literary aim of producing a structure of words for its own sake."[8] Frye seems to assert that there is no important truth relation between literature and reality. I agree that the truth of literature cannot be reduced to the truth of any explicit propositions or beliefs. But may not the truth relation of literature to reality be simply more fundamental than propositions and beliefs? Cleanth Brooks comes closer to acknowledging such a fundamental, unique truth relation. According to Brooks, the poet "must return to us the unity of experience itself as man knows it in his own experience. The poem if it be a true poem is a simulacrum of reality--in this sense, at least, it is an "imitation"--by <u>being</u> experience rather than any mere statement or abstraction from experience."[9] For Brooks, the criterion for judging poetry is not correspondence, but coherence, and the criterion for judging coherence is "our basic pattern of human nature, not necessarily as reshaped by Freud or Adler, or as summarized in some textbook, but a living pattern actually experienced."[10] One of my central aims is to develop more fully and explicitly the distinction Brooks here begins to make. I hold that we do have a primary acquaintance, through perception, with human nature. Our perceptual acquaintance, while in many ways vague, paradoxical, and elusive, is nevertheless powerful and insistent, and provides the only basis for all of our propositional interpretations of human nature. This acquaintance is an experience of truth but not of definite belief. The essential aim of literary art is to communicate such acquaintance. The dilemma of correspondence versus coherence is false: an artwork is coherent if the perception it embodies has a deep identity with our actual perception of the world, and brings to life our sense of the actual depths of the world. Through coherence, it achieves its own kind of correspondence, to be distinguished from the truth of correspondence that explicit propositions may possess. But Brooks's assertion that "the revelation that poetry makes is primarily a revelation of ourselves,"[11] it seems to me, is too narrow. I agree with Brooks that poetry does not provide ultimate answers, but I hold that it can pose ultimate questions, not only about human nature, but about the world and reality as a whole-- questions we may call 'cosmic' or 'metaphysical' or 'religious.'

Sallie McFague TeSelle, in her study <u>Literature and the Christian Life</u>, suggests the essential distinction between feeling and commitment that I take as my starting point. She opposes Tillich's notion that commitments are implicit in all great cultural creations. For her, literature is a kind of knowing--the knowing of the human situation that Cleanth Brooks describes, a knowing that cannot be reduced to propositions and that falls short of ultimate answers. Literature is a kind of knowing, but commitment is a kind of doing. Aesthetic knowing does not directly imply or compel the action of commitment. As TeSelle points out, "what Kierkegaard saw better than perhaps anyone before or since was that knowing and doing, contemplation and commitment, thought and being are related only through an agent, only through the decision of the self to interiorize the truth."[12] Aesthetic experience may offer a vision of the concreteness of life, and may also suggest commitments, but aesthetic knowing itself never amounts to the honest acceptance of a commitment.

My study differs from TeSelle's in that I develop a detailed philosophical treatment of the issues she raises, drawing on William James, Whitehead, Heidegger, and Husserl (in addition to Kierkegaard and H. Richard Niebuhr, who do enter into her argument); in that my argument is based on a detailed treatment of four novels, instead of on a survey of a variety of works of literature and of criticism; and in that my perspective is basically the philosophy of religion rather than Christian theology.

The aim of the present study is to contribute to the justification of the notion that perception has a truth of its own that is prior to commitment and explication. In particular, I will argue that the meaning of a novel is the truth of a perception, and that while perception may have a religious dimension, the religious dimension must be distinguished from religious commitment. At each stage, I draw attention to evidence against opponents who, on the one hand, hold that perception involves implicit commitments, and on the other, who do not accept that perception has its own kind of truth. I present my evidence and develop my theory through a project in practical criticism. My aim is not so much to develop a new interpretation of each work I treat, as to study the nature of interpretation itself, and its relation to literary and religious experience, through concrete examples. I want to suggest an interrelation between a certain way of interpreting literature, and a certain philosophical understanding of human experience. I argue that if my literary interpretations are plausible, their plausibility lends support to a certain philosophical position; and if my philosophical position is plausible, its plausibility lends support to a certain way of interpreting. I try to show how literary interpretation can be a form of phenomenological reflection, and how such reflection can lend support to a certain way of distinguishing and relating different kinds of truth. The kind of reflection I suggest is not primarily an argument on the propositional level, but is essentially an attempt to draw the reader's attention to certain aspects of experience that are prior to propositional experience. If the reader shares my intuition of these aspects of experience, he may agree that the explicit interpretation of them that I offer is accurate.

The overall strategy of the present study is to substantiate the approach to the problem of belief outlined above through a detailed treatment of four novels: Faulkner's <u>Light in August</u>, Dostoyevsky's <u>The Idiot</u>, Franz Werfel's <u>Embezzled Heaven</u>, and Georges Bernanos' <u>The Diary of a Country Priest</u>. Each of these novels illustrates a distinct type of religious meaning, and a different approach to writing a religious novel. In Part One, which is devoted to <u>Light in August</u>, I develop the critical and philosophical concepts that form the basis for my entire study. The three chapters cover the three levels of meaning I find in the novel: our concrete experience of the characters; our experience of the implied author and of universal issues; and our experience of the religious feeling that grows out of the novel's total structure.

In Chapter One, I explore the techniques Faulkner uses to evoke the concrete current of Joe Christmas' experience, through an analysis of the flashback that occupies the central third of the novel. I attempt to relate various ethical and psychological statements about Joe's situation and the meaning of love to the literary meaning Faulkner evokes, emphasizing both their relevance to that meaning, and their inadequacy. I base my literary interpretation on a philosophical account of the relation between abstract and concrete experience, of the nature of empathy, and of the relation of imagined perceptions to actual perceptions.

In Chapter Two, I call attention to patterns that our experiences of different characters have in common. These patterns evoke the sense of universal issues all the characters face, and appear in a convincing way because of an implicit sense of identity with our own actual experience. At this point, I introduce the notion of the 'implied author' as a perspective of concrete experience beyond empathy with individual characters, through which the common patterns appear. This discussion takes place within a philosophical interpretation of the way universality enters intrinsically into concrete experience. The moral significance of the universal issues in Faulkner illustrates the way the unity of concrete feeling essentially includes tendencies that lead beyond itself to judgment and commitment.

The second chapter centers on the characters' and the implied author's experience of the universal issue of love, and the third chapter begins with a discussion of the characters' experience of the universal issue of meaning, which I have defined as the uniquely religious issue. The issue of meaning appears through the experience of humiliation that Joe and Byron share. Each responds to that issue with a decision--Joe to kill Joanna, Byron to commit himself to Lena. Joe's and Byron's decisions appear as alternative possibilities only--we do not relive the validity of Byron's decision through empathy, but only experience a tendency to affirm that validity. The entire novel is unified through the scene in which Lena gives birth in Joe's cabin. In this scene, the bringing together of all the narrative strands of the novel, and the juxtaposition of the worlds of Byron and Joe, evokes the religious feeling of the problem of the meaning of a world in which such drastic contrasts are possible. But the scene does not involve any implicit resolution to that problem. It is through empathy with the implied author that the reader relives this religious feeling. In conclusion, I relate this religious feeling to Heidegger's notion of 'world' and James's notion of 'more,' distinguishing this feeling from religious commitments to which it may give rise.

In Chapter Four, I review my analysis of evocation and commitment, and introduce the new issues, to be treated in Part Two, that The Idiot raises. An expanded discussion of the nature of religious commitment, based on the work of H. Richard Niebuhr, forms the basis of my discussion of commitment in Dostoyevsky. Like Faulkner, Dostoyevsky works into his novel comprehensive scenes that evoke the feeling of the problem of the world's meaning--but unlike Faulkner, Dostoyevsky includes that feeling within the experience of certain characters in those scenes, such as Myshkin or Nastasya. In Chapter Five I explore the ways Dostoyevsky suggests the presence of such a feeling in Myshkin, and how he presents Myshkin's religious commitments as responses to that feeling. I argue that Myshkin's commitments function effectively as elements in the novel because they appear only as alternative possibilities--as only possibly the truth about the world, and as only one possible account of Myshkin's true spiritual state.

In Chapter Six I explore more deeply the religious feeling in *The Idiot*, as it contrasts with that in *Light in August*. Myshkin's and Nastasya's reflection upon the human condition creates in them a radical discontent and a longing for an unimaginable resolution. Dostoyevsky presents the possibility that such a longing is meaningful, and really may lead somewhere, as a lively one. In *Light in August*, only Joe experiences a similar longing of equal intensity, and Faulkner presents that longing as simply hopeless and aimless. The concluding image of *The Idiot*--in which Myshkin and Rogozhin are at the bedside of Nastasya whom Rogozhin has murdered--plays a role analogous to that of the birth scene in *Light in August*. Both sum up the radical juxtapositions that run through each novel as a whole, and both evoke the sense of the problem of the meaning of a world in which such contrasts are possible. But the image in *The Idiot* differs from the one in *Light in August* in that it involves, within the experience of the implied author, a conflict between the possibility of a religious commitment and the possibility of nihilism, as well as an indescribable longing to resolve or transcend that conflict. But here again, the truth of the religious commitment, and the meaningfulness of that longing, appear only as alternative possibilities. The overall meaning of the novel is the perception of the human situation as including the possibility, and perhaps the necessity, for commitment; but the novel's meaning is not that a particular commitment is true.

In Part Three, I deal with the question of the 'committed novel.' Chapter Seven reviews my conclusions so far and shows how they may be relevant to that question. I define the committed novel as one in which the author attempts to use the form of the novel itself--including characterization, plot structure, and language--to avow a definite commitment. The authors of *Embezzled Heaven* (discussed in chapter 8) and *The Diary of a Country Priest* (discussed in chapter 9) betray their rhetorical intention by including conversion scenes and avowals of commitment by characters, and failing to suggest any real possibility that the conversions are not authentic and that the commitments are not valid. I argue that the authors of these novels, by attempting to force evocative devices to function rhetorically, compromise the believability and aesthetic unity of their works. Their novels seem to be novels basically like *Light in August* or *The Idiot*, and yet, the selection and mode of presentation of character and incident do not make sense in terms of the truth of perception alone. We sense the presence of an implicit commitment at the heart of the work, but since we cannot relive that commitment through our imaginative experience of the world of the novel, the novel itself fails to achieve aesthetic unity.

A definite religious commitment can be the meaning of a literary artwork if the author respects the distinction between imaginative experience and his own direct avowal of commitments, even as he attempts to relate the two. But such a work would not be a novel. Works in which imaginative elements are subordinated to the direct confrontation of author and reader include apologues, allegories, satires, and sacred texts such as the narrative books in the Old Testament and the Gospels. Such works accept the distinction between the taking of a position and our perception of an imagined world, rather than trying to use the latter alone to express the former. How such works can succeed is a significant problem and deserves a study in itself. In the following chapters, I will be concerned only with problems of the novel: with how the novel can succeed when it aspires to communicate the truth of a perception, and with how it fails when it tries to communicate the truth of a commitment.

NOTES TO INTRODUCTION

[1] Paul Tillich, *Theology of Culture*, ed. Robert C. Kimball (New York: Oxford Univ. Press, 1959), p. 70.

[2] See H. Richard Niebuhr, *Radical Monotheism and Western Culture* (New York: Harper, 1970).

[3] See Alfred North Whitehead, *Adventures of Ideas* (New York: Macmillan, 1967), p. 267.

[4] Nathan Scott, Jr., "The Collaboration of Vision in the Poetic Act: The Religious Dimension," in *Literature and Belief*, ed. M. H. Abrams (New York: Columbia Univ. Press, 1958), p. 132.

[5] Roy Battenhouse, "The Relation of Theology to Literary Criticism," in *Religion and Modern Literature: Essays in Theory and Criticism*, ed. G. B. Tennyson and Edward E. Ericson, Jr. (Grand Rapids, Mich.: Eerdmans, 1975), p. 93.

[6] My point here may be related to E. D. Hirsch's distinction between *Sinn* and *Bedeutung*, or meaning and significance, in literature. I would identify meaning with the imagined perception in which the artwork consists, and significance with the judgments and commitments that grow out of our experience of meaning. Hirsch would distinguish between our interpretive judgments about meaning and the various kinds of judgments and commitments we make as we relate our experience of meaning to the particular circumstances of our lives at particular times in history. Hirsch is interested in establishing objective criteria for interpretive judgments; I am trying to point out the ways that all objective judgment essentially depends on the non-objective. See E. D. Hirsch, "Objective Interpretation," in *Validity in Interpretation* (New Haven: Yale Univ. Press, 1967), pp. 209-44.

[7] See Jacques Derrida, *Of Grammatology*, tr. Gayatri Chakravorty Spivak (Baltimore: Johns Hopkins Univ. Press, 1977).

[8] Northrop Frye, *Anatomy of Criticism: Four Essays* (Princeton: Princeton Univ. Press, 1957), p. 74.

[9] Cleanth Brooks, *The Well Wrought Urn* (New York: Harcourt, 1947), p. 212.

[10] Cleanth Brooks, "Implications of an Organic Theory of Poetry," in *Literature and Belief*, ed. M. H. Abrams (New York: Columbia Univ. Press, 1958), p. 71.

[11] Ibid., p. 76.

[12] Sallie McFague TeSelle, *Literature and the Christian Life* (New Haven: Yale Univ. Press, 1966), p. 199.

PART ONE

CHAPTER I

Empathy and Characterization in *Light in August*

In this chapter I will treat the question of the reader's experience of fictional characters in *Light in August*, and of the relation between that experience and explicit propositions. I will argue that our concrete, empathetic experience of fictional characters is different in kind from our experience of propositions, and that no set of propositions can ever be adequate to such concrete experience. But that they are inadequate should not imply that they are never valid. My method will be, while developing an interpretation of the character of Joe Christmas in *Light in August*, to constantly call attention to and specify the various kinds of inadequacy that are inevitable in the interpretive statements I offer. The statements I will discuss include descriptions of experience, literary analyses, psychological explanations, and statements of moral ideals.

In *Light in August*, Faulkner is interested in how each of his main characters succeeds or fails in being loyal to another human being. The ideal of loyalty or fidelity to be found in Faulkner can be compared with the Christian ideal of unselfish love. Such fidelity or love is more than a warm inner feeling. It involves making promises and abiding by those promises even when it is difficult or unbearable to do so. Love and fidelity are not abstract. They consist not in rigid adherence to the terms of an agreement or to definite moral rules, but in a willingness to do whatever the good of the person to whom one is loyal requires. Finally, fidelity and love have not only an ethical, but what we might call a religious or spiritual aspect. While love may impose unbearable burdens, to be incapable of giving or receiving love has often been seen as a spiritual horror identical with hell itself.[1]

The main characters of *Light in August*—Lena Grove, Byron Bunch, Joe Christmas, and Joanna Burden—along with minor characters such as Lucas Burch and Doc Hines, impress me as nearly exhausting the possibilities people have of failing one another, or of being true to one another. Lena is loyal almost to the point of absurdity. She is willing to set off on foot in search of Lucas even though she does not have the slightest idea where he might be, and persists for a month until she finds him, unswerving in her conviction that "a family ought to all be together when a chap comes," and that "The Lord will see to that."[2] Literary critics have accused her of selfishness and stupidity; but the fact remains that she does find, not only Lucas, but a good husband and father for her child, and that she was willing to face almost impossible circumstances in order to do so. The dominant feature of her character is the loyalty of a mother to her child.

Byron is the kind of person who is capable of committing himself to another, but whose fear of doing so leads him to withdraw from human involvement. Hiding behind his rigid routine at the planing mill for seven years, he believes that such a life will prevent him from ever hurting anyone. In fact he sticks to it to be sure he will never be hurt. The arrival of the pregnant Lena shocks him out of his self-absorption, forcing a decision upon him. He falls in love and makes a commitment. His is obviously the kind of love that is willing to do without any reward. He is willing to endure the pains and humiliations his commitment imposes. He abandons his former security and stands up to the disapprobation both of the town and of his closest friend, Hightower, in order to ensure that Lena's child is born in peace, and that she is reunited with Lucas. He even tries to enlist Hightower's support in a desperate plot to save Joe from prison or execution.

Hightower is the kind of person who is capable of committing himself to another, but willfully refuses to do so. As a young man, he learned to live for the sake of his own private enjoyment of a fantasy culled from his family's past. Hightower, in a sense, does participate in the world--but only in terms of his personal fantasy. Byron is more honest--he honestly withdraws. Hightower's view of the world of other people and of his vocation as a preacher became grotesquely distorted by his vain obsession. His self-absorption drove his wife mad and drove the community of Jefferson to utterly reject him. And yet he is capable of a genuine friendship with Byron. For all Hightower's overt disapproval of Byron's course of action, in the end he is really proud of Byron; and Hightower's involvement with the destinies of Byron, Lena, Joe, and the Hineses leads him both to recognize the selfishness of his life and to accept it without despairing.

Lucas represents the absurd extreme of irresponsibility. He is utterly incapable of making commitments, of keeping promises, of aspiring to any kind of integrity. The very idea of such things seems to have never crossed his mind. Joe is also incapable of real fidelity to another human being. But maintaining a certain kind of consistency is extremely important to him. When Lucas asks him, at one point just after Joe has threatened his life, "aint we buddies [. . .] cant you trust me?", Joe answers, "I dont know. I dont care, neither. But you can trust me." (p. 88) The dependability Joe aspires to is inseparable from a kind of cold contempt. Joe is hardly able to even imagine what love is. Yet he secretly knows something is terribly wrong, and he cannot bear that knowledge. Joe is a serious and tragic character, while Lucas is comical and inconsequential. Joe's inner unease prods him relentlessly to search for a sense of identity, but his quest only drives him further and further into spiritual chaos.[3]

The foregoing discussion of Light in August in terms of an ideal such as Christian love may be useful insofar as it begins to call attention to patterns that really do hold the novel together. But it is also very misleading. Such a discussion can give the impression that Faulkner is trying to use his novel to express his commitment to a moral ideal, or to some form of Christian or quasi-Christian religious faith. A paraphrase of the meaning of the novel such as the one I have given is possible and valid because feelings are relevant to ideas and commitments. But such a paraphrase is misleading because it suggests that the meaning of the novel is a statement or assertion about reality. It is true that, in some sense, the novel "says something" about reality. But what the novel says is inseparable from the way the novel says it, and cannot be reduced to any supposedly implicit theological, philosophical, or psychological assertions.[4] My overall purpose is to demonstrate that the aim of Light in August is to evoke feelings, not express commitments. But before I can show that the meaning of Light in August is something other than an assertion or a commitment, I need to map out the area of experience suggested by the phrase 'evoked feelings.'

I think that the statement 'because Joe was deprived of love as a child, for the rest of his life he was unable to even imagine the possibility of really loving another human being' is true. But it seems that as long as we are concerned only with such statements, and the kind of thinking they represent, we have not even begun to understand the novel. Such statements are objective: they attribute certain qualities to certain situations and postulate connections between the situations in terms of the attributed qualities. 'Joe was deprived of love' is a statement <u>about</u> Joe. But in reading even the first few pages of the story of Joe's childhood, we are reliving Joe's experience itself--we are reliving the reality the statement is about. Something beyond predication and assertion is going on. A dimension of reality, accessible in no other way, is opened up to us. It might be better to say that <u>the</u> dimension of reality is opened up. Objective statements do refer to reality, but their function is merely to attribute particular, isolated qualities to various segments of reality. Literature has to do with the indefinable difference between a thing, a person, a life, and statements or facts about things, people, and lives. To illustrate this point, I will examine in detail the empathetic experience evoked by the first few pages of Chapter Six, contrasting that experience with the statement 'Joe was deprived of love.'

The style of Chapter Six seems to be fairly straightforward narration, but the impression the manner of description creates is manifold. At times the description suggests the way the world appears to Joe; at times the way Joe would appear to the reader if the reader were there; at times the narration moves toward a more factual description of the actions and thoughts of other characters--and all of these approaches are at times intermingled. The description of the orphanage in the first paragraph creates a vivid, dismal scene in the reader's mind. But the description suggests not simply dismalness as it would appear to an observer, but the impression it would make on a child. The building appears as a threatening, confusing power, a dark presence. The phrase "big long garbled cold echoing building" has a remorseless hammering quality. The whole paragraph is full of adjectives that suggest a feeling of being dwarfed by things you cannot make sense of that constitute a sickening threat. Joe is surrounded by things that tower above him and enclose him. The compound is "surrounded by smoking factory purlieus and enclosed by a ten foot steel and wire fence," which is later to appear to Joe to be "like a parade of starved soldiers." That the fenced-in compound should be compared to a "penitentiary or a zoo" suggests a feeling of being trapped, punished, and humiliated. The use of the word zoo adds an overtone of the grotesque. Above all, Joe's environment is described as dirty, bleak, and abrasive. The word bleak occurs three times in the first paragraph, and the word soot twice. The very repetition of these words helps suggest the numbing, depressing quality of the world Joe faces. The building is "sootbleakened," the playground is "grassless" and "cinderstrewnpacked," the fence is made with wire, the air is full of smoke, the orphans all wear "identical and uniform blue denim."

Soot and dirt take on an added significance when we consider the way Doc Hines, the janitor who we later learn is his grandfather, is described. He sits, watching Joe, in the "sootgrimed doorway" of the furnace room that looks out on the playground. His eyes are "quite cold" and "icecold." His face is "quite dirty, with a dirty stubble." When Byron Bunch and Hightower meet him thirty-one years later, he is described as being "incredibly old, incredibly dirty" (p. 361).

In the second paragraph, we are given a description of Joe, "sober and quiet as a shadow," and we learn that he has been sneaking into the dietician's apartment for a year to eat toothpaste. The images and feelings associated with the dietician are in direct contrast to those associated with the building, the compound, and Doc Hines. While everything in the first paragraph is dirty and abrasive, the things Joe links with the dietician are all clean, or have to do with cleaning or washing. The toothpaste sitting on the washstand is the obvious example. Toothpaste is also smooth and sweet. The sentence "he was watching the pink worm coil smooth and cool and slow onto his parchmentcolored finger" has a smooth and soothing quality in its very sound and rhythm. The dietician's things are also soft--Joe slips behind a cloth curtain when he hears the dietician and intern approach, and squats "among delicate shoes and suspended soft womangarments."

Instead of saying that Joe was deprived of love, Faulkner tells us that Joe lived in a dirty, ugly, confusing place, that he was watched by a dirty man who sat at the entrance of a furnace room, that he was like a shadow, and that he ate toothpaste. Faulkner does not so much describe Joe as make us experience the world as Joe experiences it. He manages to evoke in a very vivid way the whole inner quality of Joe's life as a child-- and the quality he evokes is beyond the ability of any mere description or objective definition to capture.

The shadow, the soot, and the toothpaste, along with all that is associated with each, attain their full suggestive power through the particular way Faulkner combines them. The likening of a child to a shadow has many evocations that seem to me to emerge especially in this context. Being like a shadow suggests that the predominant bleakness has somehow entered into Joe, intruded into his life and taken residence there. A person who was like a shadow would appear to be drained of something essential, somehow worn out, exhausted, and insubstantial. Shadows are also furtive, elusive, and evasive. They slip around corners, and suddenly vanish. And most of all, shadows are blank. They do not speak to you; they do not respond; nothing comes out of them. Joe's shadowlike quality is not one of many appearances he can take on--it is dominant, constant, and indelibly impressed upon his nature. This becomes clear in many ways. He is isolated from the other children. They are like sparrows, not shadows. Joe is always silent and alone. He does not respond to or try to resist even the worst mistreatment. He simply stiffens up and waits for it to be over, waits to be released. He knows that Doc Hines is watching him and that Doc Hines hates him, and, we are told, "he accepted it."

In the above paragraphs, I have been attempting to call attention to various aspects of the inner current of Joe's feeling that objective statements cannot begin to capture. Reliving someone's inner life in its concreteness is an experience of a different order from merely entertaining propositions and facts. I would suggest that there are certain things that can be known only through such concrete experience. Thinking merely in terms of objective facts cannot experience the <u>difference</u> between fact and reality; it cannot experience the <u>importance</u> of reality; it cannot experience things and people as <u>presences</u> and <u>powers</u>; and it cannot experience the vague but insistent <u>background</u> of feeling inseparable from things and people experienced in their importance as presences and powers. It is often said that empathy can give us an understanding of people's actions obtainable in no other way. If we assume that the reason people do what they do is that certain things <u>matter</u> to them, then by reliving the qualities of mattering, of importance, in their experience, we do gain a unique understanding of their actions. This quality of mattering is not accessible in the abstract. It can only be reached through empathy. The words power and presence suggest the deep involvement of things that are important in the lives of those who experience them as such. Values do not simply exist; they matter to people. Importance is inseparable from power.

The primary aim of literary technique is to convey this sense of the importance of things.

But what is importance? No matter how exhaustive a list of directly experienceable qualities one ascribes to a thing, one will never hit upon the one quality that can be identified with the importance of the thing. Only when people and things are considered concretely, in their particular connectedness, does the sense of their importance and power emerge, and then only indirectly, in the background. However insistent the feeling of importance may become, it remains something ungraspable and elusive.[5]

The central point I wish to make is that through literature we gain a kind of knowledge of reality that merely objective discourse cannot communicate. I am claiming that literature is communication of a certain kind, but that it must be distinguished from the kind of communication that directly confronts the reader with objective propositions. Literature is based on the fundamental human capacity for empathy. Empathy in literature must be distinguished from empathy with the actual human beings we face. But since literature represents the development of a natural capacity we are simply given, I must first define that natural capacity, and the kind of knowledge it represents. Empathy is the reliving of the concrete experience of others. The issues surrounding the notion of empathy arise from the interplay of the notions of 'concreteness' and of 'reliving,' themselves highly problematic.

What does it mean to say that the reality of the world and of human consciousness is concrete? It means that the world is essentially more than even an infinite collection of propositions. Our awareness of any set of propositions cannot be equated with our awareness of reality. Propositions only select and isolate qualities of things and represent the abstract possibility of their connection. But in reality, actual things, the qualities of things, moments in time, and points in space, are connected, are together. Awareness merely of propositions would not include perception of the beings and the togetherness of beings with one another in space and time. The meaning of 'togetherness' includes the aspect of continuity. The difficulties in conceptually dealing with spatial and temporal continuity are notorious. It is in a sense meaningful to speak of periods of time, or of definite distances, but there is an incommensurability between such concepts and the reality of temporal and spatial continuity.[6]

Consciousness is, first and foremost, a concrete temporal stream. Through the concreteness of that stream, the concreteness of the world appears to the conscious being. Perception involves sensitivity to the concrete reality of the world. Concrete reality involves a vague background through which importance presents itself. Importance also elicits an emotional response in the perceiver, and that response is an essential part of any concrete perception. The capacity to frame propositions and make judgments is an essential aspect of human consciousness, and concrete perception can legitimately be interpreted by means of propositions. If propositions interpret reality, their relation to reality cannot be simply that they refer to reality. There must also be a sameness that reality shares with the meaning or sense of the proposition. Yet the meaning of the proposition and the meaning in reality are not simply identical. Rather, I think, there is, between the two meanings, a sameness within a difference.

Concrete reality always includes a vague horizon open to further propositional explication. There is always more meaning in a concrete perception waiting to be made explicit through additional propositions. But a concrete experience cannot be defined as simply the potential for even an infinite set of propositions. It is not as if a concrete experience is transformed into a proposition or set of propositions, by being explicated. I think this is so for two reasons. In the first place, the actual togetherness of qualities and beings is essentially more than the potentiality our experience of beings contains for explicit articulation of their structure. In the second place, experience is full of qualities that, while transcending the particular, cannot really be entertained in isolation from the concrete. 'Importance' and 'person' are examples of such qualities, and contrast with qualities such as 'red' or 'circular.' The former qualities always involve a sense of 'more' that cannot be brought into the foreground.[7] I can exert myself, for example, to remember the color of my house. Before I remember the color I sense only a determinable, vague background, and in remembering, I determine the background, bringing the color into explicit awareness. But the vague background through which we sense 'importance' does not contain this possibility of being made explicit.

But that experience contains qualities which cannot be made explicit does not mean those qualities are indeterminate. That which cannot be made explicit about any concrete experience—its particular mood or atmosphere—is inseparable from the feeling of importance in that experience. We can begin to specify what is important about that experience, and in what way, even though the mood or atmosphere of an experience is always something indefinably more than any objective specification. There is a sameness shared by the meaning of the propositions and the meaning in the experience to which they apply, but that sameness is a sameness within a difference.

What constitutes that difference in each case is precisely what cannot be made explicit. I think that atmosphere is in fact the essence of our perception of the concrete reality of a situation, of the togetherness inseparable from a vague background, through which alone the sense of importance arises. The particular mood or atmosphere of an experience is always something recognizably unique--it is not a characterless haze, a horizon utterly indeterminate and hence utterly meaningless. Rather such an atmosphere is recognizable as the atmosphere of <u>this</u> particular experience, and is recognizable <u>as</u> the experience of importance. The atmosphere of importance presents itself as an insistent aspect of reality that yet recedes from all efforts to make it explicit.

In perceiving the world, we experience other perceivers of the world. Empathy is, first and foremost, the concrete perception of other experiencing subjects like oneself. Our awareness of other minds is not the result of an inference. The standard argument for inference runs: when we see other bodies doing things we do, we infer, by analogy, that those bodies have minds like ours. The problem with this argument is that it fails to account for the concreteness of our experience of other minds. The appearance of others involves not simply a series of events from which conclusions can be drawn in the way that conclusions can be drawn from scientific measurements. Rather, the appearance of others expresses an inner reality, and evokes empathy with that reality. One does not experience others as objects or postulates, but as real presences, and as subjects like oneself. Were the inference theory the whole truth, we might be able to reasonably postulate that others had intentions and purposes, but the concrete reality of their inner lives would be inaccessible to us: the physical appearance would not reveal inner reality, and metaphor would be meaningless.[8]

The things people say, their tone of voice, their facial expression, the way they move, and what they do, taken together, express the inner reality of their experience. Our knowledge of their thoughts and intentions is imperfect, and our empathy with their feelings often inadequate, but the presence of other experiencing subjects with their own streams of consciousness is unmistakable. Typically, the word empathy is used to refer to our experience of this or that feeling or emotion in another. An angry or sad facial expression evokes an empathetic feeling of anger or sadness. It is in fact the ability of certain spatial configurations to evoke such empathy that makes the configurations expressive. But empathy is more than the experience of others' emotions. The physical presence of another evokes not simply a series of empathetic feelings, but the presence of the conscious being to whom those feelings belong, and the continuous stream of experience that makes up that being's conscious life. Emotions are only elements in a subject's concrete perception of the world. That concrete perception, including emotional reactions, tendencies toward action and belief, a horizon of past and future, and an indefinable background that cannot be made explicit, may be referred to as feeling, in the deepest sense of the word.

There is always the danger of experiencing others only as objects, and of experiencing the world merely objectively. We tend to concentrate on what is explicit, what is in the foreground, upon what we can clearly and distinctly intuit with the five sense, or can define clearly and distinctly, through deliberate effort, in terms of abstractions. We tend to allow the ever-present background to become so familiar and obvious that it practically ceases to exist for us. The function of art is to make this familiar and pallid background strange and importunate. Art distracts us from our preoccupation with the objective and clearly explicit and intensifies our experience of background as background. But a sensitivity to background as background is already essential to our empathetic experience of actual human beings. The feeling of anger a face may express cannot be located anywhere on that face, but emerges only in the background of the total appearance of the face.

But empathy does not distract us only from the objective reality of things in the world. In a sense, it distracts us from our own actual existence. I tend to be concerned with what I must actually do, say, and believe, and with what may actually happen to me. Yet through empathy, my existence is somehow identified with another's. I experience another person's feeling, desiring, and intending as if it were my own. At any point, I am a certain person, I have certain concerns, feel certain emotions, and know I must act. Yet at the same time, my stream of consciousness can be identified with that of another, who feels different emotions, has different concerns, and whose actions I cannot perform. It is through my own stream of consciousness that the other stream is revealed. The role of my own actual existence in empathy is highly problematic. In a sense, I am distracted from my own actual existence, or at least lifted out of my exclusive preoccupation with it. Yet my identification with another conscious stream cannot be so complete that my awareness of my own existence simply disappears. If such a situation is even conceivable, it represent not empathy, but insanity. Empathy *means* taking my own existence in two ways at once: as my own and not someone else's, and as someone else's and not my own.

My own actual existence plays an essential role in my empathy with actually existing others, since that empathy involves not only the evocation of background, but the actual confrontation of being with being. But while I actually confront another, actually believing that he or she exists and in my actual believing affirming my own actual existence, I simultaneously deny myself. I take the fact of my own existence equally in two ways: as my own and as not my own. But as I empathize, my stream of consciousness, insofar as it is my own and insofar as it is not my own, are not on an equal level. Certain elements of consciousness that relate directly to my own actual existence constantly tend to move into the foreground, but empathy pushes them into the background. They include my tendency to act, to speak, and to believe, and my anticipation of what may happen to me. The suspension of these tendencies, with the exception of the tacit judgment that the other person exists, is the precondition not only of empathy, but of all evocation of background as background. They recede into a background that can again become foreground, in contrast to the kind of background that cannot. These tendencies become like an object in my visual field to which I am not attending.[9]

A minimal empathy is a constant aspect of consciousness, and remains present even in moments of intense concern over what I shall do or what may happen to me. Though empathy is always present, it also represents a capacity which may be exercised to a greater or lesser extent. Some individuals may make but limited use of their capacity for empathy, and scarcely be able to relegate their self-concern and concern with action to an insignificant background. Such individuals may even be very conscientious, but their very eagerness to act well may prevent them from pausing to consider the feelings and perceptions of those around them. We may or may not enter as deeply into empathy as we can: to empathize is both inescapable and an ethical imperative. Deep empathy, with its suspension of self-concern, inevitably awakens a tendency toward concern for others, and imposes upon us the responsibility to fulfill that tendency. Actual empathy returns us to actual existence and prompts us to act.

Fictional characters are non-existent people. Empathy with such non-existent people is remarkably like empathy with existent people, but differs in several important respects. In empathy with a fictional character, I take my existence in two ways: as my own, and as the character's. But the character does not exist. I actually know the character does not exist, but this knowledge, along with my self-concern and concern for action, is suspended--relegated to a background that is not part of the meaning of the work. In empathy with actual human beings, tendencies for action and self-concern are also suspended, but my own actual existence directly confronts the actual existence of the other. In empathy for a fictional character, the fact of my actual existence, including all judgments I make, is itself suspended. I now take my stream of consciousness simultaneously not only as my own and as another's, but as existent and as non-existent. This complete suspension of my own actual existence, and of my capacity for actually making judgments, is the condition of the unique kind of objectivity and autonomy a literary artwork possesses.

None of the statements made in a novel about a character refer directly to any real person. The author has created the character, who 'exists' only in our imagination. Our empathetic experience of the character is in an ideal realm of meaning that is available to all, and not only to those who are acquainted with certain specific actualities.[10] An author may write evocatively about existing people, but he then has the disadvantage of not being in control of the meaning he presents. Since he refers to actual people, the truth of his presentation depends on external reality. The reader may well want to investigate that reality himself to determine the accuracy of the author's report. And very few may be in a position to test that accuracy. The author cannot be sure that the meaning he finds in his subject matter is the meaning it truly has--the uncovering of new facts may radically change that meaning. But a writer of fiction is in full control of his presentation of character, and any reader is in a position to verify the validity of the meaning the writer presents.

The ability of novels to evoke a sense of reality, power, and importance is relevant to the question of truth in fiction. Our empathetic experience may be said to have a unique kind of truth. It is true if it is believable--if we experience the things that matter to a character as being things that might indeed matter to someone. But the sense of importance evoked includes more than the feelings of importance the characters experience. The author must make us feel that the characters themselves are important. The characters and their predicaments must become powers the reader confronts. Evocation really has two senses: evocation of the characters' inner lives, and evocation of an emotional response to the characters' lives in the reader. Faulkner's presentation of Joe is truthful not only because it is believable, but because it calls attention to what really matters in Joe's life: the need for love, the inability to love, and the consequences of being hated. The writer of fiction, unlike the historian, can select his details on the sole basis of their ability to evoke the reality of universal issues such as these. This freedom allows him to create a world of imagination in which all may share and that is not disrupted by direct references to the particular way the world actually happens to be.

Faulkner's literary technique enables us to experience Joe's experience as Joe experiences it. Through Joe's mind, we experience the orphanage with its bleakness and soot, the dirty Doc Hines, the smooth and sweet toothpaste, and the unpredictable dietician, as beings full of importance, as threatening or seductive presences and powers. In calling attention to the content of our empathetic experience, I have had to resort to psychological descriptions, which are still objective, however open and tentative they may be, or to my own metaphors, which are certainly feeble and inadequate. My descriptions have the advantage of claiming only to be descriptions of feelings, rather than statements of the meaning of the novel. The method of attempting to focus attention on the content of evoked feeling is useful because it helps us to understand how feeling is different from other kinds of mental activity. But such a method is also somewhat artificial, and even misleading. While I have tried to explicitly focus attention on the feelings, and to some extent analyze them--our experience of importance, presence, and power emerges in the background, on the fringe, of consciousness. But as soon as one attempts to focus on the background, it is no longer background. To examine literary meaning directly is to distort it--for it is of the essence of literary meaning to be indirect. If a critical method is to avoid heavy-handedness it must recognize the elusiveness of literary meaning--the elusiveness even at the immediate level of the characters' subjectivity.

No objective statement can begin to capture an evoked feeling. However valid that statement may be. But the elusiveness of feelings is not confined to their ability to elude objective definition. It is not as if evoked feelings were clear, luminous, fully self-present intuitions that are ambiguous only because they defy logic. A feeling of background, of the fringe of consciousness, is in itself elusive and ambiguous. Such a feeling has a quality of being on the verge of something never grasped, a quality of almost but not quite. A closer study of a few of the metaphors Faulkner uses will help illustrate how such a feeling is evoked.

In likening Joe to a shadow, Faulkner is not trying to call attention to some quality Joe and a shadow have in common. Shadows themselves, as we see them and remember them, are capable of evoking a wide variety of subtle feelings. But Faulkner is not singling out some of those feelings and associating them with Joe. The purpose of metaphors is not to predicate qualities but to evoke a feeling of background, of depth, of life. The imaginative writer faces the problem that sentences are almost inevitably predicative. Evocative language must find a way to frustrate the predicative function of language.

The sentence "in the quiet and empty corridor, during the quiet hour of early afternoon, he was like a shadow, small even for five years, sober and quiet as a shadow," frustrates predication over and over, through the use of the inappropriate ascription of qualities, and implicit identifications which are impossible. The words 'sober' and 'shadow,' taken literally, do not belong together. "He was like a shadow" is really more like an implicit identification of Joe with a shadow than a comparison of Joe to a shadow. Literally being both a shadow and Joe is obviously impossible. Our minds are not allowed to focus on the literal, objective meanings of the words; but we are not allowed to dispense with the literal meanings either. Rather, when 'shadow' and what we know of Joe from the rest of the sentence, and, finally, from the rest of the novel, are considered together, a unique feeling of background emerges, possessing unusual intensity and liveliness.

I do not think it is quite accurate to say that the background is a third element that resolves the tension between the literal meanings. The evocation depends on the tension between the literal meanings. The evocations of 'shadow' upon which the metaphor relies are not abstracted from what we literally mean by 'shadow.' The metaphor loses its power if we forget about shadows themselves, and concentrate on the feelings we associate with shadows. The metaphor allows our attention to rest neither upon the literal meanings of 'shadow' and 'small, five year old boy,' nor upon the feelings the metaphor evokes, but is somehow suspended between the two. The feelings have a quality of openness, of potentiality, of just beginning to be. In addition, the incongruity is not limited to the literal level of meaning. There is something perplexing and shocking in the very thought that a five year old child should be "as sober and quiet as a shadow," especially when we consider all the connotations the words 'sober' and 'quiet' and 'shadow' have for us. The connotations themselves do not blend harmoniously. Feeling cannot come to rest upon the connotations of any one word, but is suspended among the connotations. The juxtaposition suggests a sense of something more, but this more is an elusive background, not a fully self-present intuition.[11]

I have been trying to indicate why the statement 'Joe was deprived of love' is valid, and yet inadequate and misleading. If evoked feelings are as open and elusive as I have claimed, then even the most exhaustive set of interpretive concepts must be inadequate to the feelings, and there will always be a certain degree of uncertainty about the appropriateness of any concept applied to the feelings. If this is true of descriptive statements, such as 'Joe was deprived of love,' it must also be true of explanatory statements, such as 'because Joe was deprived of love as a child, for the rest of his life, he was unable to love others.' In what ways may such explanatory statements be valid, and in what ways inadequate and misleading?

Our empathetic understanding of Joe has two basic limitations. In the first place, the main features of Joe's personality are simply given from the start. We are presented with the fact that he is a shadow set apart from the other children. We relive his experience of that fact. Our reliving of his experience does not explain that fact to us. In the second place, Joe performs certain specific actions. For example, he eats toothpaste. Insofar as we can relive his feelings about toothpaste, we can begin to understand why he wants to eat toothpaste. His action is plausible. But his action is an action and not a feeling. Our reliving of his feelings about his actions does not enable us to clearly see that because he had these feelings, he had to perform these actions. The spontaneity of human action places an essential limit on empathetic understanding. I think that Faulkner is always trying to bring this spontaneity to our attention. He does not simply open up the depths of empathy to us--he also forces us to confront the limits of empathy. In Joe Christmas, Faulkner has given us a character who is at once equally plausible and baffling, convincing and inexplicable. It is this combination of plausibility with incomprehensibility that lends power and mystery to Faulkner's characterization.

The continuation of the first scene of Chapter Six, which I have been discussing in detail, provides an excellent illustration of the way Faulkner manages to combine plausibility with inexplicability. Joe enters the dietician's room, finds the toothpaste, hears people coming, and hides behind a curtain. As Joe listens to the dietician and the intern having sex, he takes not just one mouthful of toothpaste, but another, and another, and another, until he vomits. When the dietician discovers him, he passively accepts what has happened. Why does Joe make himself vomit, announcing his presence to the very people he is hiding from, calling down upon himself the punishment he fears? I think it is possible to frame a valid explanation for Joe's action. While Joe's action does appear "automatonlike," Faulkner also suggests the possibility that Joe wants to vomit. All that we know of Joe suggests that he is full of repressed hostility, submerged outrage, desperate need, from which there is no relief. We also know that he is attracted to the dietician. His vomiting might be interpreted as a desperate attempt to gain some kind, any kind, of attention from her. Yet the only thing he can ever expect is punishment. Even though he thinks he has accepted his grim situation completely, an inner protest arises that he cannot comprehend or control. The desperation that is too intense for him even to feel expresses itself through inexplicable compulsions.

Such a psychological account does, in a certain sense, explain why Joe makes himself vomit. But however valid I may recognize such a psychological interpretation to be, I still find the scene to be as baffling as it is believable. The primary fact is Joe's action. It cries out for explanation, and yet refuses to be explained. Psychological explanations, particularly when applied to scenes such as this one, are both inadequate and misleading. They are inadequate because of their abstractness, and misleading because they suggest that we can see the connections between things with a clarity and a certainty we do not have. The connections between things in mathematics, by contrast, can be seen with a high degree of clarity. By making abstractions, such as scientific descriptions and laws, we can clearly see why connections between certain events must be as they are. Empathy does suggest connections between feelings and actions to us--but the connections are vague, uncertain, and multifarious. Connections are suggested between feelings and actions, between environment and individual, but the feelings do not add up to the actions, and the environment does not add up to the individual. The connections are not clear, certain, definite, or necessary. Joe's vomiting is an outstanding example of an action that strikes us because of its arbitrariness and unpredictability. The way Faulkner presents the action forces this unpredictability on our attention. Environment, feeling, and action are in abrupt juxtaposition.

Even authors who present mainly actions that give the impression of naturalness and rationality cannot dispense with a certain element of unpredictability. Too much predictability is unconvincing and unlifelike. But our overall impression of Light in August is not of a natural flow from feelings to actions, or from environment to response, but of abrupt juxtapositions. Somehow, it is not enough even to say that the connections between feelings and actions are tenuous. It seems to me that no matter how deeply we might be able to penetrate into the emotional depths of a character, there is a sense in which we get no closer at all to the reason he does just what he does, and is just what he is. Faulkner's abrupt juxtapositions of feelings and actions do not simply call attention to the many-sidedness and ambiguity of empathetic understanding. The sense of mystery Faulkner creates has to do not merely with the depth of his characters, but with the impenetrability of the inner core of their personalities, of the final source of their actions and decisions. While

Faulkner enables us to empathize with even the most irrational feelings, at the same time he forces us to confront the sheer givenness of what people do.

Throughout the flashback, the basic pattern in Joe's experience we find in the first few pages of Chapter Six is repeated over and over again. Faulkner also maintains the same stylistic pattern of presentation of character, in which feelings and actions are abruptly juxtaposed in a way that is at once highly convincing and strikingly incongruous.[12] Just as, within one episode, certain parts of Joe's experience shed light on, but do not explain, his actions, earlier episodes shed light on, but do not explain, later episodes. The function of the flashback is to give us a sense of the presence of the past in Joe's experience, as a power he constantly confronts and is forced to respond to. His past cannot be interpreted as anything so simple and straightforward as a cause or an explanation.

Faulkner employs three basic recurrent elements in his characterization of Joe. We begin with a sense of Joe's experience of the powers and presences that confront him with hatred, fury, or indifference. Faulkner also, much more indirectly, evokes a sense of the submerged feelings of outrage, sorrow, self-pity, and overwhelming need that Joe experiences. Finally, we are confronted by Joe's actions, which are often compulsive, incongruous, unnatural, and violent.

The power Joe confronts is primarily that of hatred and indifference. Faulkner suggests to us a special quality this power has. Even the word contempt fails to express the penetrating, unbearable quality of what Joe faces. One might say, in terms that are somewhat abstract and feeble, that Doc Hines, the dietician, McEachern, and even Bobbie, Max, and Joanna, fail to recognize Joe's existence as a human being. They lack the ability to recognize human beings as human beings. What we may take to be Joe's experience of this indifference is often evoked through descriptions of the sheer appearance of the characters, especially of their eyes. And the eyes so described are always watching Joe. Again and again we are told that people are watching him, and that he feels himself being watched.[13]

Doc Hines' eyes are described as "quite clear, quite grey, quite cold." During Hines' first confrontation with the dietician, we read that "though he was looking directly at her face, he did not seem to see her at all, his eyes did not. They looked like they were blind, wide open, icecold, fanatical." I sense that those eyes are the real source of the coldness and terror of the orphanage for Joe. Joe thinks: "That is why I am different from the others: because he is watching me all the time." While Doc Hines' attitude toward Joe is clearly one of ferocious hatred, McEachern's attitude is clearly one of indifference and contempt. But McEachern does not neglect Joe. Rather, he sees Joe as something he is responsible for training in a certain brutal manner. The difference between Hines' hatred and McEachern's responsible indifference is brought out by the consistent association of Hines with dirt and McEachern with cleanliness and order. But McEachern's eyes are "lightcolored, cold." The first time Joe and McEachern are together, we read that Joe "did not look at the man because of the eyes." McEachern's stare, which Joe could feel, was "cold and intent and yet not deliberately harsh." He stares at Joe as he would at a horse or a plow he has decided to buy. McEachern's attitude involves more than responsible indifference. It also includes a kind of conceited vanity, even superciliousness.

Joe's reaction to McEachern's callousness appears with the same startling simplicity and directness that his earlier actions do. McEachern attempts to force Joe to learn the Presbyterian catechism and Joe refuses, despite the most brutal punishment. His strange quietness and acceptance of punishment parallel his earlier acceptance of Doc Hines' hatred and of the cruel environment of the orphanage. Joe's dogged refusal is starkly juxtaposed not only with McEachern's violence and coldness, but with Joe's own submerged feelings. While Joe believes of the day on which he won his test of wills with McEachern that "<u>on this day I became a man</u>," (p. 137) his relations with Mrs. McEachern suggest that his attitude toward such manhood is ambivalent. As he lies in bed the same night, utterly exhausted, Mrs. McEachern timidly brings him a tray of food that he serenely carries to the corner and dumps on the floor. Again, the description is not so much evocative of Joe's inner life as it is factual, external, direct: "While she watched him he rose from the bed and took the tray and carried it to the corner and turned it upside down, dumping the dishes and food and all onto the floor" (p. 145). His final action is even more startling and paradoxical. An hour later he gets up and consumes the food on his knees "like a savage, like a dog" (p. 146). The juxtaposition of his stubborn refusal with his desperate eating begins to evoke a terrible sense of starved desire. He clings to the impersonality and dependability of McEachern's brutal regimen to escape having to feel this unbearable, overwhelming need. But he cannot escape it.

It is not the punishment that Joe cannot stand. It is the possibility of love. "It was the woman: that soft kindness which he believed himself doomed to be forever the victim of and which he hated worse than he did the hard and ruthless justice of men" (p. 158). His response to the brutality of his upbringing has been to shut himself off from the world, to keep himself enclosed within himself where he is safe. He is blank, silent, drained, a shadow. From the very beginning he has learned to desperately cling to his own sheer independence, and at the end he feels he has made himself what he chose to be. But his situation is impossible. He shuts himself off to escape from the penetrating power of hatred and indifference, but hatred and indifference are themselves unbearable only because he needs love, the same as anyone. Mrs. McEachern awakens in him the inevitable desire for kindness and comfort, but she is utterly powerless against McEachern's brutality. The desire reminds him that his situation is impossible, that he really has nowhere to turn. He hates her both for awakening that desire and for being unable to fulfill it.

At the end of Chapter Seven Faulkner evokes Joe's feelings about Mrs. McEachern not primarily through metaphor but through the simple and direct expression of Joe's inner thoughts. Faulkner achieves his effect through the remarkably apt use of colloquial language. Joe's first experience of Mrs. McEachern's kindness is described in this way: "He was waiting for the part to begin which he would not like, whatever it was, whatever it was that he had done. He didn't know that this was all. This had never happened to him before either" (p. 156). As Joe lies in bed, years later, listening to McEachern arrogantly chastize his wife for lying for Joe about the cow, we again overhear Joe's thinking: "'She is trying to make me cry,' he thought, lying cold and rigid in his bed. [. . .] 'She was trying to make me cry. Then she thinks they would have had me'" (p. 158). The feeling of resentment all mixed up with desperate need and desire that is evoked by these phrases sheds a great deal of light on his earlier actions--particularly his dumping, but then eating, the food she brought.

The story of Joe's relations with Joanna is extremely complicated, and

I will consider it in greater detail in the next chapter, in connection with the patterns of tension between men and women that run through the entire novel, and with the problem of identity. But the first few days of Joe's experience with Joanna do clearly illustrate the continuity with what has gone before. There is one obvious difference in Joe's personality. His earlier proud, naive, and strangely idealistic rebelliousness has changed into a contemptuous cynicism. He has tried to adopt the self-sufficient, coldly indifferent attitude of Max, Bobbie's pimp. But the same old desperate need continues to hide beneath his cynical self-sufficiency. The earlier pattern is repeated. He climbs into Joanna's kitchen through a window, though he could have taken a door. He is again described as "a shadow." He walks directly to the food, and finds it in spite of the darkness. His superior indifference finds expression in a phrase he learned from Max, that he utters when he sees the open kitchen window: "Well. Well. Well. What do you know about that. Well. Well. Well." (p. 216). But as he eats he suddenly stops as a vivid memory returns, a feeling of desire and sad perplexity that is hard to square with his attitude of indifference. He recalls waiting to eat while McEachern says grace: "<u>and I thinking How can he be so nothungry and I smelling my mouth and tongue weeping the hot salt of waiting my eyes tasting the hot steam from the dish</u> 'It's peas,' he said, aloud. 'For sweet Jesus. Field peas cooked with molasses.'" (p. 317).

After he has had sex with Joanna for the second time, he decides that he had better leave. But when he gets up to go, he finds himself heading straight for the house. "It was as though, as soon as he found that his feet intended to go there, that he let go, seemed to float, surrendered, thinking <u>All right All right</u> ..." (p. 224) Again and again in the next three years he tells himself that he is going to leave, and yet he remains. There is something he needs from Joanna, and something about her he cannot overcome, that traps him. On that early night, when he finds the door locked, he is outraged. When he discovers that the other door, the kitchen door, is open, and that he had wanted it to be, he is doubly outraged. He cannot stand the fact that he should be compelled to stay, should half accept the compulsion, and then be tricked by her in this small way. He cannot stand the fact that she should have such control over his feelings and actions--but his very outrage makes it impossible for him to simply forget about her and leave. That he should desperately need what women have to offer, of which food is a symbol and a part, he finds incomprehensible and unendurable. He picks up the dishes of food set out for him in the kitchen and deliberately throws them, one at a time, against the wall. This scene is clearly parallel to the ones in which he dumps the tray of food Mrs. McEachern brought in, and in which he vomits the toothpaste. As in the earlier scenes, Joe's compulsive actions are abruptly juxtaposed with evocations of his own emotional depth and of the depth of the powers and presences that surround him.

In this chapter, my primary purpose has been to explore the ways the author of Light in August has made it possible for the reader to empathize with a certain character, Joe Christmas. I have tried to define and illustrate the various dimensions of empathy, and the kind of understanding of human action and motivation that empathy provides. The dimension of depth I have considered is equivalent to what Philip Wheelwright refers to as meaning in "soft focus." Wheelwright sees our experience of the character Hamlet, for example, as "an aura of highly significant obscurity around a bright focused center."[14] Wheelwright's account leaves out what I have called impenetrability. I would like to suggest that our experience of mystery is indeed like peering into depths--but it can also be like the confrontation of one's head with a brick wall. Walter Slatoff has a real sense for what I have referred to as the arbitrary juxtaposition of actions and feelings. He appreciates the fact that no adequate definition of Joe or explanation of his actions can be worked out. But Slatoff believes that we, as readers, ought to be able to "move beyond the feeling we have about uninterpreted life itself, that there is a highly complex set of relationships that we cannot quite grasp."[15] I have tried to argue that literary meaning itself is something that is never quite within our grasp. Literary meaning is neither objective knowledge nor a fully self-present subjective intuition.

NOTES TO CHAPTER ONE

¹For my definition of love as loyalty I am drawing on H. Richard Niebuhr, The Responsible Self (San Francisco: Harper, 1978). Nicolas Berdyaev is one author who has identified hell with the inability to love. See his Dostoyevsky, tr. Donald Attwater (London: Sheed, 1934). William May, in an article on medical ethics suggests in passing that Hemingway espouses a codal ethic, while Faulkner espouses a covenantal ethic. A covenant "require[s] a fidelity that exceeds any specification" (p. 70). "Code and Covenant or Philanthropy and Contract?" in Ethics in Medicine: Historical Perspectives and Contemporary Concerns, ed. Reiser, Dyck, and Curran (Cambridge, Mass.: MIT Press, 1977), pp. 65-76.

²William Faulkner, Light in August (New York: Random House, 1959), p. 18. All subsequent references are in the text.

³I am attempting to work out in detail the brief suggestion Lawrence Bowling offers that love is the unifying theme in Faulkner's works, including Light in August. Bowling observes that for Faulkner love means fidelity, sacrifice, and endurance rather than romance, and that Faulkner often emphasizes the importance of love by showing us the results of its absence. Bowling remarks that the opposite of love for Faulkner is not hate but doom. "William Faulkner, the Importance of Love," in Faulkner: Four Decades of Criticism, ed. Linda Wagner (East Lansing: Michigan State Univ. Press, 1973), pp. 109-17.

⁴I am attempting to apply what Cleanth Brooks says about poetry to the novel. However, I intend to place much more emphasis on exploring the nature of the relevance of literature to religion than Brooks does. See The Well Wrought Urn (Cornwall, N.Y.: Cornwall Press, 1947).

⁵I have derived the notions of importance, presence, and concreteness primarily from Alfred North Whitehead. See especially Adventures of Ideas (New York: Macmillan, 1967), and Modes of Thought (New York: Macmillan, 1958).

⁶See Whitehead, Adventures of Ideas, pp. 244-45.

⁷For my notion of background I am partly relying on William James, The Principles of Psychology, vol. 1 (New York: Dover, 1950), esp. pp. 249-60; and on his concept of the 'more' developed in The Varieties of Religious Experience (New York: Random House, n.d.), esp. pp. 497-509.

⁸Edmund Husserl, in Cartesian Meditations: An Introduction to Phenomenology, tr. Dorion Cairns (The Hague: Nijhoff, 1973), secs. 54-55, also denies that our knowledge of other minds is a result of an inference. For a more general discussion of the nature of empathy that influenced Husserl, see Theodor Lipps, Ästhetik: Psychologie des Schönen und der Kunst (Hamburg: Voss, 1906), e.g. vol. 2., pp. 22-28.

⁹Andrew Paul Ushenko, in Dynamics of Art (Bloomington: Indiana University Press, 1953), develops a theory of aesthetic experience and of human consciousness in terms of "vectors" or tendencies, and "vector fields." The vector field of consciousness is normally egocentric, that

is, vectors extend directly between the field of perception and the perceiving subject. But the aesthetic vector field is "completely detached from the background of the egocentric field," and, most clearly in the case of the perception of a visual work of art, "does not occupy any particular place within that field." Ushenko also states that "whereas outside of art a <u>Gestalt</u> is the figure that appears against a background, the aesthetic <u>Gestalt</u>—the work of art—rules out the figure-background contrast except as a detail of differentiation within itself" (p. 81). Ushenko also relates the aesthetic vector field to empathy, in that for both, "the antithesis between myself and the object disappears" (p. 118). I would think it more accurate to speak of the <u>suspension</u> of the egocentric vector field, since that field must still operate as the context within which the work of art appears as a work of art—as the context that distinguishes aesthetic experience from dreaming. I think the simple foreground-background distinction is not sufficient to explicate the aspect of suspension of actual existence essential to empathetic and imaginative experience.

[10] See Lipps, vol. 2. pp. 32-38.

[11] Jacques Derrida also points out the elusiveness, not just of literary, but of all kinds of meaning. I claim, in opposition to him, that the feeling of background is not itself a signifier. In aesthetic experience, the mind holds meaning in suspension and does not try to make explicit what seems to be signified—does not see the signified feeling as itself a sign to which attention is to be deferred. I will claim that a unique kind of truth emerges when we let the background appear as background. See <u>Of Grammatology</u>, tr. Gayatri Spivak (Baltimore: Johns Hopkins Univ. Press, 1977).

[12] In "The Phenomenological Approach to Literature," <u>Language and Style</u>, 5 (Spring, 1972), pp. 79-99, Robert Magliola offers a good account of how phenomenological criticism uncovers "patterns of experience" in literary works.

[13] Francois Pitavy, in a study I have found useful in many ways, points out how Faulkner uses descriptions of physical appearance, and especially of eyes, to suggest the essential traits of a character. <u>Faulkner's "Light in August"</u>, tr. Gillian E. Cook (Bloomington: Indiana Univ. Press, 1973), pp. 61-64.

[14] Philip Wheelwright, <u>The Burning Fountain</u> (Bloomington: Indiana Univ. Press, 1973), pp. 63-64.

[15] Walter Slatoff, <u>Quest for Failure: A Study of William Faulkner</u> (Ithaca, N.Y.: Cornell Univ. Press, 1960), p. 185.

CHAPTER II

Light in August and the Question of Universality

In the preceding chapter I suggested that the essence of a novel as a literary work of art is to make it possible for the reader to relive the experiences of the characters, rather than simply providing information about the characters. But the meaning of a novel involves more than sheer empathy with characters. The way a novel is written consistently draws attention to certain kinds of things in certain ways, and the consistent patterns of emphasis the reader perceives obviously cannot be included in the consciousness of any single character. The patterns do not simply offer themselves for objective discernment, but evoke certain feelings above and beyond the feelings the characters themselves experience. How are we to understand these higher-level feelings evoked by consistent patterns of emphasis? In some way, they must reflect what the author feels is important. But how do the patterns reflect the author?

One answer is that the consistent patterns in a work express the author's beliefs, or at least his feelings. People may well be tempted to identify the meaning of Light in August with statements such as, 'I believe in fidelity,' or 'I believe people should be loyal to one another,' or 'I judge that Byron's character exemplifies the ideal of fidelity.' The 'I' in these statements is the 'I' of the author. Many literary critics are quick to criticize such interpretations. Many of the standard objections have a great deal of validity. I will consider three. First, the meaning of a work should be apparent through the work itself. The beliefs and even feelings the author would have had even had he not written the work cannot be the meaning of the work.[1] Second, statements such as 'I believe in fidelity,' or 'I feel Byron is a good man,' or 'the happy ending warms my heart,' are in fact expressions only of the reader's response to the work. Third, terms like 'fidelity' denote abstractions. Novels deal with the concrete reality of life. The overall aim of a novel is not to express ideas, even in the case of a novel in which ideas are somehow embedded.

My response to these objections is, first of all, to willingly concede that a novel such as <u>Light in August</u> does not express the author's beliefs. The author is not directly present in his novel. He does not confront the reader with an unambiguous message the reader must accept or reject. Rather, the novel expresses a concrete feeling that is ambiguous, many-sided, paradoxical, elusive. This feeling is not one the author has experienced through the actual circumstances of his life, but is embodied in a perception that grows out of the language and fictional structure of the work alone. The perception belongs not directly to the real author, but to the implied author. The implied author is the stream of consciousness that unites the work, encompassing and exceeding the individual streams of consciousness of the characters.[2]

As I will illustrate in this and the following chapter, a novel definitely can evoke feelings that do not belong to the characters. We do not merely re-experience Joe's sufferings; they also evoke pity and fear. And we do not experience Joe in isolation--Faulkner has set up all sorts of parallels and contrasts with the other characters. Someone will surely object that pity and fear are not the implied author's feelings, but the reader's response. My reply is that 'response' can mean two different things. In one sense, response is primarily a receptive experience. Because the current of evoked emotional response in <u>Light in August</u> is so subtle and so intimately tied to the details of plot, character portrayal, and language, I question whether the term 'response' is adequate or entirely appropriate. The emotional response is an inseparable part of the work itself. The response is in fact a reliving of an experience created by another. It is an empathetic experience. The empathetic response is subtle, unintentional, inexplicit. It is the elusive flash of insight that comes as the meaning of some aspect of the novel first dawns on us. We feel this flash is something we must be true to--we cannot dispose of it according to our whim. But this empathetic response must be distinguished from another kind of response that is not a part of the novel. 'Response' might also mean explicit reaction. One may formulate an objective judgment about how a novel is put together. One may make a moral judgment about a character. One may attempt to describe the feelings one has undergone through reading a novel. One may attempt to express one's emotional reactions to the various episodes and characters in a novel. The meanings of none of these statements will be identical to the meaning of the novel, or to the emotional response that is an inseparable part of that meaning. All of the explicit judgments and expressions are based upon something prior. The prior experience does not arise out of a purposive effort, but out of something more like listening, noticing, being willing to receive. As Joseph Conrad observed, the artist's appeal

> is made to our less obvious capacities: to that part of our nature which, because of the warlike conditions of existence, is necessarily kept out of sight within the more resisting and hard qualities--like the vulnerable body within a steel armour.[3]

The prior experience has the subtlety, the elusiveness, the shyness, of empathy, not the directness and definiteness of a judgment or the expression of a reaction.[4]

In reliving the emotional responses I described above, we are empathizing with the implied author. Empathy with the implied author is not really empathy with a particular person, such as empathy with a character. And what the author's own sincere feelings are in real life is not the issue. 'Empathy with the narrator' is hardly the right way of putting it either. In some novels, the narrator himself is a character whom the author may undercut in many ways. The narrator must be included in a perspective much larger than his own. In Light in August, the narrator is not even vaguely a character. 'Narrator,' applied to Light in August, becomes a merely technical term that does not refer to a person in any sense. On page 200, the sentence "He opened the door" appears, not in quotes or italics. It might be convenient to say, "The narrator tells us that Joe opened the door." The way the narrator describes things also evokes certain emotional responses. But dialogue and interior speech also evoke responses. The narrator does not provide the overarching perspective I am interested in. Our empathy extends beyond empathy with characters because it includes emotional responses to each episode and feelings that bring together all the different parts of the novel. We empathize not with a mere collection of feelings but with a unified emotional perspective.

Light in August does not express any definite attitude or stance taken toward abstractions, but the consciousness of the implied author does include universals. To say that something is universal is not to say that it is abstract. The mind recognizes universality, first of all, as an intrinsic aspect of concrete experience. We are able to perceive that distinct individual objects--for example, blades of grass--can be in some respect the same: they are all green. This sameness is something in the individuals that transcends the fact that they are separate and distinct.

The primary reality is our experience of this sameness. The status of 'color' or 'green' as concepts abstracted from perceptual experience is what is problematic.

When we notice anything and ask the question, 'what is this?' certain qualities of the thing present themselves to our attention immediately and unambiguously. These qualities include color, shape, size, and location. They can be clearly and distinctly known and quantitatively measured. They are the evidence of the senses upon which science is based. But what of the more significant universals such as love, fidelity, justice, good and evil, the human condition? These universals are also present in concrete experience. They are not present clearly and distinctly, but vaguely, in the background. As Whitehead would put it, we are aware of them as vague but unavoidable generalities fused with the particularity of experience.[5] The devotion of a mother to her child is always the devotion of a particular mother to a particular child that expresses itself through particular physical movements and particular thoughts and feelings. But when we allow ourselves to notice the importance of such devotion, when we allow ourselves to notice what it really is, we recognize its universality. There can be something deeply the same about millions of particulars although that sameness cannot be clearly defined or separated from the particularity through which it appears. To recognize that something is profoundly important is always to recognize that it is not merely particular. The perception of importance is concrete, but is also inseparable from the feeling that 'yes, this is something men and women face over and over again; it is basic to their lives.' Such a perception is not abstract. Thinking merely in terms of concepts makes it impossible.

What does it mean, then, to speak of a concept of love or an ideal of fidelity? I would propose that a concept of love does indeed arise from a concrete, vague perception of universality such as I have described. But a concept is an attempt to make a perception manageable, to use it for a particular purpose. One might define love psychologically for the purpose of explaining what people do, suggesting solutions to problems, and predicting outcomes. Such a definition will attempt to be as objective as possible; it will attempt to relate love to observable events. A psychologist might say that 'a loving environment will be consistent and predictable for a child; it will be one in which the child's needs are met; it will be one in which nurturing figures spend a large amount of time with the child. Children who are not loved tend to become either malevolent or withdrawn.' The abstractness and explicitness of such statements make them practical. They are directly applicable to reality as recommendations. We also have a right to expect directness and explicitness from a moralist. We look to him for clearly and rationally understood concepts we can apply to our lives. If he states, 'I believe people ought to be loyal to one another,' we expect him to try to spell out what he means by loyalty. We want him to answer questions about possible objections and exceptions. If we are in the business of deciding what actions to perform, we expect more than vague hints about the concepts and rules we may use to help us make those decisions.

But thinking merely in terms of concepts also removes us from reality. Concepts limit our experience of reality for specific purposes, be they practical, moral, or intellectual. Literature presents reality for its own sake. The universals in literature are not concepts or ideals but the vague and insistent generality upon which concepts are based. This generality is never quite within our grasp; it is in the ambiguous background of experience. Any conceptual definition of universals will be both inadequate and inappropriate--although some definitions may be more appropriate than others.

We perceive universality through empathy. In fact, empathy depends on universality. If we are successfully to empathize with a character, the character must be compellingly real. We recognize the reality of a character through empathy itself, not through objective reasoning. We must experience what a character faces as what someone might really face, and the way he reacts as the way someone might really react. But we are convinced that the character faces what someone might really face because we recognize, in what he faces, something we also face. Through empathy, we recognize people as human beings like ourselves. Such a recognition is not the discovery of a single definite quality or set of qualities that we can attribute to a person by stating a proposition. The recognition is a concrete experience. Empathy depends on the implicit recognition of an indefinable sameness. The fact that another person can become so much a part of me that I relive what he lives means that we must have something in common. If an author is to make a character believable, he must bring to life a feeling of sameness that unites the reader to the character. However bizarre or foreign the events and persons in a book may be, the reader must feel, 'yes, I have faced what they face; it is in me to do what they have done.'

Empathy itself depends on the author's selection and emphasis. If a character is defined by what matters to him, then a character's recognizable identity will emerge through consistent patterns in his experience of importance. The patterns I isolated in the previous chapter are of this sort. Our ability to empathize with, say, Joe, and not simply with a series of experiences, depends on consistent patterns in his experience that establish his particular identity. Those patterns suggest not only what matters to Joe but what matters about Joe. They evoke a response to his life in addition to making it possible for us to relive his experiences. In responding to what is really important about Joe's life, we are also responding to something universal. Through empathy, we sense that we have something profoundly in common with Joe. When we consider the various characters together, patterns emerge among them. These patterns suggest certain universal issues.[6] Through the implied author we feel our way into the depths of each character, and also stand back to survey all of the characters together. Both depth and panorama suggest the same universality.

Light in August is indeed about fidelity and the importance of love. The unifying theme is not a concept or an ideal, but the elusive sameness amid difference that I have been discussing. Of course, the mere statement that Light in August is about love is not very informative or interesting. When we try to specify the universals in a work, the result can easily sound commonplace, flat, and hopelessly vague. If we try to isolate the universals from the work, they do seem characterless and hazy. What we mean by 'love' or 'fidelity' or 'life' is necessarily vague, but a literary work can endow that vagueness with power and importance.

In Light in August, the central problem each character faces is the problem of that character's relation to his or her lover or spouse, and often to a child. Almost every character is paired off with a member of the opposite sex. In every case, Faulkner emphasizes some basic conflict between man and woman. The most obvious conflict, between Joe and Joanna, ends in murder. Love between man and woman is the central issue of a great many novels, but the single-mindedness with which Faulkner pursues this theme, and the extreme variety of situations through which he presents it, are striking.

Light in August is a story that is largely either told by its own characters, or presented to us through the minds of the characters. The story is presented through many characters in these ways, but Joe and Byron stand out as central. Joe's flashback emphasizes two essential problems in his life. First, he faces the problem of being a child with a hostile grandfather, an arrogant foster-father, and a servile, powerless foster-mother. Second, he faces the problem of women. Joe's life is a recurring pattern of impossible relations with women: with the dietician, Mrs. McEachern, Bobbie, a whole series of whores, and finally, Joanna. Faulkner presents much, if not most, of the remaining two-thirds of the novel through Byron. We experience part of Byron's story directly through his mind. But we learn most of Byron's story through his conversations with Hightower. We even get some of the story twice--as Byron experiences it, and as he later describes it to Hightower. I think it is significant that Byron's point of view is presented mostly through his conversations with Hightower, while none of the story is told by Joe. We experience Joe as an isolated consciousness. Joe is doomed to be walled-up inside of himself, while Byron and Hightower together gradually learn to appreciate the reality of other people's lives. The central problem Byron faces is, of course, Lena. Hightower's life has been determined by his disastrous marriage. The progress Byron and Hightower make involves their coming to terms with their problems with women.

Light in August criticism sometimes poses the question of the unifying center of the novel. Pitavy, among others, claims that Hightower, as he is presented, cannot bear the weight the novel imposes upon him.[7] I feel that the center of any novel is the implied author's consciousness, and cannot be identified with any particular character's consciousness. Even the perspective of a first person narrator cannot be identical to the all-encompassing perspective of the implied author. Yet the perspective that Byron and Hightower share does approach that of the implied author. Their perspective is far wider than that of any other character. The only major characters Byron and Hightower do not know or know of are the McEacherns and Bobbie. Byron and Hightower together struggle with all the major problems in the novel. They alone gain a sympathetic understanding of the fates of the other major characters. The broadest synopsis of the plot would be: how Byron and Hightower, who know and respect one another, but are withdrawn from the world, gradually become involved in the lives of the other characters, who are separated by time, place, circumstance, and psychological isolation.

Byron and Hightower confront not the problems of single individuals, but of men and women who are locked together in various ways. By bringing together, in Byron and Hightower's experience, the situations of Byron and Lena, of Hightower and his wife, of Joe and Joanna, and of Doc Hines and Mrs. Hines, Faulkner suggests a comparison to us. The patterns set up among these characters that suggest universal issues appear within Byron and Hightower's shared experience as well as from the perspective of the implied author. The viewpoints Byron and Hightower bring to the comparison are also complementary. Byron is a withdrawn man whose life is still ahead of him, and Hightower is a withdrawn man whom life has already passed by.

We know the experience of Byron and Lena, and of Joe and Joanna, the most intimately. Their situations are the center of our attention. The situations of the Hightowers, the McEacherns, and the Hineses form a kind of background. Our empathetic experience of their lives is not as thoroughgoing or complex, but the relative simplicity of their presentation makes certain issues stand out all the more clearly. The patterns that cut across all the male-female relationships in the novel are more obvious in the case of these characters.

For all their differences, Hightower, McEachern, and Doc Hines do have several things in common: pride, vanity, stubbornness, a readiness judge others, obliviousness to women, and hatred of women. Their wives represent three different responses to male arrogance: mad protest ending in suicide, utter capitulation, and steadfast endurance.

Hightower, as a young man, is shut off from other people; their reality is not important to him. He does not choose to be oblivious, so much as shrink from acknowledging the very possibility of a choice. His consciousness somehow rushes away from reality before reality can sink in. He has used religion "as though it were a dream. Not a nightmare, but something that went faster than the words in the book, a sort of cyclone that did not even need to touch the actual earth" (p. 56). Sitting with his wife on the train headed for Jefferson where he is to become a minister, Hightower breaks out into one of his overblown eulogies of his grandfather's questionable exploits, that he manages to get all mixed up with religion. Faulkner devotes over two pages to Hightower's speech. His wife is painfully embarrassed, but he will not stop. We hear: "_Shhhhhhh! Shhhhhhhh! People are looking at you!_ But he did not seem to hear her at all. His thin, sick face, his eyes, seemed to exude a kind of glow" (p. 459). Living in a world of imagination, he is unable to notice what is important to others.

Hightower's wife married him in an attempt to escape the to her intolerable confines of the seminary where her father taught. She is clearly unstable from the start, but Faulkner strongly suggests that Hightower's exalted indifference pushes her over the edge. After about a year with Hightower, she "began to wear that frozen look on her face" (p. 57), "as if she were not seeing what she was looking at" (p. 58). She stays in Memphis for long periods, probably committing adultery. The first crisis occurs one Sunday when she finally attends church.

> In the middle of the sermon she sprang up from the bench and began to scream, to shriek something toward the pulpit, shaking her hands toward the pulpit where her husband had ceased talking, leaning forward with his hands raised and stopped. (p. 59)

He leads her away. She is sent to a sanatorium, and apparently recovers. But she keeps returning to Memphis and finally dies there, having jumped or been pushed from a hotel window. This disaster drives Hightower into obstinate and complete isolation. The Hightower Byron knows has hardened his attitude toward women. He claims Byron's actions are inspired by the devil, and that Lena does not deserve the sacrifice Byron is making for her:

> "For the Lena Groves there are always two men in the world and their number is legion: Lucas Burches and Byron Bunches. But no Lena, no woman, deserves more than one of them. No woman." (p. 299)

Hightower's relations with his wife illustrate four recurring themes: a man's unreachable obliviousness, a woman's outrage because of that obliviousness, the attempt of a woman to stifle a man and of a man to stifle a woman, and the willingness of men, and of a community, to condemn women they consider sinful.

Both McEachern and Hightower are very vain and self-satisfied men. McEachern's vanity expresses itself in the violent domination of others and in the enjoyment of catching them in sin. Hightower's vanity consists in the unexamined conviction that he does not owe anybody anything.

Although Hightower is vain and aloof, he is also very compassionate. McEachern is an instance of vanity absolutely untempered by compassion. But in both cases that vanity means shutting oneself off from others, depriving them of something they desperately need. The vanity of both men also makes them stubborn. McEachern insists on beating Joe beyond his endurance, in order to force him to learn the catechism. Hightower endures humiliation, hounding, and beating, but absolutely refuses to depart from Jefferson.

McEachern lives in a dream as much as Hightower does. He is totally absorbed in his own self-sufficiency. He clings rigidly to the plan he imposes on the people around him. Others exist only as components to be fitted into his plan. In all of this there is a vain self-satisfaction, and a shutting out of other people's lives.

With a few exceptions, Faulkner consistently associates arrogant self-confidence with men. McEachern represents the complete victory of such self-confidence over love. McEachern has driven all of his wife's mothering impulses, any concern she has for Joe's needs, into secrecy. What she wants counts for absolutely nothing. She has acquiesced in this situation. Her only outlet is a kind of innocuous deviousness. Both Joe and McEachern are oblivious to her. When they march out together to the stable where Joe is to be whipped for not learning the catechism, she tried, ever so timidly, to interpose. "'Pa,' she said. Neither of them so much as looked at her. They might not have heard, she might not have spoken, at all" (p. 139). This sentence recalls Hightower's obliviousness: "But he did not seem to hear her at all" (p. 459).

The stifling in the McEacherns' marriage takes a far more extreme form than what we see in the Hightowers'. We listen with Joe as McEachern chastizes his wife for lying to save Joe from punishment: "'You are a clumsier liar even than he,' the man said. [. . .] 'kneel down. Kneel down. KNEEL DOWN, WOMAN. Ask grace and pardon of God, not of me.'" (p. 155) Faulkner suggests, again and again, that there is something in men that is unable to stand women and all that women represent. McEacherns' "KNEEL DOWN, WOMAN" is a strikingly clear and unmitigated expression of something latently present in all of the male characters.

Eupheus or "Doc" Hines represents the extreme of callous self-absorption. His personal fantasy has taken him to the point of actual madness. Hightower is detached and aloof from others; McEachern willfully manipulates others; Doc Hines savagely destroys others. Believing himself to be the instrument of God's wrath, he is assured that God speaks to him and tells him what to do. Hines murders his daughter's lover, lets his daughter die in childbirth, and kidnaps her child, Joe, placing him in a barren orphanage where Mrs. Hines can never find him. It is not really sin that Hines so ferociously hates. Rather, he seems to be guided by a hatred of all things living. Woman herself is an abomination in the eyes of God.

Faulkner communicates Doc Hines' imperviousness largely through descriptions of his eyes, and of the way he looks at people. When Hines confronts the dietician in Chapter Six, his eyes "looked like they were blind, wide open, icecold, fanatical" (p. 120). There is something unbearable about those eyes. As Hines sits in Hightower's study, "the stare of his apparently inverted eye is as uncomfortable as though he held them with his hand." Mrs. Hines' story strongly suggests that Doc had the same stare on his face as he watched his daughter die, and as he refused to tell her where Joey was: "He looked at me like he looked at Milly that night when she laid on the bed and died" (p. 360).

The stifling of a woman by a man is the tragic theme of the Hineses' story. Doc strikes women down three times. When Mrs. Hines tries to keep Eupheus from pursuing Milly, he strikes her down with his hand. He strikes Milly down after bringing her back to the house. When Milly goes into labor, they send Eupheus out for a doctor, only to discover him guarding the door with a shotgun. Mrs. Hines runs to the back door, and Doc hits her with the barrel of the shotgun.

Mrs. Hines is very nearly the opposite of Mrs. McEachern. She is as much the image of tragic fortitude as Mrs. McEachern is of cowardly spinelessness. She is not corrupted by Hines. She resists him to the end. She knows he is wrong and is not afraid to tell him so. She tried every means to discover what Eupheus has done with Joey, and she never flags in her tragic devotion to her grandson.

Mrs. Hines is persistent in spite of incredible outrage and utter hopelessness. She does have to contend with something very like what Mrs. Hightower has to contend with: a man caught up in his own fantasy, a man shut off from love. Mrs. Hines is patient, enduring, and weary. Yet the picture of Mrs. Hightower shrieking and shaking her hands toward the pulpit is an apt image for what Mrs. Hines must also feel. Mrs. Hines attempts to stifle Eupheus in a scene remarkably similar to the one in which Mrs. Hightower tries to get her husband to be quiet on the train. Doc has been insensible for most of the day, after madly having tried to stir up a mob to lynch Joe. They are now waiting for the two a.m. train to Jefferson.

Suddenly he breaks out in another tirade, yelling "Bitchery and abomination! Abomination and bitchery!" She tries to quiet him, saying "Shhhhhhh. Shhhhhhhhh." (p. 341) We are reminded of Mrs. Hightower, as she and her husband took their first trip to Jefferson by train.

The Hineses, the McEacherns, and the Hightowers are not presented to us in the same way as Joe, Byron, Lena, and the Hightower Byron knows. The three couples might be called archetypal. The function of each couple seems to be primarily to represent a certain possible response to the situation in which men and women find themselves. The characterization of the Hineses and the McEacherns especially has intense symbolic value, but their significance is focused in a single, relatively clear-cut way. The universal almost outshines the particular, even as it shines through the particular. We do not get inside these characters in the way we do Joe and Byron. The archetypal characters do not interest us as individuals so much as for the background of human possibilities they represent.

What gives these characters symbolic value? Faulkner's descriptions confront the reader with the essence of human situations. His presentation enables us to see what the situations really are, what is really important in them. As I have suggested, whenever we confront the essence of something, we are confronting something universal. Whenever we perceive what something truly is, what is really important in it, we are also perceiving it as a symbol. Symbols, at least of the kind I am discussing, are not symbols "of" universals. Symbols _are_ "concrete universals." They point to a universality that cannot be separated from their own particularity.[8]

Doc and Mrs. Hines, with all they do and suffer, are symbolic in themselves. Certain scenes and actions seem to get at not only the essence of their own characters and of their own particular situation, but of an aspect of the human situation. Two outstanding examples are Doc sitting on the front step with a shotgun as his daughter dies, and Mrs. Hines pleading again and again for Doc to tell her where Joey is. When the Hineses, the McEacherns, and the Hightowers are considered together, certain resonances occur. The juxtaposition of the symbols calls attention to something deeply in common as well as to significant differences. Through such juxtaposition, Faulkner evokes an even deeper sense of universality than the symbols create in isolation. In each case there is something at issue that is the same. This sameness, this issue in common, is very difficult to define. In abstract terms, one could say that Doc Hines, McEachern, and the young Hightower are confronted with the reality of other people's lives, and shut themselves off from that reality. In some sense, the three really do not know that other people exist. They may be able correctly to report the fact that some other person exists, but such merely factual knowledge is abstract, and essentially trivial. Through empathy we relive not simply a character's awareness of a fact, but his confrontation with concrete reality. It is indeed possible for perfectly sane people to be unable to acknowledge the concrete reality of the lives they confront around them.

Empathy is a given in all human consciousness, but empathy also represents a capacity that may be fulfilled to a greater or lesser extent. We face the choice of neglecting our capacity to perceive the reality of other people, or of allowing that reality to appear in its true depth. To be shut off is to be unable or unwilling to relive the experiences of others. Apart from such reliving, the objective importance of other human beings cannot begin to make itself known.

The universal issue that resonates through the symbols is the issue of whether one is to be open to, or shut off from, other people. The reality of this issue is experienced through the concrete, particular images. The symbols are not symbols "of" an abstract problem separable from the symbols themselves. The symbols suggest the complexity of love: that fantasy is a withdrawal from love and is associated with vanity; that love involves a recognition of reality external to oneself; that fantasy and vanity prompt people to control and repress others; that there is something indescribably unbearable about confronting someone who is shut off from others.

I have attempted to trace certain patterns in Faulkner's characterization of the Hightowers, the McEacherns, and the Hineses that I claim evoke a feeling for the universal issue of love. By 'pattern' I mean simply a perceptible network of similarities that has a certain evocative effect as a whole. I do not mean to suggest that a pattern is a specifiable entity that is repeated over and over again. The patterns do evoke a feeling that there is something deeply the same in very different situations and personalities, but this feeling emerges only in the background of consciousness. To attempt to focus on this implicit sameness, to bring it into the foreground of consciousness, is to lose touch with it. Even the attempt to define a pattern in terms of a single definite feeling or metaphor of which the many instances of the pattern are mere "appearances" or "surface manifestations" strikes me as somewhat misleading.[9]

The network of patterns related to love I have dealt with has three aspects: the spiritual reality of being oblivious to others, the kinds of specific attitudes and actions this obliviousness leads to, and the reactions of others to this obliviousness. Such obliviousness is a kind of self-enclosed vanity. We experience Hightower, McEachern, and Hines as somehow above and apart from others. They never get inside other people, and never allow others to get inside them. The kind of action to which their obliviousness leads is designed to keep others on the level they belong. Hightower's inner flight from others, and the blows and violent commands with which Hines and McEachern stifle others all have this purpose. The third aspect of oblivious vanity is the reaction it evokes in others, such as Mrs. Hines and Mrs. Hightower: unbelief, outrage, and an unbearable feeling of anguish.

The issues the McEacherns, the Hineses, and the Hightowers represent are also present in the portrayal of Joe and Joanna and of Byron and Lena. Through the central characters, the reader experiences those issues from the inside, as part of a more complex and many-sided reality. The universal becomes an overtone of the particular, rather than dominating the particular. And the contrast between the two couples is much more radical than the contrasts among the other characters. Byron and Lena are capable of love and their love has a chance of success. For the other men and women in the novel, love fails, or never has a chance.

Faulkner's characterization is successful because it evokes a sense of the essence of personalities. This essence emerges in the background--it cannot be conveyed by a statement or identified with any particular detail of aesthetic form. The essence of a person is what makes him recognizable as what he is--it is the atmosphere of his life that pervades his every feeling with an indefinable light or an indefinable gloom. A character may perform a series of actions we judge to be good; another character a series of actions we judge to be bad. But over and above these many actions, Faulkner suggests the inner reality of people. He gives us a sense of something true and right at the core of one person, and of something profoundly twisted and wrong at the core of another. The personal disasters Faulkner portrays are not simply unfortunate turns of events. The real disasters and successes are personalities. Faulkner wants to make us aware of a contrast between kinds of people, and to make us feel the importance of that contrast.

The essence or core of a person touches upon universals. It is at the essence or core or heart of a person that he is open or shut off, warm or cold, sensitive or blind, peaceful or turbulent. Faulkner suggests that Joe and Joanna lack something essential that Byron and Lena do not lack. One name for this essential thing is the ability to love.

Faulkner communicates the moral status of a character most obviously through actions, and through the character's long-term approach to life. But we owe our concrete sense of a character's spiritual reality to the particular way a character performs those actions, and the particular way Faulkner describes them. How our minds are able to pass from these details to an abiding essence is a mystery, perhaps incomprehensible. But certain details do stand out as particularly illuminating, and certain patterns and contrasts are evident.

The two couples' first encounters illustrate the essential contrast between what I have called openness and being shut off. The scenes are apparently designed to suggest a comparison. Joanna and Byron are both hermit-like people whose lives are abruptly disoriented by the arrival of a travelling stranger. Lena walks through the door of the loading shed where Byron is working alone one Saturday afternoon, and Byron, with a stack of staves on his shoulder, turns and sees her. Joe slips through Joanna's kitchen window in the middle of the night and stands eating a dish of peas he holds in his hand. He suddenly turns, sees the light under the door, and then Joanna holding a candle. In both cases, a woman walks in on a man who is holding something, and who turns around to see her. It is strongly suggested that both men fall in love at that moment. Byron and Joe's vivid experiences have something in common--but the contrast is painfully ironic.

Joe is utterly locked inside himself; the presence of other human beings is for him a seduction or a threat and nothing else. His eventual obsession with sexual relations with Joanna reflects his inability to trust others and to see them as an objective reality independent from his needs. The only thing he can depend on is what he believes he has wrested, or stolen, from others. The only thing that can warm his heart is the enjoyment of pleasure that he can take for himself, that can be under his control like the tube of toothpaste. He struggles to wrest that pleasure from Joanna.

He in fact comes to depend on Joanna to the point of slavery, but he is unable to admit his dependence. Such a fusion of utter dependence with complete isolation is already foreshadowed in the first scene. Joe and Joanna appear as powerful presences to each other, yet they do not seem to react at all. Joe, apparently self-absorbed, only gradually stops eating his peas, and Joanna stands with her candle. When Joanna finally speaks, her words reflect the paradoxical attitude toward giving that typifies their relation: "If it is just food you want, you will find that" (p. 218). She gives, but she will not admit that she gives. It is as if she were carelessly throwing something aside and remarking, 'Oh, that? Take it if you want.'

Their whole living arrangement reflects this attitude. She sets out food in the kitchen for him to eat alone. She gives him a cabin to live in, from whence he steals into the house at night to rape her when the desire takes him. Deep down, Joe wishes there was a way he could really get into the house and belong there, but he knows he never can, and he cannot stand the thought of wanting to. The house and the cabin are a powerful symbol of their mutual pride, isolation, and dependence. This symbol, with the tragic standoff it suggests, is one of the focal points of the novel.

Joe and Joanna are both walled up inside themselves. There is an indefinable distance between them that cannot be crossed. Both are clutching something within that neither knows how to begin to let go of. In the first scene, each is literally holding on to something as they contemplate one another. Faulkner emphasizes that, for all their sexual involvement, they talk very little, never sit down together, and remain like strangers. During their first four or five months together, they would talk occasionally on the back porch of the kitchen, though never while he ate. "They would stand and talk for awhile almost like strangers. They always stood. . . . They never sat down to talk. He had never seen her sitting save one time. . . ." (p. 220)

Byron and Lena's meeting is essentially different. One's immediate impression is of a natural human situation, in contrast to the eerie tension of the other pair's encounter. Their reactions are unfeigned, spontaneous, and uncalculating. The feeling of walls and of the tension of inward clutching is absent. When Lena sees that Byron is not Lucas, her face fades "like the dying agitation of a pebble in a spring" (p. 45). They immediately start to talk, and Lena begins her story, calmly and innocently. Faulkner's description of the details of Byron's behavior communicates a feeling of letting go, of removing barriers, of directing attention away from oneself. Joe and Joanna stand holding their dish and candle, but Byron sets down the staves. When Lena makes a move to sit down, Byron immediately rushes to her assistance.

> "Wait,"Byron says. He almost springs forward, slipping the sack pad from his shoulder. The woman arrests herself in the act of sitting and Byron spreads the sack on the planks. "You'll set easier."
> "Why, you're right kind." She sits down.
> (p. 47)

Lena and Byron immediately sit and talk, while Joe and Joanna stand and stare. Their sitting expresses an unselfconscious surrender, not in the sense of submission to the will of another, but in the sense of accepting the possibility of giving and receiving. Joe and Joanna fear, and cannot admit to, giving and receiving, but Byron and Lena allow it to happen without thinking.

Byron's small courtesy of offering Lena the towsack is a kind of symbol for all that he eventually does for her, and of the way he does it. Byron tries to accomplish two things: to see that Lena's child is born in peace and safety, and to keep her away from Lucas for as long as possible. He is willing to care for her with no reward, and yet he is in love with her. His actions are hardly disinterested. He agrees to move Lena out to Lucas' cabin not only because she insists upon it, but because he knows he can be alone with her there.

By having Lena move out to Christmas' cabin, Faulkner is clearly suggesting a comparison. From the cabin, Joe sneaked into the house to rape Joanna by night. She left food for him in the kitchen. He was held there by a compulsion he could not understand. Byron moves out there with Lena after the house had burnt down, and lives in a tent a good way from the cabin. He brings food to her. He moves as a result of a conscious decision. He reflects, calmly discusses the matter with Hightower, and decides to go against the advice of his friend, even though he still respects him. The night Byron stops by Hightower's house to tell him what he has done, his arms are full of food parcels he is taking to Lena. Joe is always secretive, but Byron pitches his tent for all to see. He knows his actions will appear either sinful or humiliating, but he does not try to hide or deny his act of giving.

Joe was in the habit of climbing up to Joanna's room whenever "the desire took him" (p. 99). He was infuriated that one early night when Joanna locked the door on him. Byron's actions are different. As he tells Hightower:

> "I aint in the house with her. I got a tent. It aint close, neither. Just where I can hear her at need. And I fixed a bolt on the door. Any of them can come out, at any time, and see me in the tent." (p. 297)

The tent is a symbol of hesitancy and courtesy. In contrast to the house and the cabin, it is temporary. He himself sets up the tent, rushing to her assistance, ready to take it down and follow her when the need arises. He has left his rooming house and moved into a tent: he does not cling to what he possesses, to what insulates him. The tent expresses his willingness to help her, and his unwillingness to violate her or take what is not his. Instead of raping Lena, he asks her to marry him.

Byron and Lena give and receive not simply help (though Lena does not help Byron in an obvious way) but knowledge of who they are and what they want. It takes months for Joe to discover the personal facts about Joanna that Byron learns about Lena in a few minutes, and Joanna always remains a maddening enigma to Joe. Lena is also something of an enigma to Byron, but his sense of her as an enigma includes genuine hope. It is as if Joe and Joanna, in contrast, were always holding something back, as if each was constantly contemplating the other with a suspicious sidelong glance.

Byron experiences Lena as a powerful presence. But her presence to him is not that of a mere seduction or threat. Rather, he feels a sense of obligation, the beginnings of a bond of fidelity, and the beginnings of hope that she will share that fidelity. But the bond that he longs for is not merely the bond of a duty; it is also personal and sexual. While Byron finds the longing and concern that are growing inside him extremely disturbing, Faulkner emphasizes that there is still something essentially quiet about the man: not the quietness of repressed rage, but the quietness that sees things as they are, and not knowing what to make of them, can contemplate its own helplessness without fleeing in panic or stubborn denial of responsibility. Byron knows that something has let go inside him. He has become deeply involved with Lena without even having had the chance to realize what has been happening. He does not run from the new reality that confronts him, or rebel against it, or proudly refuse to see it. Byron knows that he cannot take Lena by force of will. He knows that whether Lena will finally accept him hangs in the balance. His happiness has suddenly come greatly to depend on what someone else does. When Byron realizes he has revealed to Lena that Joe Brown is Lucas Burch, his chagrin is due not so much to the fact that he has gotten Lucas in trouble, as that he has found his rival for her, and has been morally obligated to let her know: "And he cannot look at her, and he sits on the stacked lumber when it is too late, and he could have bitten his tongue in two" (p. 51). Byron sits there quietly, in pain, knowing he has unwittingly let go of something he can never retrieve, his mind clearly focused on the situation he has gotten into, moved equally by hope and regret.

Joe, by contrast, knows no hope. He is simply unable to live with the fact that he depends on someone else. He tries by force of will to overcome that dependence, to somehow destroy the fact that Joanna is able to withhold something from him. There is something he feels he has to prove to her. The second time he rapes her, we learn,

> he did not go in eagerness, but in a quiet rage. "I'll show her," he said aloud. [. . .] He began to tear at her clothes. He was talking to her in a tense, hard, low voice: "I'll show you! I'll show the bitch!" [. . .] 'At least I've made a woman of her at last,' he thought. 'Now she hates me. I have taught her that, at least.' (pp. 222-23)

His inability to live with dependence goes hand in hand with a strange kind of vanity and arrogance. His sneering air of superiority and indifference glosses over a desperate inner need he cannot face. Joe's vanity is a frantic, desperate flight from reality. His vanity contrasts with Byron's mild quietness, "compassionate and troubled and still" (p. 93). Whereas Joe's vanity makes him violent, didactic, and judgmental, Byron is essentially humble and unwilling to judge others, and his humility and unwillingness to judge are linked with independence and scepticism.

Most striking in the context of the whole novel is the fact that Byron does not judge Lena for being what the town would call a fallen woman. Faulkner very clearly invites us to contrast Byron with the other men in the novel in this respect. Milly is originally in almost exactly the same situation as Lena. She becomes pregnant by a circus hand and secretly leaves home with him. But Doc Hines, absorbed in his righteousness, condemns her, kills her lover, and allows her to die. As she is giving birth, Hines sits on the front steps with a shotgun to keep Mrs. Hines from getting a doctor. But as Lena is giving birth, Byron is frantically rushing to find a doctor. McEachern delights in condemning his wife for covering up for Joe, booming, "KNEEL DOWN, WOMAN." Hightower's wife was also a fallen woman. Hightower's attitude at the time was oblivious rather than overtly judgmental. But he is willing to condemn women, telling Byron that Lena does not deserve the sacrifice Byron is making. Joe does not care very much for traditional moral dictates, but he is certainly capable of utterly rejecting others, of reducing them to insignificance because of some failure or lack. Joe realizes, standing before Joanna, that she is not pregnant, but has only passed menopause. After striking her, he says, "There is not anything the matter with you except being old. You just got old and it happened to you and now you are not any good any more" (p. 262).

Faulkner does not overtly assert that Byron is a moral man, capable of recognizing the importance of other people's needs. Rather, Faulkner invites us to contrast different ways of experiencing. We relive both Byron's and Joe's experience of the presence, power, and importance of other people, and we cannot fail to notice an essential difference. One description of that difference is that Joe is locked in a fantasy world, unable to appreciate the objective reality of other people, while Byron is able to let that reality dawn on him. Joe experiences importance only through the lens of his own needs, so to speak, while Byron experiences importance as an objective reality. Byron's experience is associated with a feeling of letting go of something, while Joe's experience is associated with a feeling of being unable to let go of something. Through empathy, we are able to recognize that Byron has a truer emotional perception of the world than Joe does. The truth we experience in Byron is not the truth of a clearly defined position or ideal, but the truth of perceptions, emotions, feelings.

Byron's function in the book is to narrate a good deal of the story and to sympathize with most of the other characters. It is through his experience that we gain the most encompassing sense of objective reality. But Faulkner does not present us with two opposing positions, moral success and moral failure, affirming moral success. Rather, Byron and Joe represent opposing tendencies. The implied author more or less identifies himself with the basic tendency in Byron's character. By empathizing with the implied author, the reader comes strongly to feel that Byron's perceptions are headed toward truth and reality. But Faulkner offers us no clear definition of reality, and his tendency to affirm Byron's perceptions and way of life, however strong, is only a tendency. Faulkner also undercuts Byron in ways I will later describe.

Again and again Faulkner leads us to sympathize with the plight of the unfortunate and such sympathy naturally contains the tendency to condemn those who cause that plight and to affirm those who relieve it. Those who are blind to that plight, we feel, are out of touch with reality. Feeling is not a self-enclosed realm, but is always verging on something more. Tendencies toward commitment, judgment, affirmation, are an essential element of feeling. Faulkner's work is aesthetically successful and morally significant because he can make us keenly feel those tendencies while preserving our sense of the ambiguity of the situations in which they arise. Our experience of <u>Light in August</u> is indeed more congruent with some moral judgments and ideas than others. But a novel as successful as <u>Light in August</u> also forces us to recognize the tension that must exist between feeling and commitment. Our exertions to commit ourselves and form definite judgments can never quite do justice to the feelings of importance that continuously assert themselves in the background of consciousness. Faulkner calls attention to the feeling of urgency, inherent in all feelings of importance, that draws us on to action and commitment. But Faulkner holds that feeling in suspension. It is just not his business as a novelist to settle down on particular commitments.

In Byron's perceptions, we recognize a deep-seated tendency toward the truth. An essential part of his experience of the objective reality of other human beings is the tendency to commit himself to them. Joe's essential experience is that of being trapped in a place where he cannot get to the truth. His perceptions are twisted, childish, wrong. Joe also experiences the urgency that leads beyond feeling--but that urgency has nowhere to go. Joe's urgency does not grow out of a perception of the needs of others, but exclusively out of his own inner need.

Any character has more than feelings of tendency--he performs certain actions, and those actions help reveal his character. But those actions represent the carrying out of a tendency, the fulfillment of a potentiality, that does not take place in the mind of the reader. A feeling is an experience the reader can get inside of, but an action is more like an external fact that simply confronts the reader. When a reader wants actually to make the commitments a character does, confusing his own position taking with his experience of the character, aesthetic distance collapses. The aim of melodramas, soap operas, and propaganda pieces is to allow the reader or viewer to dispense with aesthetic distance. The tendency within feeling to go beyond feeling and make a commitment needs to be held in suspension. I dwell on this point because the real moral significance of _Light in August_ can so easily be exaggerated or misinterpreted. Byron is not a paragon. Lena is not a nature goddess. The aim of Joe's story is not to incite us to judge and hate McEachern, Doc Hines, and Joanna. It is not Faulkner's aim to communicate implicit judgments of actions and characters, nor to espouse a moral ideal. Yet, the contrast between Byron and Joe is certainly moral.

NOTES TO CHAPTER TWO

¹The classic statement of this position is, of course, W. K. Wimsatt and Monroe Beardsley, "The Intentional Fallacy," in *Critical Theory since Plato*, ed. Hazard Adams (New York: Harcourt, 1971), pp. 1015-21.

²Wayne Booth, in *The Rhetoric of Fiction* (Chicago: Univ. of Chicago Press, 1961), calls the implied author a novel's "core of norms and choices" which is essentially involved in "the intuitive apprehension of a completed artistic whole" (pp. 73-74). Booth notes that the term 'narrator' is not an accurate one for this core. I agree with Booth that our beliefs are relevant to our experience of the novel, and that our experience of the novel is relevant to our beliefs, but I do not think it correct to assert, as Booth sometimes seems to, that the implied author is committed to anything. I owe my conception of the implied author more to George Poulet than to Booth. For Poulet, reading is empathy with the author, "yet the subject which presides over the work can exist only in the work." In reading "I am on loan to another, and this other thinks, feels, suffers, and acts within me." "Phenomenology of Reading," in *Critical Theory since Plato*, pp. 1215-16.

³Joseph Conrad, "Preface to *The Nigger of the Narcissus*," in *Discussions of the Novel*, ed. Roger Sale (Boston: Heath, 1960), p. 91.

⁴Wolfgang Iser, in *The Act of Reading* (Baltimore: Johns Hopkins Univ. Press, 1974), holds that literary meaning arises out of the interaction of author and reader. The author juxtaposes various elements, such as points of view, that do not fit together in any obvious or conventional way. The reader is incited to ask why. But at this point, Iser does not clearly recognize the distinction I make between two kinds of response. For him 'response' is too much like the formulation of an objective interpretation.

⁵According to Alfred North Whitehead, "One characteristic of the primary mode of conscious experience is the fusion of a large generality with an insistent particularity. . . . The basis of our primary consciousness of quality is a large generality. For example, characteristic modes of thought, as we first recall ourselves to civilized experience, are--'This is important,' 'That is difficult,' 'This is lovely.' . . . The generality, when stated, is too obvious to be worth mentioning. And yet it is always there, just on the edge of consciousness. . . . Words, in general, indicate useful particularities. How can they be employed to evoke a sense of that general character on which all importance depends? It is one function of great literature to evoke a vivid feeling of what lies beyond words." *Modes of Thought* (New York: Macmillan, 1958), pp. 6-7.

⁶The patterns I will be concerned with are analogous to the "patterns of authorial experience" that, according to Robert Magliola, one branch of phenomenological criticism aims to discover. The phenomenological critic examines literary works as symbols of reality and as symbols of the author's experiential patterns. To determine whether the work succeeds as a symbol of reality, the critic "asks whether the "world" (characters, theme, plot, etc.) presented in a literary work is "made present" or "vitalized" through language so that it can "live" in the reader's

imagination" (p. 88). "The Phenomenological Approach to Literature," <u>Language and Style</u>, 5 (Spring, 1982), pp. 79-99.

[7]Francois Pitavy claims that Hightower is supposed to be the "moral center" of the novel, but that "he is not quite coherent enough to bear the weight imposed upon him by the structure of the book," and that "Faulkner was probably wrong to caricature him in fact." <u>Faulkner's "Light in August"</u> (Bloomington: Indiana Univ. Press, 1973), p. 83.

[8]See W. K. Wimsatt, "The Structure of the Concrete Universal in Literature," in <u>The Verbal Icon</u> (London: Methuen, 1970).

[9]Compare Magliola, p. 93.

CHAPTER III

Light in August and the Mystery of the Human Condition

Light in August is about the importance of love, as Bowling claims. The novel evokes a feeling for the universal issue of love that does have moral significance. But the contrast between Byron and Joe suggests an even deeper issue that has not merely moral, but what I am willing to call religious, significance. The religious issue comes out most clearly through Faulkner's treatment of the experience of humiliation. Both Byron and Joe are humiliated. Joanna seduces, threatens, and humiliates Joe; Lena humiliates Byron, but also gives him reason for hope. The feelings of being seduced, threatened, or obligated have to do with one's perceptions of importance, be they moral or amoral. But over and above such perceptions is another issue that finds expression in questions such as: Do I have it in me to face these threats and obligations? Am I worthy of taking a place in the world? Is it even worthwhile trying? Humiliation cuts deep because it forces just such questions upon one's attention. The issue behind such questions is essentially the issue of whether one can believe in the meaning of one's existence. The issue of meaning is distinct from and beyond the question of importance, and, of all the issues people face, may well be considered the uniquely religious one.

From the beginning, Joe had been surrounded by powers announcing to him the fact that he was detestable, contemptible, or insignificant. The hatred he confronts reaches into him in an indescribable way; it poisons the very center of his life. His experience of other human beings is that of being stifled. It is as if the world is out to convince him that his life is worthless and pointless. There may be something going on out there in the world, but Joe does not deserve to have a part in it. Joe rebels against this threat, but is unable ever to escape it. He walls himself up in his pride in order to protect himself, yet pride itself demands the presence of others to whom it can show its indifference. Unlike McEachern, he is unable to be satisfied with his pride. It is as if he cannot endure the walls he himself has built, and is constantly striving to break through them even as he makes them stronger.

The central crisis of the novel, leading directly to Joanna's murder, is her humiliation of Joe. In the long run, Joe is overcome by the terrifying thought that Joanna, and not he, is in control. For Joe, dependence represents a danger and a humiliation he is unable to face. The ultimate humiliation for him is to have to admit a need for love. He attempts to avoid humiliation by demonstrating independence, yet his need for Joanna binds him to her against his will.

After their first encounter, Joe and Joanna withdraw into their respective dwellings, each waiting the other out. Joe gets a job and no longer takes her food. Six months later, he returns from the mill one day to find Joanna sitting on his cot. He believes she has given in. "Christmas thought, 'She is like all the rest of them. Whether they are seventeen or fortyseven, when they finally come to surrender completely, its's going to be in words'" (p. 227). But the passionate fury of the "second phase" that ensues is not at all under his control. "Soon she more than shocked him: she astonished and bewildered him" (p. 224). She makes him pick up secret notes, search through the house for her, come to her through the window. He is at her mercy and his dependence makes him deeply anxious. He believes that he is going to leave, but he keeps putting it off.

His anxiety becomes terror as she withdraws from him, as the "third phase" begins. At first, it seems to him that the desire to withdraw is his, in aversion from her plans to have a child and perhaps marry. But when she realizes she is not pregnant, the situation changes. The first time she sends for him, she refuses him sex, putting aside his hand "with the calm firmness of a man" (p. 253). While at first she had only been refusing him, now she wants to change his life. The first two times she sends for him, Joe believes she has given in, and he is more relieved and expectant than he realizes. But she presents a threat each time more humiliating, more dangerous, more unbearable. She wants him to join her in her business of advising Negroes, to "make of him something between a hermit and a missionary to negroes" (p. 257). This cuts him to the quick, so much that "he would have died or murdered rather than have anyone, another man, learn what their relations had now become" (p. 256). After he has become utterly dependent on her, she attacks the very core of his pride. He had used his uncertainty about his race to keep his distance from humanity in general. He tells people he is a Negro in order to provoke hatred, so that he can believe that at least the hatred is his own doing, and that any respect he receives is out of fear alone. His relationship to Joanna is based in part on Joanna's deeply ambivalent attitude toward Negroes. She now uses his Negro identity against him.

The second time she discusses her plans, her real aim becomes clearer. She is out not only to make him into a missionary to Negroes, but actually to make him into a Negro. He is to admit his race, study at a Negro college, and become a Negro lawyer. But to be a Negro is to be at her mercy: it is to be something she is to raise out of darkness, and therefore inferior to her, under her control.

The third time she sends for him, he waits to enter the room until she has finished praying, and "it would seem to him that he could distinguish the prints of knees and he would jerk his eyes away as if it were death that they had looked at" (p. 264). McEachern was the first one to force him to kneel down and pray, the night after he had failed to compel Joe to learn the catechism, and it had then seemed to Joe, as he lay in bed, that if he had looked he could have seen "in the rug the indentations of the twin pairs of knees without tangible substance" (p. 144). Now Joanna tries to force him to pray and to repent. Two nights before the murder she had demanded again and again, "kneel with me." Her demand is an intolerable threat. He responds to that threat with the ultimate form of stifling.

The power of these final scenes and their resonance with Joe's earlier experiences evokes an empathetic feeling that has more than moral significance. We begin to sense the feeling of the utter insignificance and detestability of one's very existence, and this is a religious feeling. And Joe has in fact taken a religious position--whether freely or not we cannot tell. His feeling that life is unbearable has overwhelmed him and expressed itself through the obliteration of someone who announced to him his insignificance.

Byron also faces humiliation. But Byron resolves to go on in spite of humiliation, while Joe tries to destroy what humiliates him. I think Faulkner wants to suggest that there is something deeply similar about the situations Joe and Byron face, even though their reactions are exactly opposite. While Byron is an admirable figure, his situation is almost ludicrous. Apparently for no reason at all he has fallen in love with a pregnant woman searching for her baby's father whom she will never find. He openly does everything he can for her, including reuniting her with her lover. When Lucas runs, he accompanies her in the vain search for his rival. She seems to be impervious to his entreaties to give up and marry him. The climax of his humiliation occurs in the last chapter of the book, narrated by the furniture dealer who gives Byron and Lena a ride in his truck, and who camps overnight with them. After the furniture dealer lies down to sleep, he hears their story, and hears Byron trying to persuade Lena to give up. He notices that Byron does not see that she is "smiling a little" (p. 475). Byron gets up and walks away and Lena goes to bed in the truck.

When Byron returns he climbs into the truck to try to have sex with Lena. She practically picks him up and sets him outside, telling him to get some sleep. But she is not angry or disturbed. She speaks to him almost as if she were simply taking care of a child. As the furniture dealer, who is very sympathetic to Byron, tells his wife, "Well, I was downright ashamed to look at him, to let him know that any human man had seen and heard what had happened. I be dog if I didn't want to find the hole and crawl into it with him." He says that if he were Byron he knows that he would feel just about as if he were "waiting for the judge to say, 'Take him out of here and hang him quick'" (p. 477). Faulkner uses similar language to describe Joe's feelings about Joanna's attempts to reject and subjugate him: "He would have died or murdered rather than have anyone, another man, learn what their relations had now become" (p. 256). Both Byron and Joe are rejected and stifled by a woman, and both undergo a terrible struggle as a result. Byron storms off into the woods, and by morning he has not returned. Byron's moral commitment to Lena is not in doubt, is not the issue. It is rather because Lena's needs and the hope she offers exert such a powerful force upon Byron that he faces a different problem. He faces the temptation to feel that his situation is senseless, that he is superfluous, that his actions are trivial or silly.

The consciousness of the implied author includes a strong tendency to admire Byron, as I have pointed out, but it also leaves open the possibility that he is just a clown. The two possibilities are held in suspension, the tension not resolved. Faulkner strongly suggests that Lena is indeed devoted to Byron, and is just being coy: the furniture dealer sees her smiling as Byron tries to persuade her. But her smile is enigmatic. Perhaps she simply depends upon whomever comes along, and really cannot tell the difference between Byron and Lucas. At one point, Faulkner describes her face as having "either nothing in it, or everything, all knowledge" (p. 409).

Byron does not know if Lena will or can accept him. But his sense of obligation will not allow him to leave her, and he has allowed his happiness to depend upon her favor. The possibilities, on the one hand, that he is foolish, and on the other, that what he has done is honorable and will be rewarded, are equally alive in his mind. He is caught between them; he cannot rest, confidently or despairingly, upon either. Byron is not uncertain only about what to expect from Lena, and whether his actions will really make much difference in the long run. These uncertainties are linked to a deeper uncertainty. The issue is not only the importance of love, but the meaning of love. What he confronts is not the question of whether or not he has obligations, or even whether his plans will work out, but whether a life spent fulfilling those obligations is a life he can endure. Can he face Lena's almost absurd coyness? Can he swallow his pride one more time? Can he stand to keep hoping rather than succumbing to grim conscientiousness or simply running away?

Byron has to make a very basic kind of decision that has to do with the most secret and mysterious aspect of human life. I would suggest that in an important sense, Byron's decision is religious. For what he faces is not simply a matter of performing or not performing certain actions, or of having or not having certain feelings, or even of making or not making certain commitments. It is rather a matter of whether he can believe a life of commitment is worth living, or whether he will inwardly flee from the awareness of a reality that demands commitment. Such a flight can take many forms--from the prideful rebellion of Joe to the inward shrinking of Hightower. Byron does not run, or rebel, but returns. We do not get inside of Byron's actual decision any more than we do Joe's. Byron simply appears around the corner the next morning as they slowly drive by, and gets into the truck. "'I done come too far now,' he says. 'I be dog if I'm going to quit now'" (p. 479). Through empathy we sense the issue he faces, but we cannot relive his decision itself. We do not really know why he decides as he does, or why Joe turns, or is turned, so tragically in the opposite direction. The mystery is not only deep, but impenetrable.

The contrast between Byron and Joe might be summed up as that between returning and running. Joe physically runs from the scene of his probable murder of his father, as well as from the dead Joanna. But Faulkner makes it clear that his running is but the reflection of another running that never stops inside of Joe's mind. After having decided to give himself up, he sets off straight through the woods and sits down beside a road. (Byron too emerges from the woods and waits by a road.) He only wants to find out the day of the week, but he manages to scare off a pair of children and a wagon. He thinks:

> 'They all want me to be captured, and then when I come up ready

to say Here I am Yes I would say Here I am I am tired I am tired
of running of having to carry my life like it was a basket of
eggs they all run away.' (p. 319)

The thought, "I am tired of running of having to carry my life like it was a basket of eggs," sums up Joe's final position, and is in poignant contrast to Byron's "I be dog if I am going to quit now." Joe is running away from the same thing Byron has decided to face, and is also tempted to run from. Joe's running originally took the form of pride, as it had for Hightower, McEachern, and Hines. But for Joe, in the end, even the pride becomes unendurable. Joe both shrinks from and tries desperately to subdue the powers that oppress him, but he cannot escape involvement with others, and he cannot escape the need for love. Dropping the eggs may be an image of the inner release involved in depending upon and trusting others, the letting go essential to openness. The eggs suggest a constant, worrisome danger: with the slightest surprise or inattention they will drop and break. For his whole life Joe has had to hold on to something and watch it every moment, as if it would break if he dropped it. The eggs breaking is something too terrible for him even to imagine. Yet he wishes more than anything that he could drop them--he wants to let go.

Joe is not simply in an intolerable situation. His mind is an intolerable situation. At the very core of his personality is an unbearable turbulence. The turbulence cannot be stilled because he is unable to make or face any attachment to another person, believing in the worthwhileness of that attachment; and yet he has literally no place to be except in the world of other people. Some critics claim that Joe "finds peace" at the end, but I do not think this is so.[1] The basket-of-eggs metaphor occurs after Joe has 'calmly' decided to turn himself in, and it is almost the very last empathetic glimpse we have of him. The peace he feels comes from weariness, starvation, and despair; not from any resolution of the awful inner tension he feels. That peace might be compared to the strange peace and emptiness he felt that night long before, laying in bed after McEachern had whipped and starved him all day.

In the depths of our empathy with Joe and Byron, we sense that we are facing a religious problem. But the religious significance of <u>Light in August</u> is not limited to the religious feelings we encounter inside our empathy for the individual characters. Faulkner is always juxtaposing characters; and the overall plot of the novel consists in the juxtaposition and interweaving of the story of Byron and Lena on the one hand with the story of Joe and Joanna on the other. Through the juxtapositions, patterns emerge that suggest certain universals such as the importance of love or the problem of meaning. As the reader senses these patterns, he begins to empathize with the implied author--he begins to re-experience certain feelings about what is important. But a novel is more than a heap of patterns, episodes, and characters. To understand what the author is trying to do, a novel's overall structure must be considered. The overall structure expresses a complex panoramic feeling that is more than the sum of our empathetic experiences of the individual characters, and of the various patterns that reach across those experiences. To re-experience this panoramic feeling is to empathize with the implied author.

The plot structure brings together and juxtaposes, in a strikingly suggestive way, characters who represent radically different human possibilities. Faulkner brings to our attention universal issues that are the most significant anyone can face--love and meaning--and contrasts the tragic with the hopeful, comic possibilities those issues involve. There is something mysterious and riddle-like about the co-existence of personalities doomed to be unable to love, with others who are able to form bonds fidelity and hope for fulfillment in the face of uncertainty and evil. Through the implied author, we sense this mystery. This feeling of mystery is religious because it involves questioning the meaning of a world where tragedy and comedy exist in indissoluble partnership.

I would like to argue that the climax of the plot is not Joe's death in Chapter Nineteen, nor Hightower's change of heart in Chapter Twenty, but Chapter Seventeen, which centers on the birth of Lena's child.[2] Chapters Eighteen through Twenty-One each deal with the fate of individual characters, while Chapter Seventeen juxtaposes all the major characters in the book. The birth scene gathers together all of the major symbols and narrative strands into one unified symbol that sums up the entire novel. Lena's child is born in Joe's cabin behind the ruins of Joanna's house. Hightower acts as midwife while Byron searches frantically for a real doctor. The Hineses are in attendance, and poor Mrs. Hines believes that Lena's child is Joe. Joe is killed the same day. Faulkner wants us to experience the fate of Joe and Joanna as the background of the birth of Lena's child. The function of the whole plot is to bring these radically disparate characters together in Chapter Seventeen. The whole book is focused into this single short episode.

Joe and Joanna seem to live in a different world from Byron and Lena. The two worlds affect one another apparently not at all--each plot runs its independent course. And yet Faulkner is constantly confronting us with the fact that these people do live in the same world. Faulkner brings his characters together mainly through coincidence--but more than coincidence is involved. Although Lena and Joe have no direct impact on each other, their destinies interweave. Lucas has sex with Lena and later comes to Jefferson, where he remains mainly because of Joe. Lena would not have become so involved with Byron if Joe had not been in Jefferson to keep Lucas there, and she would not have found Lucas if Byron, whose last name sounds like Burch, had not been in the same town as Joe. As it happens, Lena arrives in Jefferson the morning after Joanna is killed. The fact that she sees the yellow column of smoke from Joanna's house as she approaches Jefferson in a wagon, and does not take much notice, may not impress the reader at first. But as we learn more about Joe, the significance of the image grows. The smoke is the result of a terrible conflict the possibility of which Lena and the quiet world of the town are unaware. It somehow represents the reality of Joe's world intruding itself upon normality, demanding to be noticed and taken account of. At the end of the first chapter, Lena and Joe are already juxtaposed. The reader can, in retrospect, stand back and survey through this image all that is to come--the opposing destinies of Lena and Joe.

Outside of the flashback, Faulkner presents episodes relating to Joe in constant alternation with those relating to Lena, both within and outside of the experience Byron and Hightower share.[3] And for the whole course of the novel, the reality of Joe's life intrudes itself deeper and deeper into Byron's and Hightower's lives. In Chapter Sixteen, the intrusion is taken a step further. Byron brings the Hineses into Hightower's study to request that Hightower give an alibi for Joe. The presence of Doc Hines in Hightower's study is the most direct and startling intrusion in the novel. Joe's flashback seems to constitute an independent world. But while Faulkner preserves the independence of that world, he links it to the world of the rest of the novel in many ways, as I have tried to show. The Hineses' intrusion may be even more shocking than the shooting and castration of Joe in the same house the next day. Through Byron and Hightower's conversation with the Hineses, the whole tragic story of Joe's childhood unfolds, and Doc Hines emerges for the first time in his full enormity. It is as if Faulkner has been focusing in step by step on the nature of evil, beginning with Hightower and Lucas; moving on to McEachern, Max, and Joe; and finally hitting bottom, as it were, with Doc Hines. By placing the Hineses' narrative after the flashback, Faulkner makes the horror incomparably more intense. The tragedy of Joe's entire life is the direct result of Hines' actions. While Byron and Hightower cannot, of course, empathize with Joe as the reader does, they are certainly aware that Hines is responsible for what Joe is. Hightower responds with an agonized denial, and Byron with that quietness of his, seeming "to muse upon one hand which lies upon his lap, the thumb and forefinger of which rub slowly together with a kneading motion while he appears to watch with a musing absorption" (p. 336).

Faulkner weaves his plot out of the natural consequences of improbable coincidences. The improbable coincidences are that Lena should find Lucas on the very morning after Joanna is killed, and that Joe should end up in Mottstown where his grandparents live. I think the coincidences are believable for the reason that they function very effectively as symbols, and that the meaning of those symbols cannot be reduced to some obvious moral imposed upon the narrative, as I will show. Also, once these improbabilities are accepted, it seems only natural that Lena should move into Joe's cabin, and that the Hineses should come to Jefferson, visit Hightower, and be present at the birth of Lena's child. The entire plot builds up to Chapter Seventeen, which brings all the major characters together, either literally or symbolically. The birth scene sums up and contains all the major juxtapositions of the novel. The birth of Lena's child is literally placed side by side with the scene of Joanna's death. Chapter Seventeen is the absolute center of the novel, not simply because of the importance of Lena's giving birth, but because of the way all of the strands of the story are symbolically brought together in the birth scene, and then unravel from there.

The birth scene, in a sense, contains the entire structure of the novel. Through this scene the reader is enabled to stand back and survey the radically opposed human destinies Faulkner has brought to life. Why Faulkner has brought these people together in the way he has is far from obvious; and yet the question insistently presents itself. The overall juxtaposition has a powerful effect above and beyond the impact of each individual character and plot line. The individual destinies are brought together like the terms of a metaphor. The whole constellation evokes something new, a feeling of background even deeper and more elusive than the aura of significance associated with an individual character or universal theme. This feeling is very difficult to describe and very easy to over-interpret. _Light in August_ definitely adds up to something, aims at something; and yet that something slips away the moment one tries to grasp it. The aim of a work such as _Light in August_ is not to state anything directly or make a definite avowal.

Art is concerned with precisely the kind of experience that cannot be straightforwardly expressed or directly communicated. Joseph Conrad wrote that the aim of art "like life itself, is inspiring, difficult--obscured by mists. It is not in the clear logic of a triumphant conclusion."[4] I want to indicate how the final aim of _Light in August_ is to evoke a feeling of mystery that has religious significance, even though that feeling does not contain, even implicitly, any triumphant religious conclusion. There is an inherent problem in such an attempt. For I propose to talk directly about what I claim can only be communicated indirectly. Objective discussion is bound to distort the meaning of a work. It is almost impossible even to remember the subtle empathetic experience in which <u>Light in August</u> consists. But surely people can make statements <u>about</u> that experience, some more accurate than others. And it is possible to make more or less accurate statements about what that experience is not.

As I have pointed out, the perspective Byron and Hightower share tends to unify the novel. Byron and Hightower have to come to terms emotionally with the very existence of Lena, Joe, and the Hineses, in addition to struggling with the problem of what they can bring themselves to do to help them. In Chapter Sixteen, Hightower can only listen as the Hineses tell their story, aided by Byron. In Chapter Seventeen, Byron and Hightower are both active, and the scene in the cabin is described twice, once from Byron's and once from Hightower's point of view. As the chapter begins, Byron is rushing to get something done: first to find Hightower and then to get a real doctor. Throughout the novel we get the picture of Byron hurrying from place to place, trying to arrange things for Lena, and in the end for Joe also. Byron's activity at this point typifies his character. The scene appears first from Byron's point of view, as he arrives with the doctor. The doctor mistakes the Hineses for the grandparents. Doc Hines is asleep on one cot, Lena is on the other, and Mrs. Hines is holding the baby. Mrs. Hines believes that Lena is Milly and the baby is Joey. The second time, the actual birth scene appears from Hightower's perspective. We learn that Mrs. Hines had

> snatched the still unbreathing child and held it aloft, glaring
> at the old sleeping man on the other cot with the face of a
> tiger. Then the child breathed and cried, and the woman seemed
> to answer it, also in no known tongue, savage and triumphant.
> (p. 381)

It is as if the tragic conflict between man and woman has finally been resolved in favor of woman. There is something archetypal about the scene. We seem to see the triumph of a mother's selfless love over death-dealing pride, the victory of an elemental principle of life.

Lena and Mrs. Hines are in many respects quite similar. Both seem to embody an elemental life-giving force in nature. Both exhibit an astounding persistence in their search for someone: Lena for her child's father, Mrs. Hines for her grandchild. Both find the person they are looking for through a series of strange coincidences. And both may well appear to be somewhat absurd. I have already described Lena's absurdly naive confidence that things will work out, and her blind trust in Lucas. Faulkner consistently describes Mrs. (as well as Doc) Hines in comic terms, with her purple dress, and the plume on her hat that bobs as she walks. The umbrella she carries adds to the effect (Lena also carries a parasol). The Hineses are "puppetlike" and absurdly fat (p. 348). Hightower cannot suppress his laughter as he first sees them through his study window. There is nothing more absurd, and nothing more poignant, than that she should get Joey mixed up with Lena's child in her mind.

The birth scene does portray something very like a victory. Even though Mrs. Hines is mixed up, her joy is real, and is really justified. But in the midst of the victory, we are not allowed to forget the tragedy. Life may have triumphed today--but only in Mrs. Hines' imagination has Joey gotten a second chance to be born. Faulkner does suggest that there is something strangely true about Mrs. Hines' belief that Lena's child is Joey--but however strangely true her belief may be, it is also pitiful and absurd.

When Mrs. Hines looks down at the baby and says, "it's Joey [. . .] It's my Milly's little boy" (p. 376), the two plot-lines are juxtaposed more subtly than anywhere else in the novel. The juxtaposition involves not two different people or things, but two different perceptions about one person. The two perceptions are juxtaposed even inside Lena's mind. After listening to Mrs. Hines all day, Lena gets confused too, starting, herself, to think that Christmas is the father, as Mrs. Hines must now be claiming.

Mrs. Hines' statement intensely focuses the novel on a single point. At most places in the novel, one plot-line is in the foreground, and the other in the background of the reader's consciousness. But here, the two worlds practically merge; it is difficult to say which is background and which is foreground. The scene is also full of more clear-cut oppositions. There is irony in the fact that Mrs. Hines should mistake the baby for Joey while surrounded by signs and reminders of the real Joe and his deeds. They are in his cabin, Lena has given birth, very likely, on his bed, upon which Joanna had sat and talked and left a note. They are right next to the site of Joanna's house, burnt down because of what Joe had done. The birth scene is infused with a background of murder and despair. This background is not simply a feeling of depth that extends back continuously from the foreground. There is a tension between background and foreground that cannot be resolved or ignored. The background does not blend harmoniously, but represents a perplexing contrast.

Joe's world is not merely implicitly present in the birth scene--the tension is increased a hundredfold by the actual presence of the Hineses.

There is something indescribably moving about the juxtaposition of the evil potency in Hines with Lena. The joy that is present is given a new dimension by our sense of the horror that has been avoided. Byron and Lena's love, however comical it may seem at times, means something more when we realize that Joey might as well have been Lena's child. We realize that the whole tragedy of the kind of person Joe was doomed to become depended directly on the lack of exactly what Byron and Lena represent. The birth scene adds a new dimension to our feeling for the importance of love. But the purpose of the scene, and of the novel, is not simply to evoke a universal meaning that recurs in the most varied circumstances. The reader is also confronted with the sheer fact that particular people, each with his or her individual destiny, exist together in the same world, the same community, the same room. The contrasting destinies seem to represent the very limits of human possibility. Faulkner is striving not only after universality, but comprehensiveness.

A novel needs to be believable and convincing. We experience a a novel's believability through empathetic feeling rather than by considering some kind of objectively definable evidence. But a novel is convincing not simply because it contains convincing characters. The novel must present a believable world. A world is somehow more than just a set of characters who do certain things. As we read any good novel, we do not somehow infer that its world is believable; rather, a feeling steals over us that the author has securely anchored his characters in a single, believable world. We take this feeling of 'being in a world' for granted, but there is really nothing more subtle and elusive. The world of a novel is convincing and aesthetically coherent if we readers, through empathy with the implied author, sense a deep, indefinable sameness that our experience of the fictional world shares with our experience of the real world. That sameness cannot be reduced to the sameness universal themes represent. The sameness can finally only be described as the quality of being a world. The total structure of Light in August does succeed in evoking this quality of 'world,' but it does so in a very unusual way.

One remarkable quality of any vivid feeling of background is that, while there is no way definitely to characterize it and distinguish it from other feelings of background, it *is* unique. The aura of significance associated with different characters and different symbols does not extend out into a uniform, characterless haze. Similarly, the feeling of 'world' one great novel evokes will be different from that evoked by another, even though we recognize that they both share a profound sameness with the real world. The remarkable fact about Light in August is that Faulkner manages to evoke at least two clearly distinct such feelings of 'world.' The metaphorical statement that Joe's flashback presents us with a different world from the rest of the novel is apt. The flashback is almost like a different novel. Observing this duality, some critics have judged that Light in August lacks aesthetic unity. I have been trying to point out many of the ways the two 'worlds' are very closely linked together. But however much the worlds may have in common, however closely they may be linked, Faulkner still wants to make it clear that they really do not fit together. The discord and tension between the two worlds are intentional.

In a more conventional novel, it is much easier to imagine all of the characters together. A certain atmosphere seems to pervade the novel from beginning to end; certain boundaries are not overstepped; the characters seem to inhabit a common world. A novel by Jane Austen or Henry James would probably fit this description. The unity of atmosphere these novelists create offers an aesthetic comfort. But Faulkner offers the reader no single, unified feeling of atmosphere. Our basic feeling for the world Joe inhabits exists in sharp juxtaposition with our feeling for the world the other central characters such as Byron, Lena, and Hightower inhabit. Such a juxtaposition lends Light in August a comprehensiveness that simpler novels lack. And the comprehensiveness has a certain religious significance: by refusing to provide the reader with the unified feeling of atmosphere he desires, Faulkner evokes a feeling of questioning about the world itself.

The feeling of mystery Faulkner evokes is not just a luminous aura naturally resting in the background. A juxtaposition forces itself vividly on the reader's attention and at the same time frustrates his powers of imagination. Faulkner creates feelings of atmosphere that are profoundly alive and convincing. But he also wants to confront us with the limits of such feelings. He wants to suggest that the world is more than can be encompassed inside a feeling of 'world' that is within our imaginative grasp.

It seems as if each world ought to occupy the whole picture, and the mind rebels at seeing them placed relentlessly side by side. The overall juxtaposition has the effect of a paradox that cannot be resolved but must be resolved. The juxtaposition evokes a sense of something more--and that more is not only deep, but also impenetrable. This feeling of 'more' might be compared to the feeling of having a name on the tip of your tongue-- except that the name is permanently and absolutely stuck there. The sense of 'more' is pervaded by expectancy and power, as well as frustration and unease, but the expectancy is held in suspension, and the thing expected is maddeningly elusive.[5]

The totality of juxtapositions, summed up in Chapter Seventeen, becomes a metaphor for the world, for the world that every man faces. The reader perceives this metaphor through the implied author. While the reader is unlikely ever directly to encounter events as bizarre as those in Light in August, he recognizes that the world he faces through empathy is the same as his own world. Faulkner has somehow managed to express the essence of the human condition. This essence is not definable, and is sensed only at the very limits of human feeling. The feeling for the human condition Faulkner evokes is accessible only through the particular symbols he uses. Were someone to ask Faulkner what the point of Light in August was, Faulkner could really do little more than point to Lena giving birth in Joe's cabin and say "life is like that." But we can ask what makes such a response appropriate. Why do statements about Light in August tend to become statements about 'life' or 'the human condition'?

The fact that Faulkner's vision is comprehensive cannot literally mean that it includes everything. Faulkner's overall metaphor has to be specific and limited in order to succeed; it is not an encyclopedic definition but a symbol that evokes a vast background. We sense the comprehensiveness as a direction in which the symbol is headed, without being able to define its destination. In basic terms, Faulkner succeeds in evoking a sense of comprehensiveness by developing two equally convincing plot-lines, one comic and one tragic, and linking them together in a convincing way. Faulkner is honest about the human situation. He does not hedge. He recognizes the extremes that are possible, and carries each to its conclusion.

Faulkner begins with a certain person, such as Joe, evoking a feeling for the essence of his character. The plot which includes his action and fate is complete and convincing because we feel that that essence has been given full expression. Faulkner allows Joe's inner destiny to work itself out--his fictional presentation is not taken off course by the intrusion of irrelevant episodes. It is unlikely that Faulkner would have been guilty of sentimentality, but it is theoretically possible that he could have spoiled the novel in a number of ways. Faulkner might have killed the McEacherns off when Joe was about twelve, and had Joe adopted by far kindlier people. After a struggle, Joe's new parents might have straightened him out, enabling him to lead a normal life from then on. There would be nothing necessarily implausible or even obviously sentimental about such a turn of events at all. Joe's story, so altered, could still be a sober and realistic narrative. But such a development would radically narrow the novel; it would destroy the novel's comprehensiveness. Even though the story might remain plausible in terms of the characters, it would become, in a sense, less honest about the human condition. The tragic possibility would not have been brought to completion. In this altered version, we would feel that Faulkner was hedging, that his story lacked bite and direction, that it did not make a forceful point. The story might avoid cloying sentimentality; but it would not be nearly as serious, and it certainly would not be great.

On the other hand, if Faulkner had left Joe's story basically intact, but had given it a happy ending, the effect would certainly be embarrassingly implausible and sentimental. Joe might have gone along with Joanna's plan to reform him, or have gone to jail and become a model prisoner. Perhaps Joe could be cured by a particularly gifted social worker or psychologist, or reformed as a result of a religious conversion. I realize that these revisions of the story would be aesthetic absurdities, but the question is, why would they ruin the novel? The problem with a happy ending imposed on a tragedy is that it is dishonest. A sentimental happy ending fails to take seriously the depth of the impact of evil, and stymies the tendency in tragedy toward comprehensiveness, the tendency to search out the full range of significant possibilities in the human condition, including the extremes. Faulkner achieves comprehensiveness by not shrinking either from authentic tragedy or authentic comedy.

Faulkner juxtaposes a tragic plot with a comic plot just as complete, as serious, and as convincing. The juxtaposition creates a comprehensiveness greater than that possible for a tragic or a comic plot alone. Neither plot overpowers the other--they exist in a kind of precarious balance. The reader may not know whether to laugh or to cry-- and he may very likely do both at once. The juxtaposition of comedy and tragedy produces a unique effect. Each seems to subtly qualify the other while retaining its own integrity. The hope in Byron and Lena's situation does not make Joe's life any less hopeless--nor does the reality of Joe's tragedy somehow spoil Byron and Lena's success. And yet neither feels quite the same to the reader for the presence of the other.

The juxtaposition of the two worlds evokes a feeling of questioning about the one world in which both belong. Neither 'world' alone is enough. Only a paradoxical contrast, a balance of opposite emotional responses, can begin to do justice to the nature of the world. But the paradox is unresolved. The juxtaposition moves in the direction of doing justice to the nature of the world, but the sense of expectancy evoked about what the world is and means is held in suspension. We experience a tendency but not a fulfillment. We experience a feeling of questioning that leads beyond our experience of the individual characters, and that our experience of the characters in their particular interrelation evokes. It may be that the questioning concerns the meaning of a world in which such characters can exist side by side.

Byron and Joe confront the question of whether they can believe their lives have meaning. But the question of meaning in *Light in August* is not limited to the problem that each character faces of the meaning of his own individual existence. Even if Byron does 'find meaning,' the fact that Joe is shut off from meaning somehow calls the meaning of Byron's life into question. The opposite is also true: the relative success of Byron and Lena calls the meaninglessness of Joe's and Joanna's lives into question, without diminishing their tragedy in the slightest. Byron's decision to endure cannot totally resolve the problem of meaning even for him. He knows that Lena, Joe, and the Hineses exist. He has allowed their lives to intrude upon his own. Through empathy one discovers not merely that people face the same universal issues. The empathy between characters that we re-experience, and the empathy that links us to the characters and the implied author, includes this deeper dimension of *intrusion*. Intrusion means not just evoking sympathy; it means that one senses another's actual fate as somehow being one's own, and not just possibly one's own. The question of meaning I face is never just the question of the meaning of *my* life. The issue of the meaning of *anyone's* life intrudes itself into mine. I cannot solve the question of meaning alone, for myself. Faulkner's juxtapositions evoke just this feeling of a common human fate. Facing a common fate means more than just facing the same universal issues. May not the subtle way the comic and tragic plot lines affect each other in our minds come down to the feeling that human fates cannot be insulated from one another? It is not just that no one can escape acting and being acted upon; the very existence of one tragic life affects or questions the meaning of every other life, however fortunate.

The panoramic feeling in the consciousness of the implied author provides yet another perspective on the question of meaning. The overall structure of <u>Light in August</u> raises the question of the meaning of the world. Through empathy, we recognize that the world of the novel is, in a profound way, the same world that we are actually involved in. The totality of what I face intrudes upon me just as deeply as the individual fate of any other human being. One cannot separate the meaning of the totality from the meaning of one's own existence.

The response to the totality Faulkner evokes is ambiguous. The tragedy and the absurdity the characters encounter, and that we encounter in the characters, evokes a tendency to feel that such a world cannot be faced, or is not worth facing. But even within a totally tragic character, such as Joe or Mrs. Hines, we sense a rebellion against this tendency. They have a blind will to endure, to refuse to succumb to the nameless threat to which everything tells them they must succumb. The tragic characters themselves do not represent the alternative of sheer meaninglessness, any more than the comic characters unambiguously represent the alternative of meaning. The possibility of hope and love in Byron and Lena's situation does evoke a tendency to feel that a world in which such things are possible can be faced, is worth living in. But Faulkner will not allow our minds to rest upon this comforting alternative. The possibility is open that Byron and Lena are simply absurd. And the tendency to which they give rise, to affirm the whole, does not cancel out the opposite tendency. We cannot understand how the two tendencies can coexist. Yet we can dismiss neither one. The paradox baffles feeling as much as intellect.[6]

The aim of my analysis of Light in August has been to show how all aspects of the aesthetic form of the novel work together to evoke the religious feeling I have just described. Our experience of this feeling depends, first of all, on our empathy with the characters. In Chapter One I attempted to show how Faulkner makes this most basic level of empathy possible, and that the understanding of a character we gain through empathy must be distinguished from the kind of understanding an objective explanation aims at. In Chapter Two, I introduced the question of empathy with the implied author, and suggested that empathy with characters already depends on this higher level of empathy. Through consistent patterns of characterization Light in August invites the reader to experience not only what is important to, but what is important about, the characters. Patterns that run through our experience of all the characters evoke a feeling for what is of universal importance in their lives: the issues of love and meaning. The sense of universality a novel evokes is not a matter of definite concepts or moral commitments the author presents or espouses, but emerges only in the vague background of the reader's empathetic awareness. Faulkner does not directly address the reader, but creates an overall emotional perspective with which the reader may empathize.

The overall perspective in Light in August is not merely universal, but comprehensive. Faulkner creates a feeling of comprehensiveness by convincingly developing the alternative possibilities inherent in the universals: the possibilities of hope versus no hope, of comedy versus tragedy. In the progression of episodes these extreme alternatives are consistently juxtaposed so that the reader always experiences either one as the background of the other. The climactic birth scene focuses all the juxtapositions into a single powerful image, and in a sense contains the entire structure of the novel. The panoramic feeling this scene evokes involves a sense of the mysteriousness of a world in which such contrasts can exist. The scene, and the novel as a whole, awaken in the reader's mind the question of the meaning of such a world, but do not resolve the question, or provide any unambiguous relief from the unease the question creates.

Some critics take a very different view, claiming that the final effect of Light in August is affirmative. Robert Slabey calls attention to some of the same aspects of Light in August that I have: the contrast between the comic and the tragic plots, the significance of the identification of Joe with Lena's baby, the issue of the meaning of the whole. Slabey also points out many analogies in Light in August to various ancient myths. Slabey has a certain theory of the meaning of myth that he applies to Light in August.[7]

In my treatment of the juxtaposition of the comic and the tragic plots, I pointed out that the two plots react with one another to produce a unique effect, while their opposition is not resolved. But Slabey claims that in Light in August, as in mythology, the opposition has been definitely transcended. The comic and tragic elements are swept up in an all-encompassing, almost mystical, world-affirmation. Slabey attaches great importance to the fact that the novel ends with Lena. Slabey refers to Joseph Campbell's book, The Hero with a Thousand Faces, in this connection. According to Campbell,

> The happy ending of the fairy tale, the myth, and the divine comedy of the soul, is to be read, not as a contradiction, but as a transcendence of the universal tragedy of man [. . .] The dreadful mutilations are then seen as shadows, only, of an immanent, imperishable eternity.[8]

For Slabey, Lena represents this eternity.

> Lena, involved in but somehow above and unmoved by birth and death, represents a primordial image and ancient and lasting truths about existence, perhaps more Oriental than Western--life as a rhythmic cycle of births and rebirths and "the peace that passeth understanding."

Slabey finds the final effect of Light in August "both meaningful and affirmative."[9] Lena reveals a deeper truth that supposedly encompasses horror and tragedy without denying them.

What kind of claim are Slabey and Campbell really making? They find, immanent in mythology and Light in August a certain kind of pantheistic, quasi-mystical religious belief, and not merely the religious problem of meaning. Apparently, Light in August is supposed to be communicating a definite affirmative stance toward the world. That stance might be expressed in a statement such as the following: The world is meaningful and the existence of and individual in the world is worthwhile. The boundless creativity and natural innocence present in the world reveal that meaning to us and point to something eternal. Evil, death, and destruction are an essential part of that meaning too. They fit into the whole in a way we cannot rationally understand, but can mystically intuit through the "totality of the revelation which is life."[10] Slabey apparently holds that the mystical message is immanent in the plot structure, with its mythic significance. And Slabey would probably also agree that the mystic significance immanent in the symbolism and plot structure of Light in August cannot be adequately captured in a consistent set of objective propositions. Slabey certainly does not claim to see clear logic in the meaning of Light in August, but he does find a triumphant conclusion.

Slabey would probably not disagree that literary meaning is communicated through empathy. In drawing his parallels to myths Slabey concentrates intensely on the characters' experiences. My question is, can a religious stance, a religious commitment, be communicated through empathy?

To affirm is to take a stand; it is to claim that the position you take is true and right. The affirmation Slabey describes involves seeing through mere appearances to the inner nature of reality. Beyond the creation and destruction of forms lies the "Peace that passeth understanding," and by loving the universe, man can sense that peace and affirm the meaning of his existence. If I read Slabey correctly, he is claiming that Faulkner's intention in writing <u>Light in August</u> is to implicitly communicate just this affirmation. In my terms, Slabey must be claiming that the affirmation is communicated through the consciousness of the implied author. The affirmation is not supposed to be an abstract statement, but a deeply felt experience that arises naturally out of the fictional form itself. But does it make sense to speak of reliving an affirmation, of empathizing with a commitment?

I have been arguing that the relation of a symbol to reality is indirect. Through empathy, one recognizes something deeply in common between a character's experience and one's own life, and between a novel's overall vision and the real world one actually confronts. This sense of something in common is what makes a novel believable and significant. It is because a symbol or a characterization can evoke a feeling of reality in the background that a symbol can be called 'true' and a characterization 'true to life.' But reality is only in the background; it is not directly addressed.

Artistic form has the remarkable ability of enabling one to relive a particular concrete experience someone else has already created and lived through. One's experience becomes simultaneously one's own and not one's own. Empathy involves the reality of one's personal existence as a human being, but shifts that reality to the background. One does not focus upon one's own identity; rather, one allows that identity to blend with another's. But in making an affirmation, one's relation to reality is direct. One is not concerned merely with the vague sense of sameness in the background of an empathetic experience. One's own personal existence moves into the foreground. One addresses reality directly, and adopts a definite position in regard to reality. Such a position may not be explicitly or conceptually definable, but it is definitely an affirmation and not a denial or an evasion or a wavering attitude. In taking a religious stance, one goes beyond the feeling of implicit sameness with another present in empathy, and asks directly, "who am I and what do I affirm?". If one should happen to take the same stance as somebody else, one may be said to 'share' a commitment--but such sharing is not a matter of empathy.

Artistic form enables us to empathize--but making a commitment is not a matter of reliving someone else's experience. This means that in reliving someone else's experience, we cannot be reliving the making of a commitment. The feeling of reality evoked by artistic form is available only through our experience of some particular aesthetic whole. But the reality one faces and affirms through a religious commitment is independent of any particular aesthetic experience. A story may seem real and convincing, but in taking a stance, one must face reality directly, and not simply through a story. In making a commitment, one must step outside of one's experience of literary meaning.

Slabey seems to be holding that the meaning of *Light in August* is an affirmation. What such a position could possibly mean is very unclear. My explication of his position would be that the implied author makes a religious affirmation and the reader, through empathy, sees the truth of this affirmation. According to Slabey, *Light in August* "reveal[s] 'the eternal joy of existence'."[11] If my understanding of empathy and commitment is correct, Slabey's position is almost nonsensical. (I refer to Slabey's literary critical, not his religious, position.) One consequence of Slabey's view may be that the empathy involved in the experience of imaginative literature is a kind of mystical experience that constitutes enlightenment. I hold that the experience of making a commitment is impenetrable. We simply cannot get that far into the author's mind through empathy.

Commitments are communicated through explicit statement. When we understand the explicit statement of a commitment, we do not relive the author's experience of making that commitment. An explicit statement of a commitment does not invite us to relive another's experience--it focuses attention directly on the reader's own personal existence and challenges him to make his own decision. Slabey's interpretation of *Light in August* in fact includes many such statements of commitment. Perhaps he has confused what may well be his own commitments with the meaning of *Light in August* because the novel has somehow inspired or confirmed those commitments. Such a reaction is natural because there is a relation between commitment and aesthetic feeling. A novel such as *Light in August* makes us feel the importance of religious problems and evokes tendencies to affirm the world as well as to despair of its meaning.

But one must be cautious even about statements such as '*Light in*

August poses a religious problem,' or 'Light in August confronts us with the the problem of the meaning of the world.' Even the statement 'There is a problem of the world's meaning, and everyone must face that problem' is a direct assertion. 'If the meaning of any man's life is in doubt, the meaning of every man's life is in doubt' is another direct assertion. In Light in August, the religious problem is only hinted at. Light in August does not focus our attention on the problem; rather, it suggests a feeling of questioning that leads away from the particular. The novel suggests a feeling of questioning, not a specific question. Posing a question involves judging that certain terms are the best ones in which to frame the question. No definite question can do justice to the feeling of questioning. The use of quasi-philosophical terms such as 'meaning,' or 'world,' or 'the nature of things,' or 'the human condition,' or 'the way things are,' or even just 'reality' or 'life' is a little misleading. All of these words represent attempts to name, to deal directly with, what a work such as Light in August only hints at.

A literary work of art does no more than hint at something that cannot be straightforwardly expressed or directly communicated. What does it mean to hint? Hinting involves no clear assertion about *what* is being hinted at. Hinting does not even involve a definite assertion *that* there is something to which the hinting points. Hinting means suggestion and not assertion. Feeling a hint is an experience of possibility, of expectancy, of tendency; it is not the belief that something is possible, that there is something to be expected. But the experience of background is not meaningless. Some explicit statements do seem more appropriate than others, even though all explicit statements are more or less inappropriate. I have tried to present such a valid interpretation. Light in August evokes a feeling for the human condition: the common human fate of living in a world whose meaning is in question, and a world that calls the meaning of one's own existence into question. But <u>Light in August</u>, as a work of art, stops short of actually posing the question of meaning.

NOTES TO CHAPTER THREE

¹For example, see Olga Vickery, The Novels of William Faulkner (Baton Rouge: Louisiana State Univ. Press, 1964), p. 73.

²Both Pitavy and Benson suggest that Hightower's change of heart is the climax of the novel. Francois Pitavy, Faulkner's "Light in August", tr. Gillian E. Cook (Bloomington: Indiana Univ. Press, 1973), chap. 2; Carl Benson, "Thematic Design in "Light in August," in William Faulkner: Four Decades of Criticism, ed. Linda Wagner (East Lansing: Michigan State Univ. Press, 1973).

³Pitavy calls attention to the "contrapuntal" structure of the plot, pp. 45-47.

⁴Joseph Conrad, "Preface to The Nigger of the Narcissus," in Discussions of the Novel, ed. Roger Sale (Boston: Heath, 1960), p. 93. In a similar vein, Goethe, discussing Faust, remarks that while his work contains many insoluble problems, "so wird es doch gewiss denjenigen erfreuen, der sich auf Miene, Wink, und leise Hindeutung versteht"--it will please whoever has a sense for gesture, hint, and subtle indication. Letter to Sulpiz Boisserée, September 8, 1831, quoted in Goethes Werke, vol. 3, ed. Erich Trunz (Hamburg, Wegner, 1959), p. 458. Goethe makes essentially the same remark in a letter to Heinrich Meyer, July 20, 1831, p. 457.

⁵I am here drawing on William James' notions of the 'more' and of religious unease, as he develops them in The Principles of Psychology, vol. 1 (New York: Dover, 1950), pp. 249-60, and in The Varieties of Religious Experience (New York: Random House, n.d.), esp. pp. 497-509. I am also drawing on the notion of 'world' Heidegger develops in "Der Ursprung des Kunstwerkes," in Holzwege (Frankfurt: Klostermann, 1950), pp. 7-68; translated as "The Origin of the Work of Art" by Albert Hofstadter, in Poetry, Language, Thought (New York: Harper, 1971), pp. 15-88. According to Heidegger, "Welt ist nie ein Gegenstand, der vor uns steht und angeschaut werden kann. Welt ist immer das Ungegenständliche, dem wir unterstehen, solange die Bahnen von Geburt und Tod, Segen und Fluch uns in das Sein entrückt halten. Wo die wesenhaften Entscheidungen unserer Geschichte fallen, von uns übernommen und verlassen, verkannt und wieder erfragt werden, da weltet die Welt" (p. 33). "World is never an object that stands before us and can be seen. World is the ever non-objective to which we are subject as long as the paths of birth and death, blessing and curse keep us transported into Being. Wherever those decisions of our history that relate to our very being are made, are taken up and abandoned by us, go unrecognized and are rediscoverd by new inquiry, there the world worlds" pp. 44-45. A work of art presences world without turning it into an object--or, we might say, allows the background to appear as background in its full liveliness. Heidegger's statement that the world worlds through "die wesenhaften Entscheidungen unserer Geschichte" may be congruent with my interpretation of plot climax as evoking the feeling of 'world.'

⁶According to Walter Slatoff, "As in The Sound and the Fury and As I Lay Dying, we are left with highly mixed feelings about the significance

and worth of the human agony and struggle we have witnessed." But Slatoff critcizes Faulkner for failing to commit himself. <u>Quest for Failure: A Study of William Faulkner</u> (Ithaca, N.Y.: Cornell Univ. Press, 1960), p. 196.

[7] Robert Slabey, "Myth and Ritual in <u>Light in August</u>," in <u>Studies in "Light in August"</u>, ed. M. Thomas Inge (Columbus, Ohio: Merrill, 1971), pp. 75-97.

[8] Ibid. p. 97.

[9] Ibid. p. 97-98.

[10] Ibid. p. 98.

[11] Ibid.

PART TWO

CHAPTER IV

From Faulkner to Dostoyevsky:

Two Kinds of Religious Experience in the Novel

The overall aim of Part One (Chapters One, Two, and Three) was to describe the way Faulkner, through his novel Light in August, evokes a certain kind of religious feeling. My central conclusion was that this feeling must be carefully distinguished from all ideas one may have about it, or objective descriptions one may make of it, as well as from all religious commitments. The aim of literary art, I have suggested, is precisely to evoke that most basic level of concrete feeling that is prior to all explicit ideas, judgments, and commitments. But the example of The Idiot, I think, shows that religious reflection and commitment may nevertheless have a role to play in the meaning of a successful novel. In this chapter, I will try to define that role.

The novel Light in August, as a whole, evokes a feeling of 'world,' or 'the nature of things,' or 'the way things are,' and also evokes a feeling of questioning about the meaning of the world. I am willing to call this feeling religious. Faulkner evokes a religious feeling, but does not include any extended discussions, either by characters or the narrator, of such ideas as 'the meaning of life,' 'the nature of things,' or of 'God' or 'the world.' Faulkner evokes only the non-objective experience pregnant with the possibility of such explicit notions. Religious experience does not begin with explicit ideas about the universe or God, or with overt statements of belief in particular philosophical or religious versions of ultimate reality. Faulkner evokes the first beginning of religious experience in our sensitive awareness of the world of other people, an awareness that comes to life prior to all our judgments, ideas, and commitments.

The most obvious difference between <u>Light in August</u> and <u>The Idiot</u> is that the latter work contains a great deal of explicit discussion of religious ideas, including many overt expressions of religious commitment. But if, as I have claimed, the aim of literary art is to evoke feeling, what role can commitments and ideas possibly play in the empathetic experience literary art evokes? The answer I propose is that, in a work such as <u>The Idiot</u>, we experience the overtly stated religious commitments and ideas of the characters as responses to religious feelings, and that this is possible partly because feelings contain tendencies toward ideas, judgments, and commitments. Through empathy, we cannot experience commitments as true; <u>The Idiot</u>, as an aesthetic whole, includes a range of alternative possibilities for the truth, including the possibility that no commitment is meaningful.[1] Dostoyevsky makes it possible for us to relive his implied author's experience of the human condition as including important and conflicting alternatives for religious commitment. Feelings of tendency, arising as an aspect of our empathy with the implied author, constitute our response to commitments, which cannot themselves be relived. Dostoyevsky does not preach to us: rather, he evokes a feeling for the concrete situation in which religious commitments arise, and he brings to the fore opposing possibilities for commitment that will not go away.

Dostoyevsky's evocation of the religious feeling of the problem of the meaning of the world is similar to Faulkner's, but with this difference: Dostoyevsky consistently includes that religious feeling within the experience of his characters, and presents their struggle to respond to that feeling with ideas and commitments. My aim in this chapter and the following is to explore the techniques Dostoyevsky employs to convincingly integrate religious feelings and commitments into his characters' experience. I will attempt to define Dostoyevsky's special techniques of characterization by comparing them to Faulkner's.

In order to understand the role of religious commitment in The Idiot it may be helpful to define religious commitment more closely than I have done so far. H. Richard Niebuhr, in his book Radical Monotheism and Western Culture, offers a succinct account of religious commitment as a universal human reality. Three basic points he makes about religious faith are especially relevant to the problem at hand:

(1) Religious faith has to do with the meaning of life. As Niebuhr puts it, religious faith is "the faith that life is worth living, or better, the reliance on certain centers of value as able to bestow significance and worth on our existence."[2] The God of Christianity and Judaism is only one such possible center of value. Other centers, other 'gods' upon which people have relied include nation, community, the home, the family, truth, beauty, and the self.

(2) According to Niebuhr, faith "is not intellectual assent to the truth of certain propositions, but a personal, practical trusting in, reliance on, counting upon something."[3] Ideas about, for example, God, or the objective assertion that God exists, must be distinguished from the experience of actual reliance upon God as the source of life's worthwhileness. Such reliance is a concrete experience: it is the definite taking of a position in the sense of devoting one's life to a cause. Such devotion is prior to all ideas and propositional assertions about that cause. Such loyalty to and trust in a cause, Niebuhr claims, is the foundation of personal identity. Unlike the mere affirmation of

propositions, loyalty to and trust in a cause inwardly shapes and directs a person's life. A question that might be raised about Niebuhr's viewpoint is that of how, and whether, we can know that the inward commitment that shapes a person's identity is the same as the one explicitly expressed through a creed.

(3) Religious faith can be our response to the human situation in its fullness, although it is not that in every case. Niebuhr emphasizes the fact that the many centers of value upon which we rely are subject to change, conflict, and destruction. For Niebuhr, the realization of the tragic relativity of all that we rely upon is the primary religious experience. The fact of the human condition we must all confront is that we are drawn toward reliance upon and fidelity to values whose fate is always uncertain and that seem doomed to ultimate frustration in death. "What is it that is responsible for this passing, that dooms our human faith to frustration?" Niebuhr asks.

> We may call it the nature of things, we may call it fate, we may call it reality. But by whatever name we call it, this law of things, this reality, this way things are, is something with which we all must reckon. We may not be able to give a name to it, calling it only the "void" out of which everything comes and to which everything returns, though that also is a name.[4]

Niebuhr is not yet referring to the God of monotheistic religions. He is rather attempting to name, and to make assertions about, what he takes to be a universal human experience, an experience of "the last shadowy and vague reality," against which "there is no defense." I think Niebuhr is pointing to essentially the same kind of experience that Faulkner evokes through <u>Light in August</u>: a sense of the problematic and mysterious nature of things. Faulkner too seems to ask, how can life be worthwhile in a world that holds out the possibility of love and meaning to some but is always ready to withdraw that possibility from anyone for no comprehensible reason? The experience of 'the nature of things' raises the question of what man can rely upon to give meaning and worth to human existence. But unlike Niebuhr in his philosophical and theological reflections, Faulkner in his novel Light in August does not reflect explicitly on 'the nature of things' or propose some form of religious faith as a response. Faulkner instead evokes the rare, elusive experience that gives rise to such reflection and response.

In Chapter Three, I pointed out that in Light in August there is a difference between the religious experience evoked through the overall perspective of the implied author and that of the characters. The entire structure of the novel evokes an elusive sense of the paradoxical nature of things, but there are only certain occasional indications that certain characters (such as Byron and Hightower) share such an experience. The central issue in the lives of Byron, Hightower, and Joe is whether they can accept involvement in the lives of others. The decision to accept or reject such involvement, I claimed, may be considered a religious one, since it involves either confidence or despair that a life of involvement can be worth living. We sense that Byron and Joe face, in an essential way, what we face in life, and we confront their responses to what they face. In a sense, their decisions are religious commitments. Byron faces the issue of whether involvement in the world is meaningful in spite of the trouble and humiliation it involves. In deciding to stick with Lena, he decides such involvement is worthwhile, and thereby decides something about the world. But there is another, more specific kind of religious commitment Faulkner does not include in the experience of his characters.

Faulkner does not emphasize Byron's experience of the problem of the meaning of the world the implied author senses; Faulkner does not present any character's (except perhaps Hightower's) attempt to respond to that experience with ideas about the nature of things; and Faulkner does not include the further kind of response Niebuhr makes--an inward, abiding commitment distinct from decisions made in response to particular situations one faces in the world. Faulkner does not assert that there is some cause that gives life meaning for Byron. Lena does not make life meaningful for him--she is not his goddess. Rather, he finds commitment to her to be meaningful, and the reason he is able to find meaning in commitment, the reason he is able to 'endure,' Faulkner allows to remain a mystery.

Characters in <u>Light in August</u> do not explicitly reflect upon the nature of things and respond with assertions, such as the following one Niebuhr makes:

> Now a strange thing has happened in our history and in our personal life; our faith has been attached to that great void, to that enemy of all our gods. The strange thing has happened that we have been enabled to say of this reality, this last power in which we live and move and have our being, "Though it slay us yet we will trust it." [. . .] And insofar as our faith, our reliance for meaning and worth has been attached to this source and enemy of all our gods, we have been enabled to call this reality God.[5]

And, to consider a very different example, no character in <u>Light in August</u> responds to his or her experience of life as Ippolit responds to Holbein's disturbing portrayal of the dead Christ hanging in Rogozhin's apartment:

> "Looking at such a picture, one conceives of nature in the shape of an immense, merciless, dumb beast, or more correctly, much more correctly, speaking, though it sounds strange, in the form of a huge machine of the most modern construction which, dull and insensible, has aimlessly clutched, crushed and swallowed up a great priceless Being, a Being worth all nature and its laws,

> worth the whole earth, which was created perhaps solely for the advent of that Being. This picture expresses and unconsciously suggests to one the conception of such a dark, insolent, unreasoning and eternal Power to which everything is in subjection." [. . .] "Can't I simply be devoured without being expected to praise what devours me?"[6]

Ippolit's commitment is a negative one; he simply refuses to rely on anything at all. His negative statement also represents an interesting response to Niebuhr's earnest affirmation. And no one in <u>Light in August</u> responds with a positive affirmation such as Myshkin's, in his conversation with Rogozhin:

> "I came upon a peasant woman with a tiny baby in her arms. She was quite a young woman and the baby was about six weeks old. The baby smiled at her for the first time in its life. I saw her crossing herself with great devotion. 'What are you doing, my dear?' (I was always asking questions in those days.) 'God has just such gladness every time he sees from heaven that a sinner is praying to Him with all his heart, as a mother has when she sees the first smile on her baby's face.' That was what the woman said to me almost in those words, this deep, subtle and truly religious thought--a thought in which all the essence of Christianity finds expression; that is the whole conception of God as our Father and of God's gladness in man, like a father's in his own child--the fundamental idea of Christ!" (p. 208)

Both Ippolit and Myshkin have something to say about Christ, but Ippolit sees 'God the Father' as an insolent, eternal Power that sent Christ to earth only to destroy him; while Myshkin sees Christ as an expression of God's gladness in man. Whatever else Myshkin's metaphors for God's love imply, they certainly suggest trustworthiness and meaning. But one question Dostoyevsky implicitly raises and leaves open is whether Myshkin is fully aware of the problems of evil and death reflected in the other two passages.

The theologian H. Richard Niebuhr, and the fictional characters Ippolit Terentyev and Lvov Myshkin experience, reflect upon, and think about the nature of things, and respond with a definite inward commitment. The reflection that leads to such commitment is not simply an objective thinking-about; it is, first and foremost, the awakening of the elusive experience of the problem of the world's meaning, an experience like the one awakened through empathy with the implied author of Light in August. When Niebuhr or Ippolit or Myshkin attempt to describe the nature of things or God, they are attempting to make something explicit--they are responding to a religious feeling with an idea. But insofar as they make commitments (whether positive or negative) they are not simply making something explicit; they are taking a position. They are claiming to actually rely on, or to reject, a reality; they are not simply interpreting their feelings.

The theologian H. Richard Niebuhr is not a fictional character. The aim of his essay "Faith in Gods and in God," from which I have quoted, is to directly present to the reader both his reflections and rational judgments about religious experience, and earnest avowals of his own faith. I think that his essay, considered as a sort of thoughtful sermon, is a successful piece of writing. But is it possible convincingly to present fictional characters who so reflect, judge, and avow? Do Myshkin's and Ippolit's statements of commitment detract from the believability of their characterization, or perhaps simply fail to play any significant role in their characterization? In general terms, I would like to ask, if the function of literary art is to evoke concrete feeling, how can judgments and commitments be a part of that feeling? Even if commitments and judgments are responses to feelings, how can commitments and judgments be parts of the total feeling the artwork evokes? To shed light on this issue, I would like to recapitulate some of my previous discussion of the nature of feeling, universality, and judgment.

As I have pointed out, the experience of feeling includes the feeling of the possibility of judgment. Feeling includes tendencies that lead beyond feeling. This is so even on the simple level of sense perception. Sense qualities such as the color green represent a sameness amid difference immanent in perceptual experience that is prior to explicit judgment. But the presence of that sameness amid difference also involves a nisus or tendency toward explicit judgments involving concepts, such as 'this is green.' The feeling of the possibility of judgment is an essential aspect of sense experience. But sense qualities do not exhaust experience. Experience also includes feelings of sameness that cannot be so easily considered in isolation from concrete instances, such as 'love,' 'the human condition,' and 'person.' These feelings of sameness also prompt explicit judgment. In their case, the difference between feeling and judgment, and the inadequacy of propositional judgment to feeling, is especially clear.

In exploring the relation between empathetic experience, judgment, and commitment, we cannot avoid the question of truth.[7] If judgments can apply to concrete experience, and if concrete experience can even contain tendencies toward judgment, does it not seem odd to suppose that judgments are the only aspects of experience that can be true or false? Judgment depends on a prior sensitivity and attentiveness--upon an emotional and personal sensitivity as well as the sensitivity of the five senses. Attentive perception--whether it be sense perception or empathy--is true perception, inattentive, false. A person who shrinks from empathy has, in an important sense, a false perception of the world. To concretely experience another human life, including the vague, indefinable background of feeling inseparable from our sense of 'person,' 'love,' and 'the human condition,' is to have a true experience of that life, or rather, to re-experience that life truly.

The readers of a novel relive the implied author's empathetic experience of the characters in the novel. A character is believable if a feeling of implicit identity emerges between the character and the reader in the vague background of the reader's experience. The reader feels, in an indefinable way, that what the character faces in life is also what he, the reader, faces, even though the character's particular circumstances may be drastically different from any the reader has actually encountered. Through empathy, the reader <u>validates</u> the author's presentation of character. Not a judgment, but the empathetic experience itself, is validated.

But the characters themselves sometimes make judgments and commitments, and decide to perform certain specific actions. The characters presumably experience the validity of their own judgments, commitments, and actions. If the reader is reliving their experience, should he not also relive their experience of the validity of their decisions for action and belief? But how many readers will experience Joe Christmas' actions or Percy Grimm's actions, as right? And it has often been pointed out that one need not agree with the judgments and convictions expressed in a novel such as Dostoyevsky's <u>The Idiot</u> in order to fully appreciate the novel. Indeed, one must disagree with some of them, since they include irreconcilable opposites. And, as I pointed out for the case of Joe Christmas, it is possible to empathize with a character whose actions appall us. It must be the case that we experience characters' decisions and convictions in a different way than we experience their feelings.

An examination of Faulkner's presentation of human action already led me, in Chapter One, to qualify the statement that readers relive the experiences of characters. For in Faulkner's (as well as Dostoyevsky's) presentation, the moment of decision represents a striking discontinuity in our empathetic experience. A character's decision seems to represent a barrier before which our reliving of a character's experience momentarily comes to a halt. Making a decision, whether for action or belief, is a process of validation that differs in kind from the process of validation empathy represents. In reading, the reader can achieve empathy or not achieve it, and if not, the fault may lie either with the reader or the author. The achievement of empathy is already the completion of a process of validation. But to carry the validation of a decision to its conclusion is to actually make that decision. If one is actually making a decision, one is, in fact, making one's own decision, and cannot thereby be reliving someone else's decision!

The basic limitation literary art cannot overcome is the basic limitation of empathy. The sensitive paying-attention empathy represents cannot relive decisions for action and belief and cannot constitute the validation of any kind of judgment. (But that empathy cannot constitute the validation of a judgment does not mean that empathetic experience cannot be the source of evidence for judgments.) Nor can empathy be the reliving of someone else's commitment to a cause--of the actual relying upon something through which that person experiences life as meaningful.

Religious commitment has its own kind of validity, to be distinguished from the validity of judgments and feelings. One may make the objective judgment, for example, that God exists; or one may through empathy with another person, sense the possibility of a commitment's validity. But through neither of these experiences of truth does one experience an object of loyalty and trust as the dependable source of the meaning of one's life. Only through actually making the commitment does one know one's cause as the true source of life's meaning. The belief _that_ a cause is a worthy one must be distinguished from _reliance on_ that cause as the power that sustains one in good fortune and adversity, and that sustains one in a certain disposition toward the world (also to be distinguished from a belief about the world). Belief-that can exist without belief-in. And though it may sound strange, belief-in may have a truth or falsity of its own. In the struggle to believe in something, one always faces the possibility that the meaning one seeks is illusory, or that the trust one remembers having had, was an illusion. A religious person may not doubt that God exists so much as whether God even matters to him, or whether God can give meaning to life in a world such as this. And it is certainly true that the experience of believing-in really is false sometimes. Believing-in can easily be a manifestation of arrogant bigotry. Many sincerely held commitments are in fact false commitments because they are made to gods that are sources only of meaninglessness, hatred, and death, however inspiring they may seem to the believer. For Niebuhr commitment, loyalty, and trust are not values in themselves, but depend entirely on their object.

If Dostoyevsky's presentation of character is to be effective, he must make his characters' commitments attractive, but also raise doubts in our minds about his characters' commitments. When a character expresses and lives out a religious commitment, the reader cannot validate the truth of that commitment. Through empathy, the reader cannot know that the character truly makes a true commitment. Since we do not validate the commitment, the character's account of himself and of his beliefs must be only one alternative--and we become curious about the other alternatives. The author must make us wonder whether their commitments are genuine, or only self-deceptions; and wonder whether they are true, or false. To experience another person's commitment as possibly, rather than actually, true, means to experience it as possibly false, and as possibly a self-deception. A convincing presentation of such possibility must include these alternatives. It must evoke a strong feeling of tension between these alternatives if it is to be true to our concrete experience of commitment as an aspect of other people's inner lives. With Myshkin, Dostoyevsky succeeds in sustaining this feeling of tension. The question that haunts our experience of Myshkin is whether his convictions are genuine or are only somehow the product of inexperience, of an overactive imagination and intellect, and perhaps even of mental illness and epilepsy. Myshkin's commitments may or may not be genuine, and may or may not be true--and the power of Dostoyevsky's characterization is made apparent by the fact that we cannot rest comfortably with either alternative.

NOTES TO CHAPTER FOUR

¹Throughout my study I am highly indebted to Mikhail Bakhtin's <u>Problems of Dostoyevksy's Poetics</u>, tr. R. W. Rotsel (Ann Arbor, Mich.: Ardis, 1973). According to Bakhtin, "The plurality of independent and unmerged voices and consciousnessnes and the genuine polyphony of full-valued voices are in fact characteristics of Dostoyevsky's novels. [. . .] In the author's creative plan, Dostoyevsky's principal heroes are indeed not only objects of the author's word, but subjects of their own directly significant word as well" (p. 4). For Bakhtin, the principle of Dostoyevsky's art is the dialogical interaction of the characters' voices, in addition to their simple juxtaposition (p. 23).

²H. Richard Niebuhr, "Faith in Gods and in God," in <u>Radical Monotheism and Western Culture</u> (New York: Harper, 1970), p. 118.

³Ibid., p. 116.

⁴Ibid., p. 122.

⁵Ibid., p. 122-23.

⁶Fyodor Dostoyevsky, <u>The Idiot</u>, tr. Constance Garnett (New York: Random House, 1935), pp. 389; 393. All subsequent references are to this edition. I would like to thank Michael Finke and Becky Moyle of the Indiana University Slavics Department for checking all of my quotations from the Garnett translation for accuracy, and for their answers to numerous questions about the sense of the original.

⁷I am here relying, to a great extent, upon Alfred North Whitehead's discussion of truth in <u>Adventures of Ideas</u> (New York: Macmillan, 1967), pp. 241-51; 265-72.

CHAPTER V

Characterization and the Experience of Conviction

in <u>The Idiot</u>

In this chapter, I will attempt to define Myshkin's character, and to show how Dostoyevsky includes reflection and commitment as a part of that character. I will attempt to distinguish four aspects of our experience of Myshkin: a feeling of openness; religious reflection; the kind of personal conviction that seems to shape Myshkin's personality and behavior; and Myshkin's explicit statements of religious conviction. I will emphasize that though these four aspects are related, they are independent, and cannot, in the context of our experience of the novel, be reduced to any single aspect. A general discussion of Myshkin's character as it first appears in Part One will introduce the basic aspects of openness and conviction, noting the contrast between Dostoyevsky's and Faulkner's aims in characterization. Then I will consider in detail Myshkin's meeting with the Epanchin ladies in Part One, and also discuss his meeting with Rogozhin at the beginning of Part Two, in order to illustrate the way Dostoyevsky weaves together all four aspects into a convincing characterization.

The feeling of openness Faulkner evokes at the center of Byron's character is similar to the openness we sense in Myshkin. Both face other people directly, accept them as they are, and are disinclined to condemn, judge, or even dislike them. But in Myshkin's case, we constantly sense the presence of something more. Dostoyevsky suggests the presence, deep in Myshkin's character, of a decision and a commitment that runs counter to the way of the world, and to much of what we would naturally expect from a person in the situations he faces.

I do not think that Faulkner suggests the presence of such a commitment in Byron. Byron's actions seem natural in a way that Myshkin's do not. Upon Byron's first meeting with Lena, Faulkner suggests a strong feeling of sympathy between the characters. Byron's particular actions--setting down the staves that were balanced on his shoulder, and immediately spreading the sack on the planks when she makes a move to sit down--seem natural responses to the promptings of sympathy, and Byron and Lena's first encounter functions as a kind of symbol of their whole relationship. Byron's commitment to Lena seems a natural response to his feelings of sympathy. Faulkner does have Byron express his beliefs on a few occasions, but he does not include anything like Dostoyevsky's constant emphasis on the possibility of an inner decision guiding his characters' actions.

The details of Myshkin's action and conversation always seem to respond to more than the simple promptings of sympathy. Myshkin represents a kind of goodness that may seem unnatural and exaggerated. His goodness is not only attractive, but challenging, disturbing, and in a way questionable. Though he becomes deeply involved with those around him, he always seems preoccupied with something other than the immediate situation he faces and the natural human feelings it involves. This preoccupation gives his character a kind of steadiness that impresses others, but also makes them uneasy.

In his characterization of Myshkin, Dostoyevsky suggests more than the gap between feeling and action present in Faulkner's characterization of Byron and Joe. Though we can empathize with Joe's inner needs, the actions that respond to the frustration of those needs appear irreducibly strange and alien. That Joe's strange rebellion can lead nowhere at all is the essence of the tragedy of his character. Myshkin's actions are also strange, and represent a problem for empathy. But Dostoyevsky suggests that there may be something meaningful in Myshkin's strangeness--that a conviction worth considering may underlie that strangeness.

It is not simply that Myshkin performs particular actions that are strange and surprising. In *Light in August*, all significant actions are in some way surprising: not only Joe's grotesque rebellion expressed through such actions as vomiting toothpaste or throwing Joanna's food against the wall of her kitchen; but Byron's sudden falling in love with Lena and his consistent loyalty to her, are surprising, and represent a gap in empathetic experience. But in our empathetic experience of Myshkin, there is no level untouched by strangeness. It is not simply that Myshkin performs definite actions that are strange; rather, his whole inner life seems controlled by a definite action we cannot reach through empathy. It may be for just this reason that referred to Myshkin as "sphinxlike."[1] The unexpectedness of action does not contrast with empathy in Myshkin's case so much as infect it. Dostoyevsky suggests the possibility of commitment as a single inward action distinct from the many decisions one makes for actions in the world. In *Light in August*, the only religious choice Byron has to make is inseparable from the choice he has to make about Lena.

Consider the scene that begins the novel, Myshkin's first meeting with Rogozhin. That Myshkin reacts to Rogozhin as he does raises a real question in the reader's mind about Myshkin's motivation. Myshkin does seem to be guided by a commitment, but we wonder what kind of commitment could prompt him to so willingly accept an individual as obviously degraded as Rogozhin. Already in this scene, Rogozhin reveals his essential features. In some ways, Rogozhin seems cynically and bitterly closed off from others: we learn that "his lips were continually curved in an insolent, mocking, and even malicious smile" (p. 3). His conversation with Myshkin betrays a definite malice, but Rogozhin also shows a genuine interest in Myshkin that is hard to reconcile with his cynical and mocking attitude. The narrator notes that Rogozhin is warmly dressed, but that Myshkin is unprepared for the long winter train ride from Switzerland to Petersburg. Myshkin must be physically uncomfortable, and Rogozhin opens the conversation with a remark about the temperature:

> His dark-haired neighbor in the sheepskin observed all this, partly from having nothing to do, and at last, with an indelicate smile, in which satisfaction at the misfortunes of others is sometimes expressed, he asked:
> "Chilly?"
> And he twitched his shoulders.
> "Very," answered his neighbor, with extraordinary readiness, "and to think it's thawing too. What if it were freezing? I didn't expect it to be so cold at home. I've got out of the way of it."
> "From abroad, eh?"
> "Yes, from Switzerland."
> "Phew! You don't say so!" The dark-haired man whistled and laughed.
> They fell into talk. The readiness of the fair young man in the Swiss cloak to answer all his companion's inquiries was remarkable. He betrayed no suspicion of the extreme impertinence of some of his misplaced and idle questions. (p. 4)

It is not enough to say that Myshkin, in this scene, is patient and cheerful. It is not that Myshkin refuses to take offense; rather, he seems simply oblivious to the fact that offense has been given. Myshkin's remarks about the cold are not complaints, but simply an honest answer to Rogozhin's question. His answer is perfectly forthcoming--Myshkin seems to be not only unaffected by, but oblivious to, Rogozhin's Schadenfreude. In fact, Myshkin is actually drawn to Rogozhin, as Rogozhin is to Myshkin.

The very crude and cynical remarks exchanged by Rogozhin and Lebedyev, who is also in the compartment, do not seem to frighten or disgust Myshkin in the slightest. It is not as if Myshkin has simply made a conscious decision to face everyone with perfect openness: his strangely consistent openness seems completely unforced. We are surprised by the apparent absence, not only of certain overtly expressed emotional reactions, but of certain inner feelings and tendencies, in Myshkin. The question that begins here and continues throughout the novel is whether Myshkin's openness is the result of a conviction held so deeply that it really forms the basis of his identity, transforming his inner life; or whether his strange openness is somehow pathological or neurotic or foolish. Does Myshkin perhaps really fail to perceive the nature of Rogozhin's character? Does Rogozhin simply enjoy taking advantage of a naive foolishness in Myshkin? Is Myshkin's attraction to Rogozhin somehow unhealthy--a kind of morbid attraction to suffering and violence?

Dostoyevsky introduces, in the course of the novel, all sorts of complicating factors that suggest that Myshkin is neither a perfect saint, nor a perfect idiot. His willingness to become intimate with the likes of Rogozhin may indicate a simple lack of prudence and knowledge of human character. Yet we soon learn that he has indeed foreseen that were Rogozhin to marry Nastasya, he would probably murder her the next day (p. 33). Myshkin is extremely naive and innocent, yet he can empathize deeply with others and grasp the essence of their situations. His naivete may concern what it is possible for others to become, rather than what they are. For, as we later learn, Myshkin believes, or at least longs to believe, that "Rogozhin too could walk in the light" (p. 217). He believes he can somehow persuade Rogozhin to give up his malice and craving for shame. Even in the first scene there are indications of Myshkin's naive, unflinching willingness to face the impossible, or what any reasonable person would consider impossible. It is in his hope for Rogozhin, and also for Nastasya Filippovna, that Myshkin is closest to Don Quixote.

The narrator's suggestion that Myshkin "betrayed no suspicion of some of [Rogozhin's] misplaced and idle questions," is, in a sense, misleading. Myshkin is not simply oblivious to the malice and pettiness in others, and he sometimes does have to struggle with his own anger and irritation. He becomes very irritated with Ganya a number of times; on one occasion Myshkin pointedly, though not insultingly, objects to being called "an idiot" and suggests that they had better part (p. 82). The violent slap Ganya later gives Myshkin when he tries to prevent Ganya from hitting his sister sets off an intense struggle within Myshkin. In Myshkin's reaction, we see the conflict between his conviction and the natural human response the situation calls forth.

> Exclamations were heard on all sides. Myshkin turned pale. He looked Ganya straight in the face with strange and reproachful eyes; his lips quivered, trying to articulate something; they were twisted into a sort of strange and utterly incongruous smile.
> "Well, you may . . . but her . . . I won't let you," he said softly at last.
> But suddenly he broke down, left Ganya, hid his face in his hands, moved away to a corner, stood with his face to the wall, and in a breaking voice said:
> "Oh, how ashamed you will be of what you have done!" (p. 109)

Here again, Myshkin does not seem to be struggling with a <u>principle</u> of nonviolence, with a conviction in the sense of an affirmation of a proposition. The personal presence of Ganya himself is an essential part of that struggle: Myshkin directly faces the person Ganya, and not some rule. Myshkin does not lash back at Ganya. To say that Myshkin <u>refuses</u> to lash back is somehow inaccurate. He does not restrain himself out of any sort of proud moralistic contempt or stoical adherence to principle. It is rather as if Ganya had broken something shared between them that ought to have been respected, and Myshkin looks back across the gap created, himself feeling ashamed by Ganya's action and undoubtedly feeling anger himself, but feeling sorrow and shame over his own anger as well. It is as if Myshkin had placed something in trust with Ganya, but Myshkin cannot and will not bring himself to withdraw from Ganya what he had placed in trust with him. There is something he wants to tell Ganya that he cannot put into words, something he wants to set right, but does not know how to set right. Myshkin's conviction here seems to be, quite specifically, his loyalty to Ganya, and not to any principle of non-violence or abstract humanity. But Dostoyevsky does not assert that Myshkin has made such a commitment so much as raise the possibility that there is a sense of commitment that goes far deeper than commitment to explicitly expressed beliefs.

Myshkin's conviction, here expressed through action, may be the conviction at the very heart of his character, at the center of his orientation toward other people. Yet Dostoyevsky does not close off the possibility that Myshkin may after all only cling to an abstract principle he cannot really accept, and that may attract him for hidden, perhaps pathological reasons. But the strength of the former possibility provides a real challenge to any attempt to reduce the moral life to rule-following, or to the choosing of one objectively considered action over another. The moral quality of Myshkin's reaction has as much to do with the *way* he turns the other cheek as with the simple fact that he does not retaliate.

In the course of the novel, Myshkin's non-resistance and willingness to forgive attain truly heroic--or quixotic--proportions. He not only overlooks Rogozhin's rudeness, he overlooks Rogozhin's attempt to kill him, and in the end, Rogozhin's successful murder of Nastasya. Myshkin's conviction expresses itself not only in non-resistance to evil, but also in the desperate attempt to convert evil to good. Dostoyevsky could hardly have invented a more extreme situation for Myshkin to confront than what he faces in Rogozhin and Nastasya. I think Dostoyevsky means to suggest that there is something absurd about Myshkin's loyalty to them, and his persistent struggle to change their hearts. Aglaia's explicit comparison of Myshkin to Don Quixote reflects not only her personal attitude, but suggests a possible interpretation of Myshkin Dostoyevsky really wants us to consider. And does not Don Quixote's character also unify nobility with absurdity?

Myshkin is a quixotic character, and his relation to the world around him is for that reason ambiguous. I think it incorrect to assert, as some critics do, that Myshkin unquestionably represents pure holiness, and that the rest of the characters constitute a corrupt and evil world that has nothing in common with him at all.[2] Dostoyevsky offers a whole spectrum of human character, and presents even some of the most degraded and desperate as possibly drawn to Myshkin. Nastasya and Rogozhin are attracted by Myshkin's idealism as much as they despise or fear it; he represents a problem in their lives they cannot dismiss. The worst characters in the novel are not those who are repelled by Myshkin, but those who are simply unmoved by him: Totsky and Lebedyev.

Totsky is not a man motivated by hatred or a desire to destroy. Rather, he is utterly complacent and self-satisfied--and utterly shut off from other human beings. He 'adopts' the seven year old orphan Nastasya and has her raised in elegant and refined surroundings for the sole purpose of cultivating her as his own personal courtesan. When she reaches age sixteen, he shows up for two months of the year in order to have sexual intercourse with her at his pleasure.

Totsky has long wished to marry, but has found that Nastasya will neither marry him nor allow him to marry anyone else. Myshkin has arrived on the very day when a deal that will liberate Totsky is supposed to be consummated. Nastasya will marry Ganya, setting Totsky free, and Totsky will marry General Epanchin's eldest daughter Alexandra. But, as it happens, General Epanchin has also, senselessly, been courting Nastasya, Ganya is scared to death of marrying her, and the whole deal is based on a generous bribe offered to her by Totsky. Totsky's amoral character is well summed up by the terms he uses to plead with Nastasya to go along with the deal:

> He blamed himself for everything; he said frankly that he could not repent of his original offense, for he was an inveterate sensualist and could not control himself, but that now he wanted to marry, and the whole possibility of this highly suitable and distinguished marriage was in her hands: in a word, he rested all his hopes on her generous heart. (p. 42)

At the other end of the spectrum, General Epanchin's wife, Lizaveta Prokofyevna, and his daughters, best represent the possibility of consistent openness to others, and are the characters most consistently drawn to Myshkin. Of all the characters in the novel, Lizaveta is the one most closely akin to Myshkin. Like Myshkin, she is childlike, spontaneous, and direct. Lizaveta comes to deeply sympathize with Myshkin's position in the world, and his unconventional outlook. The absurdity, hypocrisy, and evil of the world are clear to her, and she is capable of seeing plenty of absurdity in herself as well. Yet she resists evil in a way Myshkin does not. She is adamantly opposed to the scheming in which her husband and

Ganya are involved, and especially to the prospect of her daughter's marriage to Totsky. Lizaveta sees through her husband, and is able to deal with him on his terms. It becomes clear that she appreciates the lowness of her husband's scheme, and it is also clear that she will never allow him to carry it out. It may be that General Epanchin's character is incompletely developed--but he seems on the whole to be a basically good, if not entirely scrupulous, man. Most importantly of all, his wife has thoroughly intimidated him.

Lizaveta represents a kind of unselfishness very different from Myshkin's: though she sees very well that the world is impure, she manages to deal with the world as it is, and she is willing to meet evil head on and fight with it. She directs her energies vigorously and at times frenziedly outward, but in pursuit of definite goals for the sake of particular persons to whom she is attached by the normal bonds of love. While she is caught up in a social game of sorts, one senses that the center of her concern really is her daughters' well being, and not simply how their fortunes in life reflect upon their mother. Even while she fights her husband and wrangles with her daughters, she is obstinately and sincerely loyal to them all. Lizaveta is the voice of common sense. Hers is the common sense that compromises with society without losing sight of love, and that loves unselfishly, but does not try to do the impossible.

The paradox of Lizaveta's character is that while she is firmly committed to a certain way of life, she cannot help listening to Myshkin. Her deep inner approval of Myshkin exists in tension with her essential canniness: she cannot resolve the conflict in her feelings, and neither can we.

In the first four chapters of Part One, Myshkin is mainly a spectator.

He meets Rogozhin, Lebedyev, General Epanchin, and Ganya, and learns of Nastasya Filippovna, but has himself very little to say. It is only in Chapters Five, Six, and Seven, which describe his meeting with the Epanchin women, that his character really opens up. The atmosphere Lizaveta Prokofyevna creates in her surroundings is strikingly different from what Myshkin has encountered so far. Dostoyevsky seems to suggest that this atmosphere is the first one in which Myshkin's character, or at least certain essential aspects of his character, can unfold. Lizaveta and her daughters take an immediate interest in Myshkin--an interest that appears to have no ulterior motive and that grows as his character impresses itself upon them. Dostoyevsky evokes this atmosphere and interest through the flow of dialogue.

In general Dostoyevsky brings human relationships to life dramatically, by recreating believable and lively conversation. But what does it mean to recreate conversation? That a dramatic, dialogical presentation of character can be aesthetically effective is founded on the fact that conversation itself tends to be evocative. The aim of everyday conversation is not simply the exchange of objective statements and claims. The basic aim of conversation is empathy, but empathy does not come about through the attempt to reflect upon, analyze, and objectively state one's feelings. Even in baldly stating a belief, one may suggest in any number of ways that one may not be quite taking the firm position one seems to be taking. Conversation communicates all sorts of half-intentions. Through irony, exaggeration, calmly paradoxical statements, pauses, enigmatic smiles, one may reflect that suspension between seriousness and play, between sincerity and insincerity, that in fact characterizes the state of mind of most people most of the time.

While Dostoyevsky gives his characters all sorts of overt and direct statements to make about themselves, his characterization is effective because he is always able to evoke in their conversation the sense of something unsaid. The something unsaid is not some other statement simply unspoken--but something elusive that cannot be spoken. The give and take of empathy involves an implicit awareness that one always means more than one directly says, that one's feelings are often contradictory and confused, and that one seldom clearly knows what one's feelings even are. Openness means allowing thoughts and feelings to emerge in the background rather than insisting that even one's feelings be defined and directly stated. Even irony and insincerity may go hand in hand with openness toward others and respect for others. Not taking oneself too seriously, and not constantly demanding of others that they be serious, is part of the meaning of kindness and respect. Playfulness is an essential aspect of openness. It is just this quality of playfulness and openness that characterizes Myshkin's first conversation with Lizaveta Prokofyevna and her daughters.

Lizaveta's openness is apparent even in the way she fights with her husband. On her first appearance in the novel, that is exactly what she is doing. Because of her anger at Ivan Fyodorovitch over Nastasya Filippovna, she pretends not to understand anything that is going on. While it is clear that she genuinely frightens her husband, and is genuinely angry, her anger lacks the bitterness and prideful outrage that erects a wall between people. The partly intentional humorousness of her performance evokes a sense in us and in her husband of the ambiguity and ambivalence of her feelings. She is furious with her husband and yet does not make the final statement that would either forgive or definitely condemn. By pretending not to understand anything, she puts her husband in an uncomfortable position, but, in a way, does not put an end to dialogue: she is waiting for him to account for himself, rather than shutting off all further development.

Lizaveta's irascibility and comic performances do involve all sorts of tensions with others, but those tensions are always on the verge of being resolved, and exist against a background of an implicit understanding and sympathy within her family. This implicit sympathy is apparent as they finally persuade her to take notice of Myshkin after the general has introduced him. In this passage, each family member has his or her say, starting with the general:

> "[. . .] I supposed it would be rather interesting to you to see him, in fact, because after all he belongs to the same family."
> "Of course, <u>maman</u>, if one needn't stand on ceremony with him. Besides he must be hungry after the journey; why not give him something to eat, if he has nowhere to go?" said the eldest girl, Alexandra.
> "And if he is a perfect child, too. We could have a game of blind man's buff with him."
> "Blind man's buff! What do you mean?"
> "Oh, <u>maman</u>, please leave off pretending!" Aglaia interrupted in vexation.
> The second daughter, Adelaïda, who was of a mirthful disposition, could not restrain herself and burst out laughing.
> "Send for him papa, <u>maman</u> gives you leave," Aglaia decided.
> The general rang, and told the servant to call the prince.
> "But on condition he has a napkin tied round his neck when he sits at the table" his wife insisted. "Call Fyodor or Mavra . . . to stand behind his chair and look after him while he eats. I only trust he is quiet when he has a fit. Does he wave his arms?"
> (pp. 47-48)

As Myshkin's conversation with the Epanchin women proceeds, a feeling of personal warmth and intimacy emerges among them. Myshkin cheerfully adapts to their playful and ironic family style, and laughs right along with their good-natured teasing. Lizaveta is intensely, and in fact exaggeratedly, interested in Myshkin, and does not hesitate to express her most personal feelings. Their whole interview has the atmosphere of a game, but it is a game willingly played, and one that fosters, rather than inhibits, intimacy.

However, Dostoyevsky's presentation of Myshkin involves something more than the evocation of a feeling of openness and intimacy. With surprising ease, their conversation moves toward a discussion of the ultimate problems of life and death. Myshkin expresses his earnest reflections, and makes what might be called a statement of religious belief. Through this scene, Dostoyevsky shows religious reflection growing out of the experience of a story, but at the same time in tension with feeling. Myshkin's discussion with the Epanchin ladies reveals, for the first time, the intensity of his reflectiveness. The juxtaposition of this reflectiveness with our sense of the strange force of his personality raises the question of the relation between the two. Both the reader and the Epanchin ladies wonder whether his reflectiveness and position taking really express an inward, life-shaping commitment, or whether his strange consistency has some other nature or cause.

The Epanchin women make a game of insisting that he tell them a story, but the stories he tells are perhaps more than they bargained for. He recounts his experiences in Switzerland and France, first just describing his feelings during his recovery, but then retelling the experience of an acquaintance there whose death sentence was lifted at the last minute, and finally describing a guillotining he himself witnessed. A character's retelling of previous experiences already involves a new complication in dramatic presentation. The situation suggests that Myshkin's hearers are listening. They have been pulled out of the immediate give and take of conversation, and have become more reflective. Such reflectiveness does not play nearly the role in Light in August that it does in The Idiot. Stories are told in Light in August, but that novel does not focus on listeners' conscious attempts to react to and grope for the meaning of the stories characters tell. Such reflection, reaction, and groping are very important for Dostoyevsky's characters.

The most remarkable aspect of Myshkin's account of both executions is his attempt to get inside the condemned man's mind in each case. Myshkin seems driven to imagine exactly how it would feel to know that in five minutes one's life was to end. The key to Myshkin's character is that he lacks the habitual obliviousness to the terrifying limitations all humans encounter, and does not suppress the indefinable feeling of rebellion those limitations inspire. In confronting these limits as he does, Myshkin faces an issue that is strange and unfamiliar in a radical sense. Myshkin faces not the issue of involvement in life, which represents an experience we all share, but confronts death, which is not in us. We cannot adequately define what we mean either by life or by death; but in facing life, we can concretely feel what we are facing in a way we cannot in facing death.

The sense of rebellion and terror Myshkin experiences is absent even from Light in August. The horror we feel at Joe's murder cannot compare to the horror in Myshkin's execution descriptions. Faulkner does not provide us with Joe's experience of facing the moment of his death. As soon as Joe arrives at Mottstown to turn himself in, Faulkner pulls away from him. We no longer intimately empathize with Joe as we have until that point. The subsequent events in his life are presented objectively, from the point of view of an observer. What impresses us about Joe's death is not so much the horror of death itself as the tragedy of a life that has ended in such a brutal and humiliating way.

In general, Faulkner's characters do not face religious issues in the same way Dostoyevsky's do. Dostoyevsky's characters reflect on the whole human situation and struggle to respond to it, while for Faulkner's characters the issue of meaning is only in the background of their immediate life-concerns. In Light in August, from the viewpoint of the implied author, a new religious perspective emerges. The complete structure of the novel evokes not only a mysterious background, but a sense of the human condition as involving opposing forces that need to be reconciled but cannot be. We sense not only a mystery, but something impenetrable. Our overall reaction to Light in August includes a sense of perplexity and unrest. But in The Idiot, it seems as if the whole presented in Light in August has been somehow telescoped into the experience of each major character, and especially into Myshkin's. One way Dostoyevsky telescopes Faulkner's whole into the individual characters is simply by the inclusion of interpolated stories, such as Myshkin's execution stories. The characters' reflection often is simply their response to these stories, both as listeners and as tellers.

The passage including Myshkin's story of his acquaintance whose death sentence was lifted, and the ensuing discussion, provides an excellent example of the way Dostoyevsky weaves reflection and belief-statements into successful character portrayal and presentation of scene. Reflection is presented, not as analysis of an idea, but as reaction to a story. Dostoyevsky does not deal with ideas directly--rather, he brings the feelings out of which ideas arise into the experience of his characters. Such feelings are exactly the ones that can be evoked by a story, such as the interpolated stories in The Idiot, or even by an entire novel such as

Light in August. Myshkin himself finally reacts to his story of the cancelled execution with a statement of conviction: that he believes he will live more wisely than other people. His statement, seen as the statement of an idea, is not only very vague, but almost empty, and taken out of context, may well appear trite or simply silly. But as a statement of conviction, falling where it does in the narrative, it has a definite force.

As Myshkin finishes his story we sense that the flow of dialogue has been interrupted. The women are no longer immersed in the give and take of conversation. It is not clear to them how they are to respond, and yet they are impressed by Myshkin and moved by both stories Myshkin tells--the story of the reprieved man and the account of the guillotining Myshkin himself witnessed. Their reaction to the second story--the guillotining-- suggests even more clearly the presence of reflection than their reaction to the first. Myshkin concludes his account with his description of the picture he urges Adelaïda to paint: a portrait of the condemned man's face just before he lies down on the plank.

> Myshkin ceased speaking and looked at them all.
> "That's nothing like quietism, certainly," said Alexandra to herself.
> "And now tell us how you were in love," said Adelaïda.
> Myshkin looked at her with astonishment.
> "Listen," Adelaïda said, seeming rather hurried. "You promised to tell us about the Bâle picture, but now I should like to hear how you have been in love. Don't deny it, you must have been. Besides, as soon as you begin describing anything, you cease to be a philosopher." (p. 61)

Alexandra's soft remark and Adelaïda's hurried attempt to change the subject both suggest their reflectiveness. What they say does not provide us with ideas so much as suggest that the story has affected them as it has the reader. Adelaïda's desire to change the subject suggests not thoughtless frivolity--but that the story has successfully evoked a kind of reflection she is afraid to dwell upon.

In the discussion that follows the first story, a new element in Myshkin's characterization emerges. The flow of dialogue evokes a sense of openness, interpolated storytelling and description suggest the presence of reflection, and the discussion of the story introduces Myshkin's explicitly stated convictions. The story of the man reprieved at the last minute evokes a living sense of an ultimate problem to be resolved. It is full of the tendency within feeling to go beyond feeling--which is to say, it evokes reflection. The story itself includes many of the condemned man's own reflections. Faced with the experience of having only five minutes to live, the thought that he might by some chance be pardoned becomes almost impossible for him to bear. He feels he would treasure each moment of his new life; he would not waste one. Myshkin abruptly ends his account by reporting that his acquaintance "longed to be shot quickly," the thought of what he would do with his life were he pardoned became so unbearable (p. 55). As Myshkin finishes, a gap in the dramatic flow occurs that suggests that the women have indeed been listening, but are now slightly ill at ease.

> Myshkin suddenly ceased speaking; every one expected him to go on and draw some conclusion.
> "Have you finished?" asked Aglaia.
> "What? Yes," said Myshkin, rousing himself from a momentary dreaminess.
> "But what did you tell that story for?"
> "Oh . . . something in our talk reminded me of it. . . ."
> "You are very disconnected," observed Alexandra. (p. 56)

Alexandra, in her attempt to keep the conversation going, thereupon offers a somewhat glib moral for the story:

> "You probably meant to show, prince, that not one instant of life can be considered petty, and that sometimes five minutes is a precious treasure. That's all very laudable but [. . .]" (p. 56)

She then asks whether Myshkin's acquaintance actually went on to live each moment to the full. As we might have expected, Myshkin answers that the man did, in fact, continue to waste time. Alexandra concludes that "it seems it's impossible really to live 'counting each moment'." Myshkin answers with what is, in fact, his response to the entire story.

> "Yes, for some reason it is impossible," repeated Myshkin. "I thought so myself . . . and yet I somehow can't believe it . . . "
> "Then you think you will live more wisely than any one?" said Aglaia.
> "Yes, I have thought that too sometimes."
> "And you think so still?"
> "Yes . . . I think so still," answered Myshkin, looking at Aglaia with the same gentle and even timid smile; but he laughed again at once and looked gaily at her. (p. 56)

On the surface, Myshkin's statement hardly differs from Alexandra's. But the purpose of their statements, their attitude toward what they say, and the position they take towards others through what they say, are all very different. Alexandra attempts, at first, to bring the discussion of the moral of the story back down to the level of ordinary conversation, to bridge the gap in their conversation created by reflection. Her attempt suggests not that she is oblivious to the impact of the story, but on the contrary, that she has recognized it clearly enough to want to get away from it. But Myshkin is always bringing them back to the gap created by that impact. Alexandra's statement tends to soften the impact of the story, but we sense that Myshkin's statement of conviction is made with the story fully in mind.

Myshkin, through his statement that he believes he will live more wisely than anyone, directly confronts the story and directly addresses his listeners. In doing so, he creates a new difficulty for conversation. The difficulty arises because, as I have tried to point out, the primary aim of conversation is not the exchange of direct statements, but the evocation of feelings and ambiguous attitudes. Myshkin's conviction that it must be possible to use the moments of his life more wisely than others is his response to the disturbing experience of facing death. He is not content with merely sensing the mystery of death as the inescapable background of life. He is not content with the background as background--he wants, somehow, to get past it. He confronts the background, questions it, and is convinced he must strive to overcome the threat it presents. Dostoyevsky gives us no clear idea of what Myshkin believes in, but he vividly evokes the situation Myshkin's conviction responds to.

Dostoyevsky's presentation of Myshkin's statement of conviction is successful because the characters are aware of, and respond to, the gap that exists between feeling and conviction. Myshkin's statement represents, both for us and for his listeners, a break in empathetic experience. When Myshkin says "Yes . . . I think so still," he is not merely sharing feelings, but directly addressing his listeners. We, and they, experience Myshkin in a different way. He is expressing a commitment that he believes to be one of the central commitments of his life. This commitment presents itself to others not as a feeling they are invited to share--such as the feeling the condemned man experienced--but as a possible decision they might also make. The situation is plausible because Dostoyevsky creates the sense that the Epanchin ladies are listening to

Myshkin without automatically agreeing with him. They do not respond to his statements of commitment with other statements of commitment, but with a questioning interest, expressions of feeling, and even mockery. Dostoyevsky handles such scenes successfully because he can evoke the state of mind of <u>listening</u>--a feeling of uneasy suspension between attraction and doubt. Commitments appear, both to the reader and to the characters, not as truths, but as possibilities that are attractive, yet questionable.

Myshkin's belief statements are not isolated, but form a convincing part of a natural human situation. They emerge as a response to a story and to reflection, and create responses in his listeners of embarrassment and perplexity. Myshkin's statement that he still believes he will live more wisely than anyone had come as a response to Aglaia's taunting, sceptical prodding. Once he has spoken his mind, she mocks what seems to her to be presumptuousness. Myshkin himself is disconcerted by the possibility of presumptuousness. He is aware that in stating his beliefs he is taking a new position over against his listeners, that he is confronting them with a recommendation, an ideal. He senses the inappropriateness, one might almost say the impoliteness, of that position. Myshkin senses the tension that exists between openness toward others and the avowal of a conviction. He states his conviction gently, and not quite as directly as he might have, not wishing to violate that openness. In a few moments he becomes terribly frustrated and embarrassed, asking whether or not they are angry because he seems to be preaching to them. The intensity of his desire to communicate his deepest beliefs has come into conflict with his desire not to impose upon others.

The Epanchin women do not simply sympathize with Myshkin, but are challenged and perplexed by the definite identity Myshkin seems to have.

It is the force of his personality, summed up in his quiet sense of conviction, that attracts them. His listeners wonder what gives him the self-assurance he has--a calm and humble assurance, and not an assurance that is always on the ready to vanquish the resistance it assumes to be forthcoming. His beliefs and his presence appeal to his listeners as a possibility. By presenting Myshkin as a possibility, Dostoyevsky also presents Myshkin as an unresolved problem. The problem is not the objective one of the truth or falsity of statements of belief; the problem is one of who Myshkin is.

Dostoyevsky distinctly focuses on the frustration Myshkin encounters in trying to communicate his convictions. One has the sense of a barrier that cannot be overcome. The Epanchin ladies do not nod in agreement to his inspiring ideas. Rather, they <u>wonder</u> whether he might be on to something, or whether he is only an idiot or a rogue. Perhaps Myshkin's sense of frustration, even more apparent in later sections, stems from the fact that the kind of communication he desires is not possible. Perhaps he is frustrated precisely because he can arouse no more than their sense of interest and wondering and cannot bring them to really see the truth in his heart. Perhaps his problem is that he wishes people could be unified through their convictions in the same way they can be unified through sympathy.

We experience the convictions of others not as experiences to be relived but as possibilities or goals for our own being. The whole novel <u>The Idiot</u> centers, in fact, upon the possibility Myshkin represents. But in centering his novel in this way on a possibility, Dostoyevsky is not even asserting that Myshkin's beliefs are real. In giving Myshkin convictions to state, Dostoyevsky is not even asserting that Myshkin has convictions, much less that they are valid. He is not asserting that people have the capacity to form convictions. Rather, he evokes the feeling that conviction may be possible. Perhaps this feeling may be understood as empathy pushing against its limits. May not empathy, considered as the attempt of one person to concretely know another, be dissatisfied with itself? If empathy can recognize that it has limits, does it not also, by that very fact, recognize that there may be something more beyond those limits? Others' convictions are experienced as a feeling of 'more'--'more' not in the sense of background, but in the sense of *telos*, of a direction in which our minds may be able to move. Dostoyevsky allows it to remain an open question whether this feeling of *telos* really leads somewhere or is only a delusion. The feeling of possibility is not a belief that something is possible. Simply feeling that something *may* be, involves the feeling that it also may *not* be. Our experience of others' convictions is limited to this sense of possibility because we can experience the reality and validity of convictions only by making our own decisions, not by reliving the experiences of others.[3]

Our sense of 'more' as *telos* rather than background is not limited to our sense of the possible truth or falsity of Myshkin's beliefs--the strength, the source, and the rational content of those beliefs remain open questions. The statement of commitment Myshkin makes before the Epanchin women, by itself, is not the statement of an interesting idea; it does not challenge the reader to reason or reflect; and it does not have any great persuasive power. But the whole scene, including the statement, evokes the concrete situation of facing death, the challenge that situation presents to one's sense of life's meaning, and the possibility of a conviction that life somehow must, or even does, have meaning in spite of death.

Dostoyevsky has provided only the barest hint of Myshkin's inner life, but in doing so he has suggested the unreachable depth of Myshkin's own experience of his convictions, a depth that may be unreachable for Myshkin himself. It is precisely the sense of a possible spiritual reality <u>deeper</u> than the mere affirmation of propositions that Dostoyevsky wants to suggest. The inadequacy of the statements is precisely what Dostoyevsky wants to call attention to. In fact, were Myshkin, to any great extent, to analyze his ideas with true intellectual rigor, or were he to deliver really effective sermons, I suspect the plausibility and narrative continuity of the novel would be compromised. Passages of clear and distinct philosophical discussion, or of eloquent rhetoric, would weaken the evocation of character, and confuse the relationship between character, implied author, and real author.

But Dostoyevsky does give Myshkin's religious beliefs a more specific content than the vague and general sentiments Myshkin expresses before the Epanchin ladies. Myshkin's most direct statement of his religious beliefs comes in the conversation he has with Rogozhin six months later, upon returning to Petersburg. Dostoyevsky places Myshkin's statement at a point of crisis in the plot, and I think Dostoyevsky means to point out the strange contrast between Myshkin's beliefs, and the situation and the world they confront. As we know, when Myshkin offered to marry Nastasya, she ran away to Moscow with Rogozhin, then she ran to Myshkin, then to Rogozhin again, then away from Rogozhin again, and then back to him. In their conversation, Rogozhin and Myshkin discuss these events, and Rogozhin tells Myshkin that Nastasya wants Rogozhin to murder her, and that she loves Myshkin, but feels unworthy of him. Rogozhin tells Myshkin that when Myshkin is absent he is angry with him at once, but he says, and we see, that Myshkin's presence softens his anger, and rekindles his former affection. Here, as before, the strange absence of certain natural responses in Myshkin suggests the possibility of a real inner commitment and loyalty in Myshkin--a commitment and loyalty to Rogozhin that, it seems, opposes, or has really overcome, fear, disgust, and vengefulness.

As Rogozhin is showing Myshkin out of his apartment, they stop before a copy of Holbein's chilling portrayal of the dead Christ. Rogozhin asks Myshkin if he believes in God; Myshkin avoids the question. Rogozhin tells Myshkin the picture is making him lose his faith, and that he likes looking at the picture. Myshkin finally tells Rogozhin four very odd stories in response to his original question. Myshkin tells of a conversation he had with a learned atheist, emphasizing that he felt all the time that the atheist really was not talking about God at all; Myshkin then retells the story of a peasant who prayed to God for forgiveness as he murdered a friend for his watch; and of a drunken soldier who sold Myshkin his tin cross as a silver one. The final anecdote concerns a young mother Myshkin encountered, who, as her baby smiled at her for the first time, declared: "God has just such gladness every time he sees from heaven that a sinner is praying to Him with all his heart, as a mother has when she sees the first smile on her baby's face." These stories lead Myshkin to make some rather direct statements of religious faith, including the clearest expression of his personal creed in the novel, which I quoted earlier:

> "That was what the woman said to me almost in those words, this deep, subtle and truly religious thought--a thought in which all the essence of Christianity finds expression; that is the whole conception of God as our Father and of God's gladness in man, like a father's in his own child--the fundamental idea of Christ!" (p. 208)

But the clarity of this statement does not resolve our uncertainty about Myshkin's inner life. In our empathetic experience of Myshkin's character, we do not verify that the source of his strength and consistency is in fact the faith he explicitly describes to Rogozhin. The fact that Myshkin says he believes in God does not put an end to our uneasy wondering about his motivation. Dostoyevsky raises the question of whether Myshkin's explicit statement of commitment has anything at all to do with the possibility of inward commitment we sense otherwise in Myshkin's actual behavior.

Dostoyevsky evokes the possibility of an inward, life-shaping commitment as one aspect of our experience of Myshkin, and also the possibility of objects of faith, but through empathy we do not verify any connection between the two possibilities. Our experience of Myshkin does not somehow imply Niebuhr's assertion that everyone lives for the sake of some cause. What Myshkin's object of faith is, whether it is real, and whether it is the power that shapes his life, are all open to question in our experience of his character. It is only through one's own actual experience, and not the reliving of another's experience, that such questions can possibly be resolved.

Dostoyevsky raises the question of the reality of Myshkin's belief in God in a compelling way by emphasizing the tension between his explicit statement and the experience it responds to. The stories Myshkin chooses to express his faith raise disturbing questions. Myshkin seems oblivious to the grotesque and absurd light in which his story of the pious murderer can be seen. Rogozhin, who laughs uncontrollably, is very aware of the absurdity. We really wonder what could have prompted Myshkin to buy the tin cross from the drunken soldier--mere compassion does not seem to be a sufficient explanation. Most striking of all is his response to the young mother. Myshkin's warm assertion of God's gladness in man is immediately juxtaposed with his own report of a grotesque crime; with the dangerous menage a trois between him, Rogozhin, and Nastasya; and with Holbein's portrayal of the dead Christ that reveals no sign of his supposedly imminent resurrection.

All of the stories suggest to us the sense of the world Myshkin lives in, and as we then hear him speak of God's gladness in man, Dostoyevsky implicitly raises the question of whether Myshkin has really faced that world. When Myshkin responds to the kind of world he faces with a belief in 'God's gladness in man, like the gladness of a mother when she sees the first smile on her baby's face'--Dostoyevsky really wants us to ask, what can Myshkin possibly be responding to? In re-experiencing Myshkin's inner life at this point, we do not re-experience his faith in God. What the word 'God' itself means to him remains uncertain. But a religious metaphor, such as the one Myshkin presents, does involve feelings the reader can share. Any experience of God is present to the reader in a negative way, as the tension created by an apparent attempt to somehow equate the feeling of the nature of things with the feeling a mother has when she first sees her baby smile. Dostoyevsky raises the question of whether Myshkin is in some way oblivious to the nature of things, or whether he is responding truthfully to something real in his belief in 'God's gladness in man.' But Dostoyevsky gives no hint of the relation between this possible reality and the evoked experience of the nature of things.

Rogozhin, like the Epanchin ladies, experiences Myshkin's commitments as possibilities rather than as truths. But for Rogozhin, Myshkin does not merely invite reflection. Myshkin represents a definite challenge Rogozhin feels compelled to face, and yet can barely endure. Rogozhin's response to Myshkin's stories and statements of commitment is a definite action and apparent commitment, rather than simple reflection. The intense struggle Rogozhin has experienced through the whole scene reaches its climax in his response to Myshkin's stories. As Myshkin finishes, and takes his leave, saying "God be with you," Rogozhin stops him, asks him to exchange crosses, takes him back to be blessed by his mother, and finally embraces Myshkin, passionately renouncing Nastasya.

The climax of this scene brings together in a very small space the three contrasting elements of the characterization of Myshkin and Rogozhin: the essential feeling of openness toward others versus that of being shut off from others; the sense of a conviction at the basis of Myshkin's character, in tension with empathy and suggested by Myshkin's actual behavior; and Myshkin's explicit statements of religious commitment themselves.

The conflict within Rogozhin concerns not only what he is to think, or even what he is to do, but who he is. In facing this conflict, he faces a kind of conflict that Faulkner's characters do not face. Faulkner evokes a sense of a character's identity by evoking an essential feeling--of openness toward others or of isolation from others. But in our empathy with Rogozhin we sense the equal presence of both feelings: neither one alone constitutes his identity, and they are incompatible. This doubleness in Rogozhin is strikingly apparent at the moment he exchanges crosses with Myshkin: "With painful surprise Myshkin noticed that the same mistrustfulness, the same bitter, almost ironical smile still lingered on the face of his adopted brother; at moments, anyway, it was plainly to be seen" (p. 209).

On one level, it may seem that Rogozhin is attracted simply to Myshkin's openness. Even Myshkin's religious stories may in fact have only a personal, emotional significance for Rogozhin. But the very depth of the conflict we sense in Rogozhin suggests a further possibility. The two incompatible, and equally powerful feelings essential to our empathetic experience of Rogozhin suggest the need for the kind of inner conviction that shapes identity. Empathy alone creates a radical problem in our minds about who Rogozhin is. Not only Myshkin's openness appeals to Rogozhin, but the inner conviction suggested by Myshkin's strangely consistent behavior. And the fact that Rogozhin chooses to exchange <u>crosses</u> with Myshkin obviously suggests the other possible kind of conviction involved: an explicitly expressed Christian faith.

Dostoyevsky does not unambiguously indicate that Rogozhin has reached any kind of decision at all. Rogozhin's decisive gestures stand in marked contrast to his "lingering ironical smile," as well as his later attempt to murder Myshkin. Rogozhin experiences Myshkin's convictions as possibilities, possibilities that inspire not only wondering and reflection, but an unbearable longing that exists side by side with a murderous hatred. This double reaction is inspired by the whole force of Myshkin's personality. Myshkin's explicit Christian statements are involved in the impact he makes on Rogozhin, but the force of Myshkin's personality cannot simply be equated with his apparent Christian commitment. The reader can neither verify that Rogozhin has made a decision, nor that he has made any certain kind of decision. The truth and content of Myshkin's beliefs are uncertain to Rogozhin, and the nature of Rogozhin's inward response to those beliefs is uncertain to the reader. That Rogozhin is responding to the inherent power of Myshkin's faith is only a possibility, countered by the possibility that he is only responding to an idiot.

NOTES TO CHAPTER FIVE

[1] Fyodor Dostoyevksy, The Notebooks for "The Idiot", tr. Katharine Strelsky, ed. Edward Wasiolek (Chicago: Univ. of Chicago Press, 1967), pp. 174; 199-201.

[2] George Panichas, in The Burden of Vision: Dostoyevsky's Spiritual Art (Grand Rapids, Mich.: Eerdmans, 1977), offers such an interpretation of The Idiot. According to Panichas, "Myshkin is the pure spirit of innocence. In a profane and profaning world, which the other people in The Idiot represent in all degrees of profanity, any encounter with innocence must needs be terrifying" (p. 57). "Even when, at times, some of the characters seem to like Myshkin, their attitude is ultimately as hard and selfish as he is selfless. [. . .] When, at times, they pay tribute to Myshkin, the tribute is composed of merely empty words" (p. 60).

[3] Sven Linner, in Starets Zosima in "The Brothers Karamazov" (Stockholm: Almqvist, 1975), raises the question of our ability to empathize with the moral and spiritual perfection of Zosima. "Being captivated by a literary character usually means, among many other things, that we somehow share his or her feelings. [. . .] But what happens when the fictional character's central quality is unselfishness or the sort of freedom from oneself of which Dostoyevsky speaks at the beginning of The Brothers Karamazov? Can one be free from oneself in one's imagination?" (p. 139) Linner concludes that one cannot, and that a character such as Zosima cannot be made entirely convincing, because, in effect, we cannot relive his central experiences. I see the problem in a slightly different way. In his treatment of Zosima, Dostoyevsky's problem is that he does not respect the gap that exists between empathy and our experience of others' convictions. In the case of Myshkin, he does respect the gap. We cannot be free from ourselves in our imagination because such freedom involves commitment and conviction. Myshkin's commitments are presented not as experiences to be relived and thereby validated, but as problematic possibilities. Dostoyevsky's characterization of Zosima is unconvincing because he tries to place judgments and assertions about Zosima at the center of the meaning of his characterization of Zosima. In a sense, he takes Zosima too seriously. Konrad Onasch, in Dostojewski als Verführer: Christentum und Kunst in der Dichtung Dostojewskis (Zürich: EVZ-Verlag, 1961), discusses the kind of "Spielernst" essential to literary art, specifically in connection with Myshkin: "Es ist einfach das Leben selbst, das sich keine Vorschriften machen lässt, welches in der Dichtung über uns kommt. In der Tat, ernst nehmen, wie man die Forderung einer Religion oder eine philosophische Einsicht ernst nimmt, kann man die Dichtung nicht. [. . .] Dichtung aber will nicht erziehen, sondern jenseits davon alle Lebensmöglichkeiten offenlassen. Es kommt darauf an, dass man die Dichtung in dieser ihrer Mächtigkeit einsieht und 'ernst nimmt'" (p. 21). It is precisely because Dostoyevsky presents Myshkin's character and convictions as 'life-possibilities' and not as unquestionably holy, pure, and true, that we cannot 'take him seriously' and that he has, at the same time, such great power to influence our lives.

CHAPTER VI

Religious Unease and the Structure of The Idiot

Perhaps the most important difference between Dostoyevsky and Faulkner lies in the way each treats the contrast between normality and aberration. For both authors, we might define the normal as the familiar, the predictable, the dependable. Familiar feelings and situations are ones we can identify with, even if only on some deep level. Earlier, I pointed out how it is Faulkner's genius to be able to find the familiar in the depths of the strange. Joe's actions are peculiar, but behind those actions, Faulkner evokes a sense of the universal human need for love. Joe is an aberration because he is blind to his situation--he cannot recognize his need for love as a need for love. We sense that Byron experiences the same need, and that for him, participating in life and forming natural human ties offers the possibility of meaning.

While Byron and Myshkin are alike in their openness and selflessness, Myshkin is, in his own way, as strange and dangerous as Joe. Dostoyevsky centers his novel on the question of the extreme of goodness, a question Faulkner ignores. While Byron is somewhat at odds with conventional society, and can see beyond the conventional, he does not represent a radical threat or challenge. But Myshkin contrasts almost as much with the average world of the Epanchins as Nastasya and Rogozhin do. Both Joe and Myshkin threaten any comforting, conventional, everyday experience of the world: Joe because he makes us ask what kind of world ours is that can include such spiritual horror; and Myshkin, because of his loyalty to a radical ideal that refuses to ignore any kind of suffering, no matter how hopeless.

<u>Light in August</u> centers on the depth of the familiar--a depth found even in the heart of the extreme. <u>The Idiot</u>, on the other hand, centers on the meaning of two extremes that are essentially irreconcilable with the familiar. Joe's extreme situation is meaningful in the sense that it is not to be dismissed. Joe must be taken into account not because he has any striking ideas or reflections of his own to offer, but because he calls into question the nature of the world. Though Faulkner takes very seriously the mystery of the existence of an extreme such as Joe represents, Joe's rebellion itself is presented as blind and meaningless. It is a tragic aberration that leads nowhere at all. Nastasya Filippovna is also a rebellious character. But the central issue of <u>The Idiot</u> is the possibility that Nastasya Filippovna's rebellion is meaningful despite its extremity bordering on insanity. Both she and Myshkin are beyond the familiar and constitute a threat and a challenge to the familiar. Both confront the limits of human life with wide open eyes. What they see, or still cannot see, sets something in motion within them that cannot be satisfied: a questioning, a puzzlement, a yearning for resolution. The problem they face is radically unfamiliar, and cannot be resolved by simply returning to what is familiar and abiding.

Each of the two worlds in <u>Light in August</u> somehow creates the impression of being, within itself, a stable and consistent world. Lena and Byron's world is rooted in fidelity, while Joe's owes its consistency to compulsive self-will. The contrast between the two worlds raises a question about the nature of the one world that contains them both. But in <u>The Idiot</u> we find not two contrasting independent worlds, but at least three worlds that are constantly interfering with one another, and constantly trying to break through to one another. Dostoyevsky does not allow the impression of any one world, with its own immanent, abiding values, to develop. In nearly every scene, one world questions, threatens, or challenges another. The two extremes are in tension with each other, and both interfere with our impression of the conventional, stable world of the Epanchins. Through such constant interference, Dostoyevsky evokes a deeper kind of questioning about the nature of the world, a feeling about the world more deeply uneasy than Faulkner's.

In *The Idiot*, there is a strangeness that reaches further than the mystery in *Light in August*, and the center of that strangeness lies in Myshkin's relation to Nastasya Filippovna. Through most of the novel, Dostoyevsky makes it almost seem as if Myshkin can find a place in the world of the Epanchins, but our sense of his affinity for that world is disturbed by a sense that something is not quite right. Myshkin always contrasts strikingly even with Lizaveta, but his relation to Nastasya Filippovna arouses the suspicion that the contrast is even greater than it may at first appear. As we read Parts Two and Three, which go into Myshkin's developing relation with the Epanchins, we remember the events of Part One: how Myshkin proposed marriage to Nastasya Filippovna on his second meeting and followed her to Moscow after she refused. The six months he spent there, largely with her, receives no direct description, and Myshkin strongly resists any discussion of his experience. The full extent and nature of Myshkin's bond to Nastasya Filippovna represents an enormous gap in the novel. Nastasya, and what she represents to Myshkin, might be compared to an iceberg, with only a few tips actually piercing the surface of the narrative. Myshkin meets Nastasya in the last three parts of the novel only twice before the final crisis, but her presence makes itself felt again and again--in his meetings with Rogozhin, in Aglaia's jealousy, and in Nastasya's letters to Aglaia that Myshkin reads.

Parts Two and Three, while dealing directly with Nastasya hardly at all, consist in large part of the responses of the whole spectrum of people in the novel to Myshkin's strangely chivalrous actions, of which his attempt to save Nastasya is the most extreme. Myshkin's bond to Nastasya becomes a kind of story that impresses the other characters and leads them to reflection. The two essential elements of the plot are, on the one hand, the working out of the tragic fate of Myshkin, Nastasya Filippovna, and Rogozhin, and on the other, the effect Myshkin's character and destiny have on the lives of the other characters, primarily Lizaveta, Aglaia, Yevgeny Radomsky, Ippolit, and to some extent, Ganya, Lebedyev, General Ivolgin, and Kolya Ivolgin. Myshkin's impact is largely to cause them to reflect. These latter characters, with the possible exception of Aglaia, do not move the plot forward, but do occupy most of the novel. They themselves are occupied essentially with Myshkin, and Nastasya's relation to Myshkin is the most remarkable thing about him. Nastasya is the most powerful force in the plot, even though she is most of the time only a scarcely perceptible voice calling for Myshkin to return.

Myshkin's entanglement with Nastasya Filippovna is strange even in the most obvious sense of the word. All in one day, he hears about her for the first time, sees her portrait, meets her twice in outrageous circumstances, and offers to marry her on their second meeting. In Part One, we see Nastasya only in two scenes which involve great dramatic crisis: in the first, Myshkin meets her, and in the second, he offers to marry her. Of the scenes in which Nastasya appears, these scenes are matched in fullness of development only by Nastasya's meeting with Myshkin and Aglaia in Part Four. Into these first two scenes, Dostoyevsky has crammed almost his entire development of Nastasya's character. In the second of the two, Nastasya's whole life is set before her, and she passes judgment on that life, taking the decisive step that finally leads to her doom. On first reading these scenes may be simply exhausting, and one may wonder why Dostoyevsky feels he must drag us through them. But I think that these scenes prove themselves aesthetically successful, and that their very peculiarity is the key to their religious significance.

The second of the two scenes, which spans chapters Thirteen through Sixteen, is crucial to the meaning of the whole novel. Nastasya has invited Totsky, General Epanchin, Ferdyshtchenko (an obnoxious buffoon very like Lebedyev), and Ganya, as well as an assortment of less important acquaintances, to a party. She has promised to announce whether she will marry Ganya, accepting the 75,000 rouble bribe offered by Totsky. Unknown to her guests, she has also invited Rogozhin, who has offered Nastasya 100,000 roubles for her hand in marriage, and who arrives later in the course of the scene. The scene begins with the arrival of the uninvited Myshkin, whom Nastasya welcomes. This aggregate of characters brings together all of the radically opposing forces in Nastasya's life. She has, in fact, brought her guests together for the very purpose of confronting her whole past life and rejecting it. This scene sums up not only her life, but almost sums up the whole novel. Most of the major characters are present, the major dramatic forces in the novel all meet together, and the events and decisions take place that will drive the novel forward to its tragic conclusion.

Earlier, I noted that an essential aspect of Dostoyevsky's technique is the telescoping of the whole into the parts. For Faulkner, confronting individual characters with the drastic contrasts embodied in the novel as a whole is not nearly as important as it is for Dostoyevsky. One may think of an exceptional scene such as Byron and Hightower's meeting with the Hineses—but even this scene lacks the sweep and dramatic decisiveness of analogous scenes in The Idiot. Dostoyevsky's novel is in fact built around a series of such scenes. These scenes not only each sum up the novel, but always include characters who appreciate the import of the radical contrasts with which they are presented. Four vast scenes in particular stand out: the two in Part One already mentioned; one in Part Two in which Burdovsky presents his case in the presence of almost all of the characters in the novel except Rogozhin, who have come to visit Myshkin as he recovers from an epileptic fit brought on by Rogozhin's attempt to murder him; and one in Part Three, in which almost all of the characters in the novel are also present, with the exception of the Epanchins, and whose center of interest is Ippolit's extended speech and attempted suicide. These scenes share a common structure: the unwanted intrusion of the chaotic, violent world of Rogozhin, Nastasya, Burdovsky, and Ippolit into the normal or conventional world of the Epanchins and the Ivolgins. But even the shorter scenes including only two or three characters embody contrasts and conflicts as radical as those in the more comprehensive scenes.

Faulkner creates a sense of world and comprehensiveness by bringing together, through the course of his whole novel, characters representing the extremes of comedy and tragedy. Dostoyevsky, by contrast, creates such a sense of comprehensiveness within individual scenes over and over again. Through comprehensive scenes that include characters who are aware of the comprehensiveness and its significance, Dostoyevsky brings the issue of the meaning of the world and of the human condition into the experience of those characters. Interpolated stories the characters tell and listen to also serve this purpose. Dostoyevsky does not assert that certain characters are aware of this issue--or even that there is such an issue. Rather, the structure of juxtapositions within his scenes suggests that certain characters experience the same feeling of mystery and enigma in the background of those scenes and stories that the reader does.

Both Nastasya Filippovna and Joe Christmas are radically rebellious characters--both find their lives unendurable in a very basic way, and long for a way out. But the great difference between them is that Joe is morally and spiritually blind, while Nastasya Filippovna is not. Joe knows no better than to respond to the threat McEachern represents than by imitating that threat. Joe simply responds to the onslaught of his environment--he does not reflect upon his environment, and is not able to sense that it might have been, and ought to have been, different. But Nastasya Filippovna sees Totsky exactly as he is, and fully appreciates his moral turpitude <u>as</u> moral turpitude. Nastasya's violent reactions to Totsky and to the world he has created for her are not automatic and thoughtless, but simply desperate. Although Nastasya's reaction to her situation is highly disturbing, we sense that her perception of her situation is basically truthful. Our sympathy for Nastasya owes much to the fact that she is so unlike Totsky, and refuses to accept the rather easy role he offers her in life. For all her insistence that she is a shameless woman, she refuses the true degradation of libertinism, opportunism, and selfish sensuality that Totsky represents. Totsky views her as a piece of property, and Nastasya madly rebels against his attempt to define away her humanity.

Nastasya has been humiliated, and she desires to humiliate in return. She has called her 'friends' together precisely for the purpose of lashing back at them for the marriage deal they have arranged. It becomes clear that she is constantly searching for ways to embarrass Totsky as well as General Epanchin, and that she sits back in despairing fascination that they will put up with it for the sake of what they want from her. She is constantly shoving Ferdyshtchenko in their faces, watching them squirm at having to accept such a low-life in order to retain her favor. But the essential feature of her character is that she can never rest content even in her vengefulness. She is somehow always asking a question of the world, even in her most extreme reactions. Her desperate vengefulness drives her eventually to self-destruction, but her flight to her murderer Rogozhin does not provide her the peace and contentment people are sometimes said to find in the decision to commit suicide.

Nastasya's behavior is contradictory in a way that suggests her basic orientation to others is really undecided. At her first meeting with Myshkin at the Ivolgin's apartment, her aim seems, above all, to be to take pleasure in her emotional torture of the Ivolgins. She encourages General Ivolgin's spiteful silliness, only to compound the shame by unmasking his lies, and encourages Rogozhin to openly bid for her hand in marriage. But her taunting has a desperate, frenetic quality. She jumps from one embarrassing question to another, hardly listening to the replies, and laughs uncontrollably. She does not leave the impression of a blank wall, as a character who is truly shut off from others does. She betrays moments of softness and introspection impossible to reconcile with her proud petulance. This softness is apparent as a kind of eddy in the narrative, and first makes itself felt when she is introduced to Myshkin.

Myshkin seems to evoke in Nastasya the same kind of pausing and reflection he did in the Epanchin ladies. Her first question to him is still somewhat taunting, and having asked it, "she waited in impatience for an answer, as though she were sure the answer would be so stupid as to make them laugh." But there is something about Myshkin that changes her attitude. When Myshkin tells how he had been impressed by her portrait and that he felt he had seen her before, she listens to him carefully, asking him to repeat himself, asking where he had seen her before. Her response to Myshkin contrasts to her treatment of the other characters, to whom she does not listen at all. Listening to Myshkin, she drops her mocking tone. Dostoyevsky suggests just a glimpse of openness between her petulant and distracted forays. At the end of this small interlude, the narrator reports that "Nastasya Filippovna looked at him with interest, but she was not laughing now" (p. 98).

Our impression of this doubleness in Nastasya Filippovna's character is confirmed by her response to the climax of the scene. Nastasya sees Myshkin prevent Ganya from hitting his sister, and sees him take Ganya's blow himself without retaliating. She seems surprised and at a loss to respond. When Myshkin asks her "Aren't you ashamed? Surely you are not what you are pretending to be now? It isn't possible!" (p. 110), she does not resist, or scoff, or maintain a cool exterior. Her behavior comes as a surprise to the reader. She goes up to Ganya's mother and tells her in a whisper "I am really not like this, he is right," seeming somewhat embarrassed and disconcerted, and immediately leaves.

Both the scene at the Ivolgin's and Nastasya's party later that night are dramatic whirlwinds of passion and fateful struggle. But again and again, Dostoyevsky suggests that Nastasya is not simply caught up in that whirlwind, that she is not simply reacting to the immediate stimulus of the situation in which she finds herself. For all of the violent and intensely emotional conflict in those scenes, they yet have their root in Nastasya's reflection upon her life. That reflection involves a sense of mystery, and of an intolerable enigma. The very occurrence of the party is an expression of her reflection--she herself has chosen to bring certain people together, and she aims for a certain definite outcome. Myshkin is her only surprise.

One of her aims in holding the party seems to be to make the evil she feels surrounded by to show itself one last time for what it really is. Her strange pride somehow triumphs in experimentally proving others' baseness. But the complication in her character is that she cannot rest in her prideful contemplation of other peoples' dirty souls. Their existence tortures her continually. It is as if, having once seen evil, she cannot take her eyes off it, but stares and stares, as if asking it a question.

Consider the first incident at her party. Ferdyshtchenko proposes that they play a game in which each participant is to describe the worst action of his or her life. Totsky and General Epanchin at first resist, but finally give in to Nastasya's eager desire to go ahead with it. It is clear that her motivation is largely to embarrass the two men. But as she listens to the stories Ferdyshtchenko, Epanchin, and Totsky tell, she does not seem to savor their embarrassment--indeed the latter two cleverly emerge with their so-called dignity intact. Ferdyshtchenko, who is up first, tells how he once stole a three rouble note and allowed a maid to be blamed and fired for the theft, enjoying the fact that he could sit and listen to her accusation, conscious of the note right there in his pocket, without feeling the slightest remorse. Nastasya is genuinely appalled, as are the rest of the company. But Nastasya's disgust with Ferdyshtchenko, especially when he crudely manifests his disappointment at their taking offense, is very powerful indeed--we read that she "positively quivered with fury" at him (p. 138).

Nastasya sits silently through all three stories, and Dostoyevsky provides a brief but highly significant description of her reaction to each. While the stories do not directly relate to her, they reveal the characters of the three men she is dealing with, particularly their attitudes toward money, possessions, and women, as well as their different kinds of moral complacency. The three stories, and especially Totsky's, in the context of the situation in which they are told, indirectly summarize her past. Even Ferdyshtchenko's story suggests a deep similarity between him and Totsky. Totsky is in effect trying to buy her acquiescence to his plan, and through the story we gain a closer acquaintance with his possessive attitude toward women in general. He sees them as a kind of toy, something existing purely for his own amusement, and does not experience a shadow of a doubt about the obvious appropriateness of his attitude. Needless to say, he does not describe his rape of Nastasya. Rather, he tells how on one occasion he had frustrated the plans of a fellow who was flirting with another man's wife. Totsky himself obtained for her the last supply of a kind of flower that happened to be all the rage at the moment. He apparently views women as hysterical, child-like creatures who swoon for such small favors as these. And he feels that his own fault, if any, was in frustrating a potential adulterer, who, as a result, joined the army and died in battle. Dostoyevsky suggests Nastasya's brooding reflection upon Totsky's character by two small hints. As she listened, she "was staring intently at the lace frill of her sleeve, and kept pinching it with two fingers of her left hand. She didn't even once glance at the speaker" (p. 142). And as he finished, "the company noticed that there was a peculiar light in Nastasya Filippovna's eyes and her lips quivered" (p. 144). The most remarkable aspect of this incident is that listening to the men is a torture for Nastasya, and yet she herself insisted that the game be played, and must have foreseen very well what sort of thing she was to hear.

A tremendous pressure is building up inside her as she listens to the stories. It is the pressure of her entire life, and is about to explode. The scene exhibits the same pattern of reflection followed by response that we find in Myshkin's meeting with the Epanchin ladies, and again and again throughout the novel. The storytelling incident suggests her reflection on her past life, and the rest of the scene portrays her explosive response to that life.

Totsky's supercilious possessiveness has been a torture to her--she feels that for the last nine years she has simply been the object of laughter. The laughter raises a question in her soul--a question Totsky does not consider. It raises for her the question of who, or what, she is. Totsky has disturbed something in Nastasya that he had not reckoned on. He has set a process in motion that will not stop. Her extreme actions which follow express that process. Her extreme responses are, on the one hand, to invite Rogozhin to her party after encouraging him to bid 100,000 roubles for her, and on the other, to fall in love with Myshkin at first sight. Behind her encouragement of Rogozhin lies another response: her conviction that she is a "shameless hussy." She actually clings to that conviction, not complacently, but precisely because it causes her so much pain. She is also disgusted by Rogozhin--she mocks and taunts him, and despises the dirty bundle of money he lays down on her table. But at the same time she craves to be swallowed up by what disgusts her--craves, finally, to be killed by it.

Nastasya's first response to Myshkin's proposal is indeed mocking. When he tells her she is an honest woman, she responds: "Oh, all those notions . . . come out of novels! Those are old-fashioned fancies, prince darling; nowadays the world has grown wiser" (p. 154). But even this remark is ambiguous. Her cynicism is biting, but somehow lacks confidence in itself. Her remark may equally be an expression of despair. Our sense of her double state of mind is reinforced by her reaction to the excitement over the revelation of Myshkin's inheritance. She is no longer laughing, but is confused and strangely taken aback, strangely reflective.

> She was still sitting down, and for some time looked about her with a strange and wondering gaze, as though she could not take it in and were trying to grasp what had happened. Then she suddenly turned to Myshkin and with a menacing frown stared intently at him; but that was only for a moment; perhaps she suddenly fancied that it was all a joke, a mockery. But Myshkin's face reassured her. She pondered, then smiled again vaguely, as though not knowing why. (p. 157)

She apparently accepts his offer, but then somehow wakes up from her confusion, and it gradually becomes clear that she intends to go off with Rogozhin after all. I do no think that Dostoyevsky suggests this was 'really' her intention all along. Rather, her contact with Myshkin seems to have momentarily drawn her into a strange kind of wavering; and once she does announce her intention, it becomes clear that she is not doing what she really wants to do. Upon emerging from her dreamlike wavering, she launches into a long speech attacking Totsky, Ganya, and General Epanchin; and she insists to Myshkin that she is a shameless hussy heading for the gutter, while he called her perfection. But why would she be so insistent if she did not wish Myshkin were right? She makes a point of her shame almost in rebellion against her own attraction to the possibility of honor Myshkin offers her. The clearest indication of her double attitude comes at the climax of her harangue:

> "Look, prince, your betrothed takes the money because she is a low woman, and you wanted to marry her! But why are you crying? Are you sorry? You ought to laugh as I do."--Nastasya Filippovna went on, though there were two large tears glistening on her cheeks.--"Trust to time; it will al pass! Better to think twice now than after. . . . But why are you all crying?" (p. 161)

It becomes clear that Myshkin really always was a part of her world as a possibility she yearned for. As her speech continues, she tells of living in Totsky's country home, waiting for him to arrive and take his pleasure:

> "Haven't I dreamed of you myself? You are right, I dreamed of you long ago, when I lived five years all alone in his country home. I used to think and dream, think and dream, and I was always imagining some one like you, kind, good and honest, and so stupid that he would come forward all of a sudden and say, 'You are not to blame, Nastasya Filippovna, and I adore you.' I used to dream like that, till I nearly went out of my mind. . . ." (p. 161)

Here again, her cynical rejection of a "stupid" Myshkin is all bound up with a despair over her own cynicism. She does not dismiss Myshkin out of complacent nastiness; rather, she appears to feel imprisoned by her own cynicism. She longs to escape, and yet laughs at her desire to do so.

Marriage to either Myshkin or Rogozhin appeals to Nastasya as an escape from the oppressive force Totsky represents. Marriage to either would not represent for her what marriage normally means. Her alternative is not a question of involvement in the world and in the rhythms of life, as it is in the cases of Byron and Joe. Rather, Rogozhin and Myshkin represent different possibilities for her own self-definition, for her own conviction of who she is. Each represents a commitment she might possibly embrace. The possible commitment is not one of involvement with and fidelity to another human being, but an inward conviction that would constitute her identity. By going off with Rogozhin, she would affirm her identity as a "shameless hussy" who enjoys her shamelessness, and by marrying Myshkin, she would accept his conviction that she is a woman worthy of respect.

Faulkner's presentation of love suggests notions such as 'openness,' 'fidelity,' and 'endurance' that are reflected in patterns of consistent action. But in Dostoyevsky, the focus has shifted: we tend to think more in terms of 'respect' and of a spiritual attitude or stance that longs to rescue others from their self-hatred, and is convinced that self-hatred is a mistake. Love for Dostoyevsky has a dimension of inward conviction that Faulkner does not emphasize. Dostoyevsky is not concerned with the juxtaposition of comedy and tragedy, but with the possibility of overcoming tragedy through love. Dostoyevsky deals with the possibility that one whose life, whose personality is a disaster can be somehow rescued from that disaster through sheer love and inner conviction, quite apart from the growth of any other hopes. Dostoyevsky's new kind of tragedy consists in the failure of Myshkin's attempt.

One may well ask, how can Nastasya be so strongly attracted to two such extremes: to Myshkin, who utterly lacks regard for his own interest, and is completely out of place in the world; and to Rogozhin, whose mad desire to possess leads him to buy her for 100,000 roubles, and finally, to murder her? Her actions do seem to be excessive, somehow out of proportion to what Totsky has inflicted on her. Her actions may seem so extreme as to be almost implausible. But I think Dostoyevsky means to raise exactly the question of whether a 'proportionate' response even exists to a world in which Totsky's are possible.[1]

In the scene from The Idiot I have been discussing, Nastasya's sudden request that Myshkin decide whether she should marry Ganya, the sudden arrival of Rogozhin, and the triumphant yet appalled welcome she gives him, are radically surprising and deeply puzzling. Dostoyevsky attempts to evoke an unfamiliar, perplexing emotion--an emotion unlike even Joe's response to Doc Hines and McEachern, or Byron's response to Lena, or, certainly, Elizabeth's response to Darcy in Pride and Prejudice. And there is also something very problematic about Nastasya's response, and Myshkin's empathy with that response. Is she not simply neurotic? Or is there nevertheless a kind of truth in her response?

E. M. Forster, in his discussion of The Brothers Karamazov in Aspects of the Novel, attempts to define a quality in Dostoyevsky he terms 'prophecy.' He focuses on the dream Mitya has as he sleeps during a break in his interrogation.[2] Mitya dreams he is riding in a cart through the cold, snowy steppes. He passes through a village that has burned down; he sees starving peasant women along the road, and a baby crying because it can get no milk from its mother's dried out breasts. Mitya starts asking the driver why, "even though his questions were unreasonable and senseless."

> "But why is it weeping?" Mitya persisted stupidly. "Why are its little arms bare? Why don't they wrap it up?"
> "Why, they're poor people, burnt out. They've no bread. They're begging because they've been burnt out."
> "No, no," Mitya, as it were, still did not understand. "Tell me, why is it those poor mothers stand there? Why are people poor? Why is the babe poor? Why is the steppe barren? Why don't they hug each other and kiss? Why don't they sing songs of joy? Why are they so dark from black misery? Why don't they feed the babe?"[3]

I think that Forster has pinpointed, in this passage, the very essence of Dostoyevsky. Mitya, in a dream, insists on asking a seemingly senseless question that yet seems desperately necessary. The question does not so much look for an answer as long for a kind of resolution one cannot understand, and that seems unreachable. It is a <u>strange</u> longing--the kind of longing one feels in a dream. This kind of longing can be evoked not only by more or less direct statements such as Mitya's, but as the cumulative effect of entire scenes, and of entire novels, including <u>The Idiot</u>.

Nastasya does not pose the kind of direct, almost metaphysical question Mitya does--but I think her reflections and actions taken together express exactly the same kind of longing. She too is strangely puzzled by evil, she too is dark from black misery, she too wants to sing songs of joy and wonders why people are crying . . . and she is a babe they never fed. (It might be noted as an aside that Nastasya fell into Totsky's hands when her father's farm was destroyed by fire.) The whole scene is indeed dreamlike in its extremity, and she at times seems as if in a dream. Her actions and speeches also seem senseless and out of proportion to the situation in which they arise. Forster notes about Mitya that "taken by himself, he seems distorted, out of drawing, intermittent. [. . .] We cannot understand him until we see that he extends."[4] The same observation could apply equally well to Nastasya. Nastasya's and Mitya's apparent distortion creates a sense of distance and extension that raises questions about life deeper than anything suggested by a character whose reactions seem 'justified.' Mitya and Nastasya "extend" not simply because they evoke a mysterious background, but because they consciously confront and question the human condition and evoke that feeling of questioning in the reader. That questioning involves not simply a feeling of depth but of a strange problem that cannot be solved, but must be.

Nastasya experiences Myshkin's love as a possible resolution to her dilemma. But she genuinely wavers between the conviction that he can save her and the conviction that her attraction to him is a stupid delusion. Her discontent includes Myshkin himself. She is not only afraid of his love, but is well aware, as we are, of the weakness of his position. Perhaps she even begins to foresee Myshkin's inability to endure in the face of the violence of her, as well as Rogozhin's spirit. Her longing seeks both Myshkin and Rogozhin, but also extends beyond both.

Myshkin empathizes with her longing and believes he finds in it an essential purity that has survived a life of hell. Unlike Nastasya, he does not waver. But Dostoyevsky presents this sense of longing, as it is felt both by Nastasya and Myshkin, not simply as an ambiguous, but as a highly problematic, emotion. While Nastasya's character "extends" or "reaches back"--she does not reach back in the same way that Faulkner's characters do. Nastasya's longing involves a sense of 'more' different from the mysterious depths of experience. Her longing confronts a wall and longs to get past it. The men she sees before her seem like a puzzle--a puzzle she must solve, but cannot. The sense of 'more' is the sense that there must be a solution to the puzzle. It is a feeling, not aroused by an object, but a feeling aroused by the lack of an object, a feeling of need for an absent object that will not become present no matter how far or deeply one searches. Such a feeling does not imply the existence of the absent object, the longed-for resolution.

Dostoyevsky is asserting neither that Myshkin __might__ have saved Nastasya, nor that some higher resolution is available. Rather, he is attempting to evoke a feeling of possibility. To experience a feeling of possibility is not to experience the truth of the fact that something is possible. A feeling of possibility is, by its very nature, also possibly a delusion or a senseless mental disturbance. We experience the double possibility that Myshkin's and Nastasya's longing really heads somewhere, or that it is only a meaningless product of madness, idiocy, disease. I would like to suggest that the aim of a successful literary work can indeed be to evoke such feelings--as long as the author is true to their problematic character, as Dostoyevsky is.

In his characterizations, Dostoyevsky centers on the tendencies within feeling to go beyond feeling--both the tendency that leads toward a definite conviction, and the tendency that longs for a resolution completely beyond its grasp. He compellingly raises the question of whether we, in reliving those tendencies, are touching upon something deeply valid, or only a senseless aberration.

Nastasya Filippovna can find no satisfaction in what a normal, conventional life might offer her; she is driven to extremes, and cannot be satisfied even there. A psychologist might, for this reason, simply call her 'maladjusted.' She needs, a psychologist might say, to learn to appreciate the limited satisfactions and rewards a normal life has to offer. But is the lack she feels so easily understood? On the one hand, it does seem that she arbitrarily clings to her shame, refusing to believe in any alternative. But it is also important to keep in mind that she is still, in a sense, a social pariah. She is not rejected; but she is looked down upon wherever she is enjoyed. It really is almost impossible for her to escape her association with Totsky. He is her only means of support, and her reputation as his concubine will follow her everywhere.

Psychologists whose ideal is 'adjustment' to life perhaps do not fully appreciate the extreme ugliness of the conditions many people must adjust to. Nastasya Filippovna faces truly ugly conditions--her suffering is not simply a neurotic invention. But whether or not some kind of adjustment is possible for her, her abrupt and drastic actions suggest exactly this question to the reader: is her unease merely a psychological problem, an inability to understand and accept the good things of life, or does she, in some basic way, see the world for what it is, so that her unease must somehow be shared by us all? Is Myshkin right in discovering something deep and true through his empathy with her, or is he basically as sick as she is? In The Idiot, the viewpoint of the implied author is one of suspension between these two alternatives rather than the assertion that she and Myshkin have an authentic awareness of religious problems, or the alternative assertion that she and Myshkin are neurotics.[5]

In the course of Parts Two and Three, even as it appears Myshkin might be able to adjust to the Epanchin's world, and may even marry Aglaia, Nastasya is constantly lurking in the background. (She briefly emerges only twice.) In Part Four, Nastasya finally breaks through and pulls Myshkin back. Aglaia, driven to distraction by the series of honeyed, covertly spiteful letters Nastasya has sent her, arranges a confrontation. In the presence of Myshkin and Rogozhin, the two women give vent to their jealousy. At the climax of the scene, Nastasya takes another sudden action. She demands that Myshkin stay with her and marry her, holding him to his earlier promise: "I've only to tell him, and he'll throw you up at once and stay with me for ever, and marry me, and you'll have to run home alone. Shall I? Shall I?" (p. 544) Myshkin looks into Aglaia's face, and cannot endure the hatred for Nastasya he sees there. He runs after her, but feels Nastasya clutching him from behind, pleading with him to stay. He does stay, and promises again to marry her. Myshkin has now left the familiar, normal world for good, even if he cannot accept that fact. He desperately wants to talk with Aglaia again, believing that he can make her understand; but the Epanchins refuse to see him.

Myshkin's last contact with the Epanchins comes in the form of a remarkable interview with Yevgeny Radomsky, another friend of the Epanchin family, and a former suitor of Aglaia's. Yevgeny is a minor character, but plays a significant and clearly defined role in the novel, as the most articulate spokesman for common sense. Yevgeny represents a kind of person Dostoyevsky personally disliked--a rationalistic proponent of Western European culture, sceptical, ironic, and occasionally supercilious. Yet, in the novel, Yevgeny is basically a positive and sympathetic character. Even though Myshkin puzzles and perhaps amuses him, Myshkin also elicits his sympathy. Yevgeny has many points in his favor: he views Totsky as a "disgusting aristocratic profligate" (p. 553), he is himself not involved in General Epanchin's scheming with Totsky, and he helps look after Myshkin's interests after Myshkin's collapse into insanity.

While Yevgeny shares the general outrage at Myshkin's behavior, he remains well disposed toward him, and their conversation has a friendly and compassionate tone. Yevgeny, encouraged by the openness Myshkin continues to show even under the present circumstances, quickly launches into a critical analysis of Myshkin's behavior, hoping, perhaps, to bring him to reason. The remarkable thing about his analysis is its real perceptiveness and plausibility. Yevgeny explains Myshkin's love for Nastasya as an infatuation, and Dostoyevsky means, I think, for Yevgeny's criticism to be a real challenge to Myshkin.

Along with most of the other characters in the book, Yevgeny has reflected upon Myshkin's personality and actions. He is able to offer the response of the normal, familiar world of the Epanchins in its most articulate form. Yevgeny castigates Myshkin for abandoning Aglaia essentially on a moment's notice. The center of his argument is not only that Myshkin deceived Aglaia, but that his love for Nastasya Filippovna is <u>false</u>. Yevgeny goes back to the fateful night Myshkin proposed marriage to Nastasya, which he knows about in detail. Yevgeny sees Myshkin returning to Russia eager to be of service, full of romantic ideas about his homeland gleaned from books. Myshkin's idealism fastens on Nastasya the moment he hears of her. And on the day of his arrival in Petersburg, he was not in his right mind. He was disoriented by the rush of new experiences—surprising, intriguing, and shocking. His epileptic condition and extreme fatigue made him especially prone to overreact. In this state of mind, according to Yevgeny, Myshkin simply became caught up in his ideas, and lost touch with reality. Yevgeny asks him rhetorically "whether there was reality, whether there was genuineness in your emotions, whether there was natural feeling or only intellectual enthusiasm" (p. 554). Yevgeny claims that Myshkin is the victim of a "huge mass of intellectual convictions," which Myshkin had taken for "real, innate, intuitive convictions" (p. 553).

Myshkin had proclaimed his love for Nastasya, and his conviction that she was worthy of respect. Yevgeny confronts this conviction, and upon reflection decides it is not real, not sincere, but only a kind of self-deception. In confronting another's conviction, every character faces the alternatives Yevgeny does. Confronting another's conviction involves a sense of a possible 'more'—the 'more' as a possibility of a definite identity, and not simply of affirming an idea. The 'more' is a sense of tendency, and the question is raised for the characters and the reader, of whether that tendency actually leads somewhere, or is only a delusion. Yevgeny opts, in effect, for the alternative that the tendency is a delusion, and carefully explains his judgment to Myshkin. Myshkin agrees with much of what Yevgeny says, and yet insists, in an unbelligerent and strangely distracted way, that Yevgeny has left something out.

> "It was true what you said just now about that evening at Nastasya Filippovna's; but there is one thing you left out because you don't know it. I looked at <u>her face</u>! That morning, in her portrait, I couldn't bear the sight of it. . . . Vera, now, Lebedyev's daughter, has quite different eyes. I . . . I'm afraid of her face!" he added with extraordinary terror. (pp. 555-56)

The narrator mentions the mysterious tone of Myshkin's voice as he says this, and the terror too comes through in the last sentence. Myshkin is horrified by Nastasya's suffering. He feels her desperate unease as if it were his own, and longs to be able to resolve the terrible inner tension she cannot escape. Yevgeny also faces the longing Nastasya and Myshkin share, as a tendency that may or may not be headed somewhere, and he concludes that it is not headed anywhere--that it is meaningless and merely pathological.

The remarkable point about Yevgeny's interpretation is that it is in accord with at least part of the impression the proposal scene in Part One really does make. I do not think Dostoyevsky wants to make it at all easy for us to believe that Myshkin is sincerely in love with Nastasya. In the proposal scene, Dostoyevsky deliberately strains the reader's sense of plausibility. In terms of normal human motivation, Yevgeny's analysis is the most plausible account of Myshkin's behavior. But to claim that Yevgeny's perception is all that the original scene suggests, would be to trivialize the novel. Dostoyevsky's aesthetic aim is to create a double, paradoxical impression of Myshkin's character. This does not mean that he is directly challenging us to choose between interpretations. His aim is not to challenge us to choose, but to make vivid the full range of possibilities involved in human life, including the possibilities of conviction and longing. These latter possibilities, Dostoyevsky suggests, can only appear in a paradoxical way, under a double aspect.

The climax of <u>Light in August</u> is the scene in which Lena gives birth in Joe's cabin with the Hineses, Byron, and Hightower in attendance. All of the radical contrasts in the novel are brought together in a single powerful symbol. But the significance of the scene is not essentially dramatic. The two plot lines, the two worlds, do not interact or conflict, but just barely touch. That momentary, tentative contact is the key to the mystery and power of the novel. In <u>The Idiot</u>, the kind of radical contrasts that emerge over the course of Faulkner's entire novel are already present in the experience of each of the main characters. The direction of the plot is determined by the characters' reactions to these radical contrasts. The climax of the plot is not simply a symbol of the contrasts, but a real dramatic conclusion: the climax is the final working out of the fate of three people who cannot accept, but cannot overcome, the barriers that divide them. The overall effect of <u>The Idiot</u> is not simply to impress upon us the reality of the human condition, but to raise the question of the meaning of Myshkin's longing, and failure, to overcome the human condition.

Dostoyevsky's plot development is successful largely because, on the one hand, he creates the convincing impression that his major characters really face choices, are really torn in two directions: Myshkin, between

Nastasya and Aglaia; and Nastasya, between Myshkin and Rogozhin. At the same time, the choices the characters make have the air of inevitability. The characters meet their tragic end not so much through the conspiracy of external forces as through the inner logic of their personalities. I think Dostoyevsky also suggests something more elusive: that Myshkin is defeated by what we might call the inner logic of the world. Dostoyevsky suggests that anyone who wants what Myshkin wants, and tries to accomplish what Myshkin tries to accomplish, must fail. Myshkin is defeated by the nature of things itself, against which he has rebelled. But here again, a caveat is in order: Dostoyevsky is not asserting that there is a nature of things and that it must defeat people like Myshkin. Rather, he uses Myshkin's fate, convincingly presented, to raise a question about what is and is not possible in the nature of things. Through the reflection embedded in the very structure of the novel, he suggests a number of responses to Myshkin's failure--not all utterly pessimistic.

Myshkin's central conviction is that he must meet the needs of everyone around him, especially their need for love. At first, it seems, he believes this is possible, and in the long run he is never able to accept its impossibility. His inability to deal with the rivalry between Nastasya Filippovna and Aglaia grows out of this conviction. A truly weak person would never have gone to the lengths Myshkin had. He fails not simply out of weakness but because of the very strength of his conviction, because of the power of his refusal to accept the limitations the world imposes on love. To the very end, he clings to the belief that he can somehow reconcile Nastasya Filippovna and Aglaia, that Aglaia would abandon her jealousy if only he could really explain "everything" to her. In his belief, Myshkin must indeed appear incredibly foolish, and in his actions, irresponsible.

In moral terms, it is hard to ignore Yevgeny's criticism of Myshkin's behavior, especially in the light of the tragic conclusion of the whole novel. While it may be tempting to see Myshkin as a kind of moral paragon, he is, in fact, an extreme moral failure. If we assume that not only an agent's intentions, but the foreseeable effects of his actions, have moral significance, then Yevgeny's arguments are cogent. If it matters not only how you feel and what you desire, but what you accomplish, Myshkin's behavior is morally very questionable. He really has played Aglaia false. From the beginning, he was in love with her, deceiving himself about the nature of the obviously romantic letter he sent her from Moscow. But now, scarcely a few days after actually proposing marriage to Aglaia, he agrees to marry Nastasya, whom he had also promised to marry six months before. For he had also deceived himself about his relation to Nastasya--about both the strength and the nature of the bond that united them. To claim that Myshkin loves Nastasya only with an '<u>agape</u>-love' and Aglaia with only an '<u>eros</u>-love,' would be an oversimplification. Is it simply out of <u>agape</u> that Myshkin raises Nastasya's portrait to his lips and kisses it? Or that he later tells her that "everything in you is perfection"? Dostoyevsky does not exclude the dimension of sheer attraction to a beautiful and fascinating woman from Myshkin's love for Nastasya. And is not the source of Myshkin's whole dilemma the '<u>agape</u>-love' he has for <u>both</u> women, making it unthinkable to disappoint either? He has ended in a morally ambiguous situation partly because he has been, to an extent, blind to his own feelings and to the nature of the situation he has gotten into. But the most striking ambiguity in his situation results from his moral ideal itself. His commitment to fulfill the needs of everyone--in particular, the needs of literally the first people to cross his path upon his arrival in Russia--results in disaster.

Even Christian moral theologians might complain, along with Yevgeny, that love for others requires some sort of calculation about what it is really possible to do for them, and a willingness to learn how to do it successfully. Myshkin's love, in the end, may well seem to have done more harm than good. The morally right act, some might suggest, is the one based on a careful consideration of what can and cannot be accomplished. By making realistic choices and compromises an individual can succeed in carrying out the course of action that is morally best under the circumstances. But Dostoyevsky suggests that unselfish love is not so simple. Myshkin's moral failure raises a question about what we might mean by moral success. Myshkin is paralyzed by the necessity of abandoning one person in order to save another. He believes Nastasya would die without him. And in the end, rather than accept the impossibility of 'saving' Rogozhin and Nastasya, he loses his mind. For this reason, Myshkin may well appear very foolish or very sick. But I think Dostoyevsky means to suggest something more through Myshkin. I think he means to suggest that moral success--achieved through calculations and compromises--really is utterly unacceptable. Dostoyevsky does this not by presenting Myshkin as some higher kind of success, but simply by presenting him as a real failure. His horror over Aglaia's jealousy, his insistence that there must be a way to reconcile the two women, his fear of Nastasya Filippovna's face--all represent the kind of feeling the person who is content with moral success, and the person who is psychologically well-adjusted, do not dwell upon.

Dostoyevsky suggests that Yevgeny's perspective is a valid one, but he also suggests that Myshkin sees something Yevgeny is blind to. Sanity and moral success may be founded upon a blindness that is also hard to excuse. Dostoyevsky seriously suggests three things about Myshkin: that he truly loves the two women with unselfish love to the very end, that he sees reality for what it is, and that his terror and even insanity are entirely appropriate responses to reality from the viewpoint of love. Myshkin demonstrates that the demands of love are impossible to fulfill, and calls into question the satisfaction one may be inclined to take in prudent compromise. But Dostoyevsky goes beyond any sentimental admonition not to forget about the heart. Through Myshkin, Dostoyevsky questions not only the compromises that are obviously questionable, but even the ones without which life is simply impossible.[6]

As the novel *Light in August* progresses, Byron and Hightower learn more and more to empathize with Joe and Joanna as well as Lena, and they are increasingly challenged to act. But the lives of the characters intrude upon one another in a way even deeper than empathy. The feeling arises in the novel that, in some sense, the fate of Joe *is* Byron's fate; that the fate of any human being is not only possibly, but actually, the fate of every other. Joe lives in a different world from Byron, but neither Byron nor the reader can exclude or dismiss Joe's world. Yet, Byron lives on in spite of the horror brought so close to him. His destiny has its own integrity; his hope survives in spite of the kind of world it is in.

With Myshkin, Dostoyevsky suggests a different possibility. Like Byron, Myshkin is brought close to deadly hatred and desperation. Nastasya longs for death as the only escape from humiliation and her own despairing outrage, and Rogozhin is willing to murder her out of greed and jealousy, and perhaps even a strange kind of sympathy for her desperation. Their lives intrude upon Myshkin's just as Joe's and Joanna's intrude upon Byron's. But, in The Idiot, it is almost as if Byron had fallen in love with Joanna and had tried to save them both as Joanna had tried to save Joe, and Byron had literally shared their tragic fate. In Light in August Joe's world intrudes upon Byron's, yet the two remain separate and somehow isolated. For Myshkin, it is not enough to sense the intrusion and perform acts of compassion: he longs to overcome the barrier itself. Nastasya's suffering intrudes so deeply into Myshkin that he finally has no life of his own. Her fate engulfs his fate. Through Myshkin, Dostoyevsky suggests both that the barrier cannot be overcome, and that life is impossible once the barrier is confronted. The climactic scene of the novel involves not the simple juxtaposition, but the tragic collision, of the two worlds.

After Nastasya Filippovna has left Myshkin for the last time, Myshkin finally finds Rogozhin in Petersburg, and Rogozhin takes him to her. The startling fact is that Rogozhin has actually sought Myshkin out--that he somehow needs to be together with Myshkin after murdering Nastasya. Rogozhin is strangely gentle and hesitant and sad, despite the malice and rage we know he harbors. And Myshkin displays a strange, docile willingness to go along with Rogozhin, despite his mounting terror. Rogozhin quietly leads Myshkin into his dark apartment, and quietly shows him the body of Nastasya Filippovna hidden behind a thick curtain. He makes a bed of cushions for them on the floor--Myshkin agreeing with him that they must spend the night together with Nastasya. Rogozhin gradually descends into delirium as Myshkin offers his hopeless comfort, himself reverting to idiocy.

Myshkin does not turn against Rogozhin with hatred or contempt even after Rogozhin has murdered the woman Myshkin loved. And Rogozhin himself was never, and is not even now in this final scene, a simple creature of malice. He is still drawn to Myshkin as much as he hates him. He is strangely distracted and confused, and even states that he still does not "understand it all yet" (p. 580). In a sense, Rogozhin has indeed simply been used by Nastasya. She has driven him to be the instrument of her suicide, and he has long recognized that death is what she desired from him. But both Nastasya and Rogozhin wavered in their desire. At one point, Rogozhin actually gave her up to Myshkin, and she herself was unable to remain with either for very long.

Nastasya does not find it easy to go to her death. The theme of Myshkin's empathy for a person sentenced to death--be he a criminal, a consumptive such as Ippolit, or even Jesus--surfaces again and again in the novel, and this theme contributes to our understanding of his empathy for Nastasya. All of these images of death and execution come together in her death. Dostoyevsky suggests that Nastasya must have experienced the same hesitation and desire to retreat Myshkin sensed in the criminal he saw executed in France.

Nastasya's feeling is complicated by the fact that the object of her terror is also the object of her desire. She desires death as a relief from the terrible tension she feels. Appalled by the injustice of her humiliation at Totsky's hands, she had, even in adolescence, longed for someone like Myshkin to arrive and tell her, "You are not to blame, Nastasya Filippovna, and I adore you." But that never happened. Nothing is more humiliating than having to cling to a slender thread of self-respect in the roar of supercilious laughter. The greatest torment is to long to believe one deserves to be loved, but to be given every day new and powerful reasons for doubt, and to be imprisoned in a world that simply smiles at one's unease. Nastasya tries to embrace guilt as a relief from this torment. The tension of doubt grows so great that the possible certainty of guilt begins to exert a kind of magnetic attraction. To simply know that she was a shameless woman would be a relief compared to her dizzying uncertainty. She also tries to escape humiliation by asserting to others that she desires humiliation. She flings Rogozhin in Totsky's face. But she flees from Totsky with Rogozhin not simply to make a point to others, but because she really wants to be murdered. The instrument of her torture had been in the hands of others--by fleeing with Rogozhin, she takes it in her own hand, and pushes it even deeper. Somehow, she finds it preferable to join forces with the evil attacking her than either to fight it or accommodate herself to it.

By fleeing with Rogozhin, Nastasya asserts that she is a shameless woman--but she is not content with that self-definition. Even degradation does not supply relief. She is somehow appalled by, and longs to escape, being torn between the reality of shame and the possibility of love. She longs to escape from Myshkin to Rogozhin, and from Rogozhin to Myshkin--but her final desire is to escape from this whole paradoxical situation, from her whole world. This is the route of escape Rogozhin's knife provides. The desire to die originates not only in guilt, but in her inability to endure the human condition as she experiences it.

The next to last chapter of The Idiot ends with a striking image: Rogozhin and Myshkin lying together by the dead Nastasya; Myshkin's tears dropping on Rogozhin's face; Myshkin stroking Rogozhin's cheeks, trying to calm his raving as they both lapse into spiritual darkness. This image plays a role analogous to the role played in Light in August by the image of Lena giving birth in Joe's cabin. Each image brings together the radical contrasts of the novel into a single scene; each seems to sum up the entire novel. Juxtaposing these two scenes brings out the essential difference between the two novels as clearly as can be: in <u>Light in August</u>, two extremes are mysteriously juxtaposed, but kept apart; in <u>The Idiot</u>, one extreme desperately strives to break through to the other. Each author has created an intense image of the human condition, but they have created two different kinds of images. In the climactic scene from <u>The Idiot</u>, the characters' own confrontation of the human condition is itself an essential aspect of the image, and the dramatic significance of the image lies in their failure to overcome what they face. Also, <u>The Idiot</u> is full of characters' reflections upon the story of Myshkin, Nastasya Filippovna, and Rogozhin, and the conclusion of the story must be seen in the light of those reflections. For this reason, the climactic scene of <u>The Idiot</u> does not sum up the novel as completely as the climactic scene of <u>Light in August</u>.

The next to last chapter of <u>The Idiot</u> ends with the observation that if Dr. Schneider had been present at the discovery of Myshkin in Rogozhin's room, "remembering the condition in which Myshkin had sometimes been during the first year of his stay in Switzerland, he would have flung up his hands in despair and would have said as he did then, 'An Idiot!'" (p. 583). This sentence might have worked as an impressive, and bitterly ironic, conclusion to the entire novel. However, Dostoyevsky does not end the novel here, but with an additional very short chapter.

The final chapter begins with a summary account of the direction the lives of the rest of the characters take after Myshkin's collapse. We learn that, for example, Aglaia has run off with a phony Polish count who has completely alienated her from her family. Once this summary is taken care of, Dostoyevsky ends the novel with a scene. Lizaveta, her two remaining daughters, Yevgeny, and Prince S. visit Myshkin at Dr. Schneider's sanatorium in Switzerland. Myshkin does not even recognize them. We learn that "Lizaveta Prokofyevna wept bitterly at the sight of Myshkin in his afflicted and humiliated condition" (p. 585). We know that Lizaveta has always loved Myshkin and respected him highly, and she seems now to have completely forgiven him. The brief impression we get of her in the closing lines of the novel is of a person who is certainly sad, but far from crushed, and certainly not bitter. Though Myshkin's fate touches Lizaveta at least as deeply as, say, Joe's touches Byron, Myshkin's fate does not engulf her as Nastasya's engulfs Myshkin. She has some source of strength that leaves her vigor and love of life unimpaired. In the final paragraph, she seems, to me at any rate, to be the same vital character she has been throughout the book. She begins by complaining about Europe:

> "They can't make decent bread anywhere; in winter they are frozen like mice in a cellar," she said; "here, at any rate, I've had a good Russian cry over this poor fellow," she added pointing to Myshkin, who did not even recognize her. "We've had enough of following our whims; it's time to be reasonable. And all this, all this life abroad, and this Europe of yours is all a fantasy, and all of us abroad are only a fantasy . . . remember my words, you'll see for yourself!" she concluded almost wrathfully, as she parted from Yevgeny Pavlovitch. (p. 586)

The tone of this final paragraph contrasts strikingly with the bitter finality of the closing sentence of the previous chapter. Her statement is ambiguous and open-ended, and contains a number of subtle and conflicting suggestions. "Following our whims" may well refer to Aglaia's infatuation with Myshkin, but Lizaveta's attack is in fact directed against Yevgeny, criticizing his preference for Europe. While she may be indirectly associating Myshkin with Europe, she says she has also had a good "Russian" cry over him.

Lizaveta has always been impatient with Yevgeny's supercilious incomprehension of Myshkin. Her outburst against Yevgeny suggests that even now, when all the results are in, Lizaveta cannot accept the sort of rationalistic dismissal of Myshkin we heard earlier from Yevgeny. Dostoyevsky hints that Lizaveta still cherishes Myshkin, with his strange earnest yearning and commitment to love, even though that yearning has ended in a disaster that directly affected her own daughter. She may suggest he is a "fantasy"--but she always exaggerates anyway. Dostoyevsky does not allow his climactic scene to be the last word on the human condition. By ending the novel with Lizaveta, he qualifies the central tragedy, both through her ambivalent attitude toward Myshkin, and through her enduring vitality itself.

The climax may also be seen in the light of another point of view developed in the novel: Ippolit's. Ippolit is a cynical and resentful, but extremely thoughtful seventeen-year-old who is dying of tuberculosis. He exhibits the same inner division between isolation and openness as Rogozhin--but he is not hardened as Rogozhin is. He is essentially naive and in his sickness and confusion can easily be drawn out of his pride-- only to later repent of his "weakness." His reflection plays a central role in Parts Two and Three of the novel--he is one of the main centers of attention in the two comprehensive scenes that dominate those sections. He is obsessed with his impending death, and cannot stop talking about it. In many ways, he is similar to Myshkin: in his alienation, in his perplexity about life, in the longing that is evident in his speeches despite the tone of cynicism he adopts. In the first scene, he tells Lizaveta that

> "I should like to have left every one friends, every one . . . but I had none. . . . I meant to do so much, I had the right. . . . Oh, how much I wanted! Now I want nothing. I don't want to want anything, I promised myself not to want anything; let them seek the truth without me! Yes, Nature is ironical. Why" he resumed with heat, "why does she create the best beings only to laugh at them afterwards?" (p. 280)

He picks up this last suggestion again, with explicit reference to Christ, in his long article he reads aloud in the second scene. Both he and Myshkin had seen Rogozhin's copy of Holbein's painting of the dead Christ, and it makes a strong impression on both of them. As Ippolit accurately reports, in this extremely disturbing painting there is no beauty in Christ's face--no hint of life or light that would suggest his coming resurrection. Seeing such a corpse, Ippolit asks, how could Christ's apostles believe he would rise again?

> "Looking at such a picture, one conceives of nature in the shape of an immense, merciless, dumb beast, or more correctly, much more correctly, speaking, though it sounds strange, in the form of a huge machine of the most modern construction which, dull and insensible, has aimlessly clutched, crushed, and swallowed up a great priceless Being, a Being worth all nature and its laws, worth the whole earth, which was created perhaps solely for the sake of the advent of that Being. The picture expresses and unconsciously suggests to one the conception of such a dark, insolent, unreasoning and eternal Power to which everything is in subjection." (p. 389)

Ippolit has his own convictions about the human condition he faces. He is convinced that life is in the grip of that Power, and he refuses to worship it. Ippolit's belief could not contrast more strongly with Myshkin's notion of "God's gladness in man" (p. 208). The climax of the novel fits rather neatly into Ippolit's way of looking at things. Myshkin is like Christ not in that he is a revelation of God or is faithful to God unto death, but that he believes in, and tries to live out, an ideal of moral perfection: of love for every human being without distinction.7 And in the end he is utterly crushed. If the climax of The Idiot is an image of the nature of things, from Ippolit's viewpoint the nature of things there represented is the dumb power that is against the best and brings all to a senseless doom.

Ippolit's reflection is part of the essential structure of the novel itself, but does not exhaust the meaning of the whole.8 Myshkin's hopes may seem to have been exposed as foolish. Ippolit's or Yevgeny's reflections may appear far more realistic. Yet if the contrasts and conflicts of the central drama are taken together with the total structure of reflection upon that drama, it becomes apparent that the implied author does not favor one viewpoint over another. Instead, the tension among the viewpoints suggests something more. Dostoyevsky once wrote that "reality is not limited to the familiar, the commonplace, for it consists in huge part of a latent, as yet unspoken future word."9 What did Dostoyevsky have in mind with his "unspoken future word"? The various viewpoints in the novel affect one another. But they do not work themselves out to reveal some inner harmony. Nor do some emerge victorious over others. Rather, the final effect of the novel is one of straining after a resolution, of "thirst after a new word."10 The reader is left in the paradoxical position of being unable to dismiss any of the viewpoints, and yet unable to resolve their conflict. The whole novel works together to confront us with the human condition, and with a comprehensive spectrum of responses to that condition, and then suggests a need for more, for an "as yet unspoken future word." But if Dostoyevsky were to speak that word, or embody that word in a character, that word would simply become another viewpoint caught in the complex paradox. The aim of Dostoyevsky's art is to express the thirst after a new word, not to express the new word itself.[11]

Myshkin, Nastasya, Ippolit, and Rogozhin all thirst after the future word, and may even have some inkling of what that word is. But while Ippolit's viewpoint may seem to be the most fitting interpretation of the novel's climax, he is undercut as a character perhaps more than any other. And it is again Lizaveta's perspective that places Ippolit in a wider context. Ippolit's world-view may be portentous--but especially in his encounters with Lizaveta, Ippolit himself can appear in a very silly and a very pitiful light. Lizaveta herself probably tends to view both Ippolit and Myshkin as two confused little boys--at one point, she tells Ippolit that "you are not too old for a whipping yourself, sir!" (p. 270) Lizaveta is not afraid of Ippolit. Rather, she is moved to compassion as soon as she forgets how offended she is, and only Myshkin has her abiding sympathy. Her complex attitude toward Myshkin and Ippolit, and her "good Russian cry" over Myshkin at the end, confirm a tendency within the climactic scene itself that runs counter to Ippolit's attempt to speak the final word.

Dostoyevsky does not draw a line for us, indicating just how deeply Lizaveta appreciates, or fails to appreciate, Myshkin's character. Her response is open and suggestive. She is sensitive to different points of view and does not herself try to speak a final word. Her openness suggests that she may be sensitive to the deeper aspects of Myshkin's character even as she views them askance. Her persistent sympathy with Myshkin suggests a refusal to simply dismiss what he stood for even in view of his grotesque failure.

The climactic scene leaves us with a paradox that inspires an unease and a questionable yet unavoidable desire for resolution. Myshkin yearned, in effect, to abolish evil through love, and he failed. The climactic scene suggests that the division between the world of Myshkin and the world of Rogozhin and Nastasya cannot be overcome, and yet remains intolerable. Dostoyevsky suggests that our sense of the intolerability and longing for a resolution may be meaningful, and may be the essence of religious feeling. While Myshkin's hopes are defeated, his aim remains compelling. That we can imagine no way for that aim to be realized only directs our attention to the radical nature of the longing his fate may inspire.[12]

NOTES TO CHAPTER SIX

¹Such a question of 'proportionate response' may be related to T. S. Eliot's notion of 'objective correlative.' In his essay "Hamlet and His Problems," in <u>Critical Theory since Plato</u>, ed. Hazard Adams (New York: Harcourt, 1971), pp. 788-90, Eliot states that Hamlet's "disgust is occasioned by his mother, but . . . his mother is not an adequate equivalent for it; his disgust envelops and exceeds her." The "adequate equivalent" would be the "objective correlative." There are no "external facts, which must terminate in a sensory experience" that evoke Hamlet's particular emotion. Because Hamlet's emotion lacks an objective correlative, Eliot believes, the play is an artistic failure. It seems to me that Eliot has pinpointed exactly the kind of feeling Dostoyevsky is trying to evoke, but that <u>The Idiot</u> is, for that reason, by no means an artistic failure.

²E. M. Forster, <u>Aspects of the Novel</u> (New York: Harcourt, 1954), pp. 130-35.

³Quoted in Forster, p. 131.

⁴Forster, p. 133. Forster, unlike Eliot, can see meaning in a feeling that lacks an "objective correlative."

⁵T. S. Eliot holds that "the intense feeling, ecstatic or terrible, without an object or exceeding its object," is "doubtless a subject for pathologists." The pathologists, or psychoanalysts, have indeed taken up the subject, and have some very interesting reflections to offer on Prince Myshkin's personality. Simon O. Lesser, in "Saint and Sinner—Dostoyevksy's Idiot," <u>Modern Fiction Studies</u>, 4 (Autumn, 1958), pp. 211-24, claims that the extremes in Myshkin's character arise simply from masochsim. He is attracted to Rogozhin and to Nastasya Filippovna because he desires to be hurt. Rogozhin is a pure sadist, while Nastasya is half sadistic and half masochistic. Myshkin suffers from a weak ego and an overdeveloped superego. For this reason he makes impossible moral demands on himself and craves punishment. The psychoanalytic viewpoint proposes an ideal of adjustment, which Myshkin fails to achieve. Elizabeth Dalton, in <u>Unconscious Structure in "The Idiot"</u> (Princeton: Princeton Univ. Press, 1979), greatly expands Lesser's interpretation, and suggests that Myshkin's radical dissatisfaction with reality itself represents an infantile regression (pp. 164-65).

⁶Murray Krieger, in "Dostoyevsky's 'Idiot': The Curse of Saintliness," in <u>Dostoyevsky: A Collection of Critical Essays</u>, ed. René Wellek (Englewood Cliffs, N.J.: Prentice-Hall, 1962), also points out the convincingness of Yevgeny's diagnosis of Myshkin's love, and the reliability of Yevgeny as a critical voice in the novel. Krieger focuses on Myshkin's self-deception, his infidelity to Aglaia, and the evil consequences of his extreme goodness. But Krieger does not unequivocally identify Yevgeny's voice with Dostoyevsky's voice. He points to the vigor of Lizaveta as a real alternative to Yevgeny's sceptical detachment. But, in my opinion, Krieger has simply sidestepped the meaning of the whole novel. The power of the novel lies in its suggestion of what Yevgeny is blind to, in spite of the real validity of his criticisms. Robin Feuer Miller, in <u>Dostoyevsky and</u>

"The Idiot": Author, Narrator, and Reader (Cambridge, Mass.: Harvard Univ. Press, 1981), draws attention to Krieger's statement that "there seems to be no irony in the credentials our author gives to Yevgeny. [. . .] Of course it is possible that our author is posing as a worldly, sensible narrator who cannot but sympathize with Yevgeny--although Dostoyevsky is hardly the sort of novelist who plays tricks with 'point of view'" (quoted in Miller, p. 235). I agree with Miller that, in fact, "the meaning of the novel hinges on just such a trick of point of view" (p. 236). Miller carefully delineates the way Dostoyevsky brings us to trust, yet also to distrust, his narrator. The result is the creation of two readers--the narrator's reader and the implied reader--who are of course at the same time the real reader. The narrator's reader agrees with Yevgeny, but the implied reader "refuses to give in to the general indignation. [. . .] One reader condemns and the other forgives Myshkin" (p. 156). The real reader shares **both** responses, and it is only through this conflict of responses that the meaning of the novel arises.

[7] According to Konrad Onasch, "Die theologisch zunächst ausserordentlich zweifelhafte religiöse Christus-Symbolizität Myschkins besteht darin, dass er nicht den dogmatisch überhöhten, dogmatisch "typischen" Christus darstellen soll, sondern, im Gegenteil, den menschlichen Jesus." Dostojewski als Verführer (Zürich: EVZ-Verlag, 1961), p. 108.

[8] Lev Shestov, in "Dostoyevsky and Nietzsche: The Philosophy of Tragedy," tr. Spencer Roberts, in Dostoyevsky, Tolstoy, and Nietzsche (Athens: Ohio Univ. Press, 1969), finds in Ippolit, as well as in characters such as the underground man and Raskolnikov, the true voice of Dostoyevsky. He tends to give Dostoyevsky's works an unequivocally pessimistic interpretation, and sees Myshkin in a totally negative light. Shestov makes much of the point that Dostoyevsky refuses to be consoled in the face of tragedy, even by the kind of ideal Myshkin represents. "Dostoyevsky prefers to beat his head against the wall to the point of exhaustion rather than find solace in the humane ideal" (p. 207). I think Shestov errs in locating the meaning of Dostoyevsky's novels in the assertion that the humane ideal and worldly hopes are vain. Dostoyevsky may suggest what Shestov asserts, but his suggestion is qualified by other alternatives.

[9] Mikhail Bakhtin, Problems of Dostoyevsky's Poetics, tr. R. W. Rotsel (Ann Arbor, Mich.: Ardis, 1973), p. 73.

[10] "L. P. Grossman speaks very well to this point, using Dostoyevsky's own words: 'The artist 'hears, senses, even sees' that 'new elements arise which thirst after a new word,' Dostoyevsky wrote much later; they must be captured and expressed.'" Ibid., p. 235.

[11] "The catharsis which completes Dostoyevsky's novels could be--of course inadequately and somewhat rationalistically expressed thus: nothing definitive has yet taken place in the world, the final word of the world and about the world has not been said, the world is open and free, everything is still in the future and will always be in the future. [. . .] In Dostoyevsky's novels everything is directed toward the as yet unspoken and unpremeditated "new word," everything tensely awaits that word, and the

author does not block its path with his own one-sided and clear-cut seriousness." Ibid., pp. 138-39.

[12] The views of George Panichas in The Burden of Vision: Dostoyevsky's Spiritual Art (Grand Rapids, Mich.: Eerdmans, 1977) contrast sharply both with those of Bakhtin and Shestov. According to Panichas, "in him [Myshkin] the finite becomes infinite; he is a revelation of the holy" (p. 83). Myshkin's worldly fate is the result of the holiness revealed through him, and that holiness transcends the apparent futility of his life. Panichas identifies what I have called Myshkin's strangeness with the "mysterium tremendum et fascinans" of the holy (p. 48). Panichas also sees The Idiot in terms of contrasting worlds. For him, they are "the world of experience and the world of revelation" (p. 61). Contact with Myshkin is "lightning contact with the eternal" (p. 57). Panichas appears to hold that, through Myshkin, Dostoyevsky is asserting the reality of the eternal, the holy, of God.

PART THREE

CHAPTER VII

Evocation of Feeling and Avowal of Commitment

as Artistic Aims:

From Faulkner and Dostoyevsky to Werfel and Bernanos

My central aim throughout Parts One and Two has been to define the notion of 'the meaning of a novel,' and to specify in what sense that meaning may be considered religious. I have distinguished two kinds of religious experience--religious feeling and religious commitment--and have attempted to relate each kind of experience to the literary meaning of Light in August and The Idiot. I have concluded that a religious feeling may be identified with the literary meaning of each novel as a whole, but that religious commitments may only form a subordinate part of that meaning. But some novels seem to be 'committed novels.' They attempt to give a particular commitment more than such a subordinate role.

In Part Three, on the basis of the conclusions I have drawn thus far, I will address three basic questions about the committed novel: How are we able to recognize a committed novel as such? What distinguishes committed novels such as Embezzled Heaven and The Diary of a Country Priest from evocative novels such as Light in August and The Idiot? And Why are committed novels aesthetically less successful than evocative novels? In this chapter, I will recapitulate my view of the nature of literary meaning, and attempt to show the relevance of my conclusions to the aesthetic problem of the committed novel. In Chapters Eight and Nine, I will apply my views to a detailed analysis of Franz Werfel's Embezzled Heaven and Georges Bernanos' The Diary of a Country Priest.

In this chapter, I shall argue that the difference between evocative novels and committed novels can only be understood in terms of the author's intention. In order to even be able to experience an evocative novel as a work of art, the reader must understand the author's intention to be to evoke a feeling. A committed novel is recognizable as such because it makes evident the author's intention to avow a commitment through the novel itself. I shall argue that if the work did not reveal the author's intention to communicate a meaning, the work would not be recognizable as an artifact created by a human mind, and would simply not be a work of art at all. In this sense, recognition of the author's intention is the precondition for the reader's experience of the work as the kind of work it is, and is not a conclusion about the author the reader makes on the basis of his experience of the work.

I have held that the function of the literary form of <u>Light in August</u> and <u>The Idiot</u> is to communicate to the reader a concrete perception, and I have called such communication 'evocation.' The analysis of the experience of reading involves two basic issues: the nature of a concrete perception, and the nature of the relationship between author and reader that constitutes the communication of such a concrete perception. The essence of my argument is that the relationship between the author and reader, in a successful work of fiction, is indirect, and that committed novels are implausible and ununified because their authors attempt to confront the reader directly with a single definite commitment, rather than to simply evoke a concrete perception. The attempt to create such a direct confrontation drains the novel of evocative power.

My view is based on a certain notion of the relation of truth to perception and judgment, and to actual, empathetic, and imagined experience. Concrete perception is the primary fact of human experience;

it exists prior to both judgment and the imagined concrete experience that literary artworks communicate. Before a judgment can be made, the things about which the judgment is to be made must appear. To affirm the reality of concrete experience is to affirm that human consciousness must be more than a sum of deliberate acts of judgment. A proposition, first of all, isolates qualities of things and suggests the abstract possibility of their connection in a merely possible situation. An actual judgment affirms that connection in an actual situation.

But what is the nature of the actual situation about which the proposition is made, such that it is possible for propositions to be made about it? Concrete experience includes the characteristics of things in their actual togetherness, as they appear to conscious beings who experience them in a spatial and temporal continuum. The structure made explicit in a judgment must in some sense already be present in the perception of the thing, so that there is an identity within a difference between the meaning of the judgment and the reality of the thing. But the meaning of the judgment cannot be equated with the reality of the qualities of the things in their actual togetherness. Any perception will always contain more meaning than can be made explicit in any set of judgments, and our consciousness of the abstract content of any proposition excludes the perception of concreteness as such. Perception includes a feeling of background--not only as a sense of more meaning to be made explicit, but a sense of meaning that cannot be made explicit. Sense qualities form the foreground of concrete experience, but other qualities emerge only in the background. Sense qualities lend themselves to precise measurement and abstract consideration, but the background qualities do not. Among such background qualities are 'love,' 'person,' and 'importance.' As long as reality is considered with the aim only of framing factual judgments, whether particular or general, these background qualities will fail to emerge.

Perception involves a concrete paying attention that is prior to explicit judgment. Judgments are based on accurate and sensitive perception--and such perception must <u>happen</u> before judgments can take place. Indeed, it is only through such perception that the need for, and possibility of, judgment, shows itself. Perception is our letting the reality that already confronts us appear. It is our realization of what is before us in its actual connectedness and depth. It involves not only sensory attentiveness, but sensitivity to the values that emerge only in the background. I share Whitehead's view that this realization represents a kind of truth, to be distinguished from the kind of truth a proposition may have.1

Our concrete experience of reality includes our perception of other persons. As I pointed out in Chapter One, we do not know of the existence of others as a result of an inference, but through our reliving of their own concrete experience, a reliving made possible by the metaphorical suggestiveness of the appearance of others to our senses. In empathy with the stream of consciousness of another, it is not that I myself feel an emotion and then ascribe it to that other, nor is it that the other consciousness is somehow a part of my own. Rather, insofar as I empathize, I take my own stream of consciousness in two ways--as my own, and as that of another. In empathy with an emotion, I do not simply form an idea of that emotion and ascribe the emotion to another; nor do I actually feel the emotion; but I feel the emotion <u>as if</u> it were my own, while at the same time recognizing that it is not. And empathy connects me not simply with the emotions of another, but with the reality of his or her concrete experience as a continuous whole.

Empathy with actually existing people essentially involves a kind of affirmation of their existence--it is the primordial experience that imposes upon me the knowledge that I am not the only being in the world. Empathy essentially involves the dimension not only of the sharing of experience, but of one existence being confronted by another. Empathy means that I simultaneously take my own actual existence as my own and as someone else's. The sense of my own actual existence, as confronting another actual existence, remains in the foreground. Empathy involves the knowledge that each personality has a core that is the source of its decisions and commitments, and which cannot be relived by another. Empathy reveals both a current of feeling to be shared, and its own limit. Empathy's knowledge of its limit involves its knowledge of the core of the actual existence of the other, which imposes the limit on empathetic experience even as it announces itself unmistakably.

Our experience of a novel is a form of empathy. This is most obvious in the case of our empathetic experience of fictional characters. In empathy with fictional characters, I take my own stream of consciousness not only as my own and as not my own, but as my own actual stream and as another, non-existent stream. That I continue to take my consciousness as my own is essential to my experience of the work as a fictional work, but my sense of my own actual existence slips into the background, and is not part of my experience of the content of the work itself.

But our experience of a novel is not simply a collection of concrete experiences of fictional characters. Our experience of the work consists in an overall concrete perception that we relive, that constitutes the aesthetic unity of the work, and that contains our experience of the characters and makes that experience what it is. This experience involves a selection of material presented that allows the implicit sense of universal issues to emerge, and that binds the characters and events together into a unified world, and may raise the question of the meaning of that world. I have called this unified perspective our experience of the implied author. That experience, I have held, is a reliving of the single current of experience that unites the novel. But it is unlike empathy with an actual person or with a fictional character, for it lacks the dimension of a definite, particular existence, of a central core that can take a position in relation to other definite beings. It is a stream of consciousness that belongs to no particular person, a perception bound to no particular perceiver.

Our own actual experience includes the dimension of depth--a depth that includes the concrete perception of universal issues, and of the sense of 'world'--of the final, elusive reality that we confront in everything, and in which everything is contained. In our own actual existence, a true perception of reality includes an awakening to these deeper aspects of experience. Such a perception grows out of the concrete and particular reality of what is directly presented to a particular individual. Individuals may more or less share such a perception insofar as they are actually involved in, and concretely face, the same particular situations. In order for an experience to be concrete, it would seem that it has to be particular and actual. But literary art overcomes this limitation and makes possible the reliving of a true perception of the depths of experience that does not depend upon actual involvement in the concrete situation through which the sense of depth emerges. Rather, those words make it possible for us to _imagine_ that situation. Literary art involves a capacity even deeper than empathy--the capacity to imagine a world we do not actually face.

Through a novel, we perceive a non-existent world. This world presents itself not as an alternative to the actual world, but as the actual world all over again. The characters do not exist, the events never took place, and yet the world of the novel presents itself as _the_ world. While it does not exist it appears in a deep, indefinable way as identical to the world we actually face. The particulars of every person's concrete experience are different, but through imagination it is possible for many individuals to share the same concrete perception, and to verify its truth. It is because the world of the novel involves no direct reference to particular actuality that everyone can share the experience of such a world.

Reading is an actual situation that reveals a non-existent world that shares the depth of the reality of the existent world. The inescapable fact about reading is that it involves actual communication: an actual author is speaking to an actual reader and both exist in the same actual world. The defining characteristic of reading a novel is that this actual situation is suspended. In empathy with the implied author, the reader relegates his own actual existence, which confronts the actual existence of the author, to the background. The actuality of the situation is not a part of the perception that constitutes the novel's meaning and unity. Yet the actual author, actual reader, and actual world have an essential role to play in our experience of the implied author and the imagined world--for it is only in contrast with the former that the latter can appear as such. Imagination depends on the presence of actuality _as suspended_. In other words, our recognition of a fictional work depends on our recognition of the author's intention to present us with a fictional work. Through fiction, the author makes available an actual situation in which the actuality of author, reader, and world are suspended--and to do this is the author's actual aim.[2]

By contrast, in a work of historiography, of philosophy, of theology, or of religious confession, the author directly confronts the reader and the world. The author makes definite claims about the actual world which the reader must then verify through his own actual investigation, reasoning, or spiritual struggle. The aim of literary art, on the other hand, is to communicate the truth of concrete perception, which is prior to all judgment and commitment. Imagination enables the reader to experience a perception that does not depend upon his acquaintance with any particular, actual situation, and that represents an opening into the depths of reality that is permanent and integral. Since the perception does not depend upon acquaintance with particular, actual facts, the reader does not have to look outside the perception to verify its validity. Through the feeling of background within the perception itself, a sense of identity with the actual world emerges. Aesthetic unity depends on the self-contained truth of the perception as a perception of a world, on the verification of the feeling that through the imagined world, we truly face a world. The truth of an aesthetic perception is verified simply through the reliving of that perception itself. The suspension of direct reference to the actual world, and the creation of a sense of identity on the deeper levels of universality and worldhood, constitute the integrity and unity of our perception of the imagined world; allow that perception to be self-verifying; and allow it to be shared by countless individuals regardless of the details of their own actual concrete experience.

The statements in a novel describing characters do not refer to actual people; they have no direct reference to anything that exists. The importance of this absence of direct reference might be illustrated by the aesthetic confusion that results when a novel pretends to be a biography. Such novels are in a sense dishonest since they fail to distinguish between the inherent truth of an imagined perception and the question of whether the imagined perception is also a true perception of a specific actuality. But a novel about truly fictional characters may contain a different kind of direct assertion: characters, or the narrator, may express definite religious and moral beliefs. Such statements refer to those aspects of reality that the fictional world shares with the actual world. A character's statement about God or good and evil refers directly to reality, even though the character does not exist. Also, the sense of universality a work evokes essentially involves tendencies toward the making of assertions that refer directly to reality. As I pointed out in my discussion of Faulkner and Dostoyevsky, the status of such assertions and tendencies within a fictional work represents a problem. Assertions tend to detach themselves from the fictional context since they inherently direct the reader toward the actual world and toward his own actual existence. Assertions bring actuality out of the background into which empathy had placed it, and thereby violate the very structure of empathy. They challenge the reader to stop reliving the experiences of others, and to make up his own mind.

In reading The Idiot, one will indeed be taken aback by the many assertions one finds there. In order to understand and appreciate the novel, one must pause and reflect upon the judgments and ideas the characters express. One must rationally analyze their meaning and consider whether one can actually make them oneself. But this activity occurs outside of one's experience of the novel itself. Once one has reflected, one must return to the novel, and allow the understanding one has gained to become part of its imaginative form. In the structure of our experience of the novel The Idiot, this separation between our own actual experience and our experience of the novel is preserved. Dostoyevsky has incorporated ideas and commitments into an imagined world that has its own integrity. The imagined world maintains its independence because the commitments within it appear only as alternative possibilities. The overall experience of the novel is one of empathy with the concrete situation of facing alternatives, and is not the experience of being directly confronted with an espoused conviction. If commitments are to form a part of a perception that is to be verified through empathy alone, those commitments must appear as commitments appear through empathy. Since commitments themselves can only be verified through the experience of actually making them, commitments cannot appear as truths through empathy alone, but must remain unverified.[3] But to experience a commitment as not yet verified means to experience it as one possibility for the truth among others. By writing a 'dialogical' novel, in which no one point of view is allowed to prevail over the others, Dostoyevsky is true to the way we perceive possibilities for commitment in concrete experience.[4] He also succeeds in suspending the actual situation of author confronting reader, in spite of the great rhetorical force of the expressions of commitment he presents.

The overall experience of The Idiot is a perception of the world that raises the question of the world's meaning, and includes an urgent sense of alternative possible responses to that question. This perception is truthful because it grasps the essence of not only a feeling but of a choice and a dilemma we all confront. But a committed novel is not unified by the sense of a universal dilemma. In such a novel, the central commitment does not appear as an alternative possibility. How then does it appear? It appears to the reader in the way a directly stated commitment appears. The reader feels that the author is confronting him directly, challenging him to believe. In the case of <u>The Diary of a Country Priest</u> this challenge seems to underlie the entire structure of the novel.

In facing a direct statement of conviction outside a fictional context, the reader experiences the commitment only as a possibility--but the aim of the statement is not to evoke empathy with an imagined situation of facing alternatives, but to direct the reader to the actuality of his own existence, to his own actual capacity for deciding and believing. A direct statement of commitment reveals the author's intention to challenge the reader in this way. Such a challenge need not be an imperious command or an urgent exhortation in order to involve a direct relationship between writer and reader. For example, H. Richard Niebuhr speaks of faith in God in the following terms:

> We have learned to say, "For this cause was I born and therefore I came into the world that I might make glorious and exhibit the power of this last cause." And we have been enabled to say it with satisfaction, with love and hope and confidence; for to have faith in something as able to give value to our lives is to love it.[5]

Such a statement, in isolation, appears directly rhetorical, and in the context of Niebuhr's essay, it remains directly rhetorical. But similar rhetorical statements occur in Dostoyevsky's novels, and do not there function in a directly rhetorical way. The fictional context in

Dostoyevsky counteracts the tendency of such statements to create a direct relationship between reader and writer.

I claim that novels such as The Diary of a Country Priest are recognizable as committed novels because their overall effect is like that of a directly rhetorical statement. Bernanos creates this effect through a number of devices. By avowing a religious commitment a character presents us both with an interpretation of himself, as truly making the commitment, and of the world, as being what the commitment holds it to be. Bernanos, in both cases, deliberately de-emphasizes alternative interpretations, so that the real tension between alternatives we find in Dostoyevsky is missing. Also, the entire plot of The Diary of a Country Priest is organized around a conversion that is itself presented unambiguously as a conversion. The novel has a plot that is recognizable as a plot, and the conversion scene is recognizable as the climax of the plot. By excluding alternative interpretations and centering his novel on an unambiguous conversion, Bernanos fails to counteract the directly rhetorical aspect the presentation of the characters' beliefs involves. Through this omission, he reveals his intention to use the novel form to express a commitment, just as Niebuhr reveals his intention to express a commitment through the essay form. The problem, I shall argue, is that the essay and the sermon are forms suited to rhetorical expression, but the novel form is not. Because Bernanos wants the aesthetic climax of his novel also to function as a rhetorical climax, the conversion scene fails to unify the plot in the way we would expect it to.

The imposition of a rhetorical aim upon fictional form compromises the integrity of fictional form in several ways. The exclusion of alternative interpretations is false to the reality of our concrete perception both of others' commitments and of the world. Our experience of characters and of the world in a committed novel is implausible and incomplete because essential aspects are eliminated from the perception the work evokes. The exclusion of alternatives has the effect of replacing, at crucial points, evocation of character and of the world with direct judgments about characters and the world. Such judgments find their place not alongside of evocation, but are somehow supposed to function evocatively. But they do not. The direct reference to actuality they involve breaks the aesthetic unity of the novel. The meaning of the novel is no longer a single, self-verifying perception, but is essentially a mixture of what is self-verifying and what can only be verified through actual experience, rather than by mere reliving.

Finally, the direct reference to actuality violates the very structure of empathy, both with the characters and with the implied author. The intrusion of the real author's position taking pulls the actual situation of actual author confronting actual reader out of the background to which it had been relegated by empathy. But that actuality be relegated to the background is an essential condition of empathy with fictional characters and with the implied author. The result is that at crucial points, empathy drops out. The reader no longer experiences the characters' commitments from the perspective of the implied author as a gap in empathy or a limit to empathy beyond which lurk alternative possibilities. Rather, the implied author dissolves, and the characters' commitments come to represent for the reader not gaps in empathy, but a simple lack of empathy.

Both Werfel and, probably, Bernanos, were influenced by Dostoyevsky, and Werfel represents an interesting transition between the two more significant authors.[6] Aside from questions of influence I think that certain similarities are evident in their presentations of religious themes and characters. The comparisons I shall make between Dostoyevsky and Werfel and Bernanos will center on the ways the latter two authors overstep the boundaries Dostoyevsky struggled with and respected.

Both <u>Embezzled Heaven</u> and <u>The Diary of a Country Priest</u> center on religious conversions, and on reaffirmations of religious faith. The question of the religious belief of one or two main characters is the central issue of the plot of each novel, and the climax of the plot is an actual conversion scene. It is with such conversion scenes that the implausibility in the novels is most evident, and their central role in the structure of the novels creates problems with aesthetic unity. It is interesting to note in this context that Dostoyevsky wanted, up to the final stages of his plan for <u>The Idiot</u>, to include such a radical conversion in the novel.[7] But despite a long struggle, he could find no acceptable way of doing so: Myshkin is never able to persuade Rogozhin to 'walk in the light,' or Nastasya that she is an 'honest woman.'

I shall argue that both Werfel and Bernanos attempt to use the novel form to convey something which it cannot convey. But the two novels fail in different ways. <u>The Diary of a Country Priest</u> has a very clear and coherent structure and the question is whether that structure can accomplish what Bernanos wants it to accomplish. At the climax of the novel, the 'country priest' succeeds in converting a woman immersed almost as deeply in bitter resentment and proud despair as Nastasya or Rogozhin, and the novel ends with the priest's victorious resolution of his own spiritual struggle in the last two days of his life. Bernanos has definitely written a committed novel--in aesthetic terms, he has made up his mind about what he is doing. But Werfel's novel <u>Embezzled Heaven</u>, with which I shall deal first, has no such clear structure. <u>The</u> <u>Diary</u> <u>of</u> <u>a</u> <u>Country</u> <u>Priest</u> has a clear pattern which fails to really jell, but <u>Embezzled</u> <u>Heaven</u> just lacks pattern. Werfel's novel is interesting because it represents a case of real aesthetic indecision. The author has simply not made up his mind whether he wants to convey a feeling of ambiguity and possibility, or to convey a definite commitment. In <u>Embezzled</u> <u>Heaven</u>, we can study the conflict of the two different aims within the same novel, and we can even begin to observe the same character presented in a relatively plausible and realistic, and in a relatively implausible and sentimental manner.

NOTES TO CHAPTER SEVEN

¹For the distinction between kinds of truth I have relied primarily on Alfred North Whitehead. According to Whitehead, "The two conspicuous examples of the truth relation in human experience are afforded by propositions and sense perception." (p. 243) A third type of truth relation is that of 'symbolic truth,' "which may be included under the second type [sense perception] as an extreme instance of it." Symbolic truth is the type of truth art may possess. Symbolic truth is a "Truth of feeling and not a Truth of verbalization" (p. 267). A symbol will be truthful if it is able to evoke the depths of reality that elude propositional thought: "The truth that for such extremity of beauty is wanted is that truth relation whereby Appearance summons up new resources of feeling from the depths of Reality" (p. 267). For Whitehead, art has to do with the re-experiencing of the depths of reality: "The origin of art lies in the craving for re-enaction. In some mode of repetition we need by our personal actions, or perceptions, to dramatize the past and the future, so as to relive the emotional lives of ourselves and of our ancestors" (p. 271). Adventures of Ideas (New York: Macmillan, 1961). Martin Heidegger, from a different perspective, also denies that propositional truth is the only kind, or even the primary kind of truth. See esp. sec. 44 of Being and Time, tr. John Macquarrie and Edward Robinson (New York: Harper, 1966). Andrew Paul Ushenko's discussion of artistic truth in Dynamics of Art (Bloomington: Indiana Univ. Press, 1953) illustrates some of the problems with limiting truth in art to propositional truth. I agree with Ushenko that aesthetic experience essentially involves "vectors" or tendencies toward propositions. But Ushenko also states that "there are essential aspects, and elements, in art that cannot even be paraphrased in a statement and therefore have nothing to do with the truth" (p. 166). I find this latter view difficult to reconcile with Ushenko's statement that when an explicit statement in a literary artwork is detached from its context "it ceases to convey the same meaning, or proposition, as before" (p. 172). Does not that context include "elements that cannot be paraphrased"? How can he justify his claim that the context matters?

²For a similar point, see Paul Ricoeur, "Metaphor and the Main Problem of Hermeneutics," in The Philosophy of Paul Ricoeur: An Anthology of his Work, ed. Charles Reagan and David Stewart (Boston: Beacon, 1978), pp. 143-45.

³Whitehead does not make the distinction between truth of feeling and truth of commitment. He makes much of the religious significance of background as background, and such awareness may be said to involve a kind of 'subjective truth.' But I have claimed that the actual reliance upon a cause that Niebuhr describes is more than mere sensitivity to a feeling of background. Religious commitment has its own kind of subjective truth, to be distinguished both from the objective truth of propositions and the subjective truth of feeling. I think that it may be such subjective truth of commitment to which Kierkegaard calls attention in his discussion of Abraham in Fear and Trembling, tr. Walter Lowrie (Princeton: Princeton Univ. Press, 1968). Kierkegaard emphasizes the fact that we cannot relive Abraham's experience as he goes to sacrifice Isaac. On the one hand, Abraham may be incomprehensible because of the absurdity of his faith. But it is possible that Kierkegaard likes to overdramatize: a more basic

interpretation may be that the "passion of faith" simply cannot be relived, whatever the faith may be attached to. The subjective truth of faith is in some very basic sense incommunicable. Kierkegaard makes much of the contrast between Abraham and tragic heroes, and of Abraham's silence in contrast to their silence. They are comprehensible to us in a way Abraham is not. One of the tragic heroes to whom Kierkegaard refers is Socrates: "In case no last rejoinder of Socrates had existed, I should have been able to think myself into him and formulate such a word; if I were unable to do it, a poet could, but no poet can catch up with Abraham" (p. 127).

⁴In Problems of Dostoyevsky's Poetics, tr. R. W. Rotsel (Ann Arbor, Mich.: Ardis, 1973), Mikhail Bahktin writes: "The plurality of independent and unmerged voices and consciousnessess and the genuine polyphony of full-valued voices are in fact characteristic of Dostoyevsky's novels" (p. 4); and that "the unity of the polyphonic novel . . . stands above the word, above the voice" (p. 37). In my terms, the implied author (which Bakhtin calls "the authorial consciousness") is the unity of the novel. The implied author's experience is that of being pulled in conflicting directions. The implied author does not have a viewpoint as such, rather, he experiences the conflict of viewpoints. Bakhtin may have been rash in claiming that Dostoyevsky 'invented' the polyphonic novel; but it seems to me that polyphony is essential to the kind of novel Dostoyevsky wrote, and that his novels may indeed represent a new departure in terms of the way they handle ideas and religious commitments. Polyphony, in my terms, is the experience of commitments as possibilities rather than as truths. That commitments are presented in the context of "full-valued" alternatives is essential to their effective presentation as possibilities.

⁵H. Richard Niebuhr, "Faith in Gods and in God," in Radical Monotheism and Western Culture (New York: Harper, 1960), p. 123.

⁶For accounts of influence and affinity, see Marysia Turrian, Dostojewskij und Franz Werfel: Vom östlichen zum westlichen Denken, Sprache und Dichtung, vol. 73 (Bern: Haupt, 1950); Temira Pachmuss, "Dostoevskij und Franz Werfel," German Quarterly, 36, no. 4 (Nov., 1963), 445-58; Willy Burkhard, "Un Dostoievsky français?" in La genèse de l'idée du mal dans l'oeuvre romanesque de Georges Bernanos (Zurich: Juris Druck, 1967), pp. 261-97; William Bush "Bernanos--un 'Dostoievsky français?'" Mosaic, 5, no.3 (Spring, 1972), 145-50.

⁷See Fyodor Dostoyevsky, The Notebooks for "The Idiot", ed. Edward Wasiolek, tr. Katharine Strelsky (Chicago: Univ. of Chicago Press, 1967), p. 161.

CHAPTER VIII

Confusion of Aim and the Lack of Fictional Structure

in Werfel's *Embezzled Heaven*

The novel *Embezzled Heaven*, taken as a whole, is both incoherent and sentimental. It is nevertheless an interesting novel for the reason that Werfel introduces elements that might have contributed to a far more serious work, which he then fails to pursue in the course of the novel. In the first of the three parts into which the novel is divided, there is evidence of a serious confrontation of the human condition, and the main character, Teta, begins to appear in a mysterious and ironic light. These effective elements have a certain affinity to Dostoyevsky's presentation of religious issues. But in the course of Parts Two and Three, Werfel systematically represses the ironic alternatives he introduced, and he loses the sense of mystery he began to evoke. Even within Part One, his characterization of Teta is not entirely successful.

Teta is a seventy year old cook employed by the Argans, a sensitive, cultured, and humane Austrian family. The main action of the novel takes place in 1936. Although the Argans have employed her for twenty years, she has always kept her distance. The Argans are puzzled and occasionally annoyed by her rigid self-sufficiency. She has humbly followed, with no complaint, a strict and limited routine her entire life, as the servant of a series of well-to-do Austrian families, and as a pious Catholic maiden-lady. The narrator of the novel is also a character in the first part. Theo is a bachelor and unsuccessful writer who has been a friend of the Argans their whole married life and has stayed with them every summer at their residence in the mountains. The first part of the novel contrasts two sub-plots: the story of Teta's life and religious faith as the narrator learns of it and retells it, and the story of the accidental and completely unexpected death of the Argan's son Philipp the summer the novel begins.

While the Argans are extremely kindly, likable, and even admirable people, they have no strong religious convictions, though they are nominal Catholics. Werfel's treatment of their reaction to Philipp's death is completely convincing. Here, Werfel really succeeds in evoking the feeling of a religious problem. But Werfel also tries to contrast their inability to come to terms with death to Teta's unwavering religious faith, which is centered on her conception of the afterlife. This contrast, it seems to me, is not presented effectively. Teta's faith does not appear as a genuine alternative to the Argan's distraught uncertainty.

Teta's ideas about religion are very honest, straightforward, and naive. In a thirty-page flashback, the narrator outlines her religious development. She has never overcome doubt; rather, she has simply known no doubt. Her central aim has always been to get to heaven, spending as little time in purgatory as possible. While she had originally felt she could accomplish this through the careful fulfillment of her religious duties, she began to sense that something was missing. Thirty years before the main action of the novel begins, the opportunity arose for a greater accomplishment, in the form of her nephew Mojmir. Her brother's widow presented Mojmir to her, asking that she support his education. After a period of hesitation, she realized that if he were to study to be a priest, she would have her own personal intermediary with heaven, and would be the cause of one more mass being said in the world every day. How Mojmir is persuaded to pursue this career Werfel does not explain. She agreed to the plan, and has been sending him most of her money ever since. She learns of Mojmir's progress through constant correspondence with him, yet she never visits him, or receives a visit. Strangely, this does not bother her. And while her involvement with him seems narrowly practical and self-interested, Werfel emphasizes that she in fact develops a very human relationship with her nephew. She keeps an idealized portrait of him in her room, waits anxiously for his letters, is proud of his successes and worried by his failures. Of course, as it is clear to the reader from the start, Mojmir is the sleaziest kind of con-artist. Although we do not learn for certain until later that he never was ordained, and has in fact led a life of lasciviousness and petty chicanery, it is clear from the beginning that he has fooled his aunt completely. He has "embezzled" the funds with which Teta wanted to buy a place in heaven.

The story of Teta and her nephew Mojmir might appear as simply an amusing tale without any deep religious significance, centering on nothing more than Teta's peculiar and extravagant naivete. But Werfel wants his novel to mean much more. He wants us to take Teta very seriously. In the completely sober account of Philipp's death, Werfel deliberately contrasts her faith with the Argan's quiet desperation. The narrator, who seems to be very close to Werfel, is impressed by "something resolute and final" he senses in Teta, and also by her cold rejection of the Nazi-atheist ne'er-do-well Herr Bichler, whom the Argans employ as a gardener.

The whole aim of the plot seems to be to test her faith and to prove that it is deeply rooted and genuine. In Part Two, after leaving the Argans (who have fallen on very hard times), Teta attempts to find Mojmir, and she finally discovers the truth about him, meeting him face to face. Though she is plunged into despair, she soon gets the idea of signing up for a pilgrimage to Rome as a form of expiation. On the way she meets Johannes Seydel, who turns out to be a real priest, a model of charity and unpretentious faith. Seydel is just the man she needs to replace the scoundrel Mojmir. She finally confesses to Seydel in the catacombs of Rome, handing over Mojmir's letters for him to read. He subsequently absolves her, saying she is guilty of no more than fear of the truth, which is not really a sin, but only a weakness.

Seydel takes Teta just as seriously as the narrator does, and Seydel is presented in a completely positive light. Werfel wants to emphasize that even though the narrator and Seydel are both very intelligent and thoughtful men, they have high respect for Teta's simple faith and resolute character. Werfel enlists the Pope himself in support of Teta. She has a stroke immediately after kissing the Pope's hand, and he prays for her during mass after she dies.

The implied author presents Teta, on the one hand, in a rather absurd light, but also, on the other, seems to take her completely seriously. The same might be said of Dostoyevsky's treatment of Myshkin in The Idiot, but the effect of Embezzled Heaven is completely different. The way Teta is presented raises doubts about her in the reader's mind; and yet, as her characterization proceeds, one senses that these doubts are not followed up. Werfel emphasizes that Teta is a very limited and credulous person, and her relationship with Mojmir certainly confirms her extreme credulity. We may well ask, may not her faith simply be the result of her need for order and her willingness to be deceived? In Teta's relation to Mojmir, Werfel introduces a powerful symbol that he simply lets drop: the situation might have suggested both an alternative interpretation of Teta's inner life and that the divine reality Teta relies on is in fact an infernal one. Mojmir might have suggested the possibility that because of the nature of things, Teta's faith is a delusion. But the whole plot of the novel works to exclude this interpretation. Teta uncovers the reality of Mojmir, is able to persist in her faith, and finds in Seydel a spotless replacement for Mojmir.

Werfel has failed to create a tension between our sense of absurdity in Teta, and any sense that her inner life represents a genuine religious possibility. He begins to suggest her weaknesses, but does not allow the impression he creates of those weaknesses to really sink in. Her religious faith appears for that reason not as one alternative account of her inner life, but as the only account. The aesthetic problem that develops in the course of the novel is not only that tendencies opposed to Teta's beliefs are smothered--but that those beliefs themselves continue to appear as simply naive, and cannot bear the weight Werfel places upon them.

In Part One Werfel begins to develop a contrast between a certain strangeness in Teta and the normal, familiar life of the Argans. This contrast is basically similar to the contrast between the strange and the familiar that Dostoyevsky develops. Unfortunately, in Parts Two and Three, this sense of strangeness dissolves. Teta's presence initially has an almost symbolic effect, suggesting the alienness of death and eternity, as well as her strange steadfastness in the face of that alienness.

In the first few pages of the novel, the narrator discovers Teta in a clearing in the park that surrounds the Argan's estate. She is in the wildest area of the park, abutting the mountains. He finds her sitting at the ruins of a stone table and bench with her favorite dog, Wolf. Wolf has been her special pet for years. He is aged, blind, and so bad-tempered that he must always be kept on a chain. She shows a deep sympathy for the beast, remarking that "He understands everything you say to him, more than some people do"[1] Teta is playing the zither in her primitive way, and Wolf is singing along. We learn later that while she plays from music, her ignorance of the meaning of sharps and flats lends a strange quality to her playing. Despite the suggestion of grotesqueness and crudity that surrounds her, the narrator remarks that she looks at him with "remarkably bright and fine eyes" that are "forget-me-not blue. Her extreme humility and politeness are combined with "something resolute and final" that attracts the narrator. A few days later the narrator, who is very lonely at night in the empty house, suffers an attack of depression, and he unaccountably feels that only Teta can save him from death. He is surprised to find her door unlocked, and opening it, discovers a room that is very modest, but full of the lifetime collection of a person who is unable ever to throw anything away. Among other cheap pictures, he sees a sentimental portrait of a kneeling saint surrounded by angels, and a photograph of a priest whom we later learn is supposed to be Mojmir. When Teta returns, her calm and humble, and yet somehow suspicious and fearful reaction to his curiosity impresses the narrator. He senses a strange connection between Teta and the picture of the priest.

I call attention to these details because it seems to me that they represent the beginning of a far more successful characterization than Werfel finally accomplishes. Teta's simplicity and even crudeness in contrast to the Argans' cultured refinement do suggest something of the power of the ultimate issues with which the Argans cannot deal. The image of her with the irascible blind dog suggests that she does have some elemental and frightening force under control, and can even make it sing, although the music is very different from the kind the Argans usually appreciate. The mystery of the image grows from its combination of a feeling of danger with a sense of kindliness, authority, and also the ridiculous.

At the end of the first chapter, when the narrator leaves Teta's room, the question of the content and the nature of Teta's faith is left open. Theo's description suggests something strong and steadfast, but also possibly grotesque and ridiculous, about Teta. But he has not told us what she believes, or the exact relation between her, the photograph, and the problem of death. After this point, the characterization loses power for two reasons. On the one hand, we lose the sense that Teta herself experiences, even in a way she cannot express, the mystery and strangeness her appearance originally suggests. Her religious commitments do not appear as reactions to her religious feelings--indeed it begins to appear that she simply has no religious feelings, but only a naive conviction that has never really faced the human condition. And on the other hand, Werfel tells us too much about her religious commitments themselves. Werfel raises no question about Teta he does not answer. The story of Mojmir and her life-plan explains the photograph. That explanation then raises the question: could she have maintained her faith without this deception? Does her faith have a real basis? The aim of the rest of the novel is to demonstrate how she does retain her faith despite her discovery of Mojmir's true nature. In the broadest terms, the novel is weak because it tries to answer all the questions it raises, and to answer them in an unambiguous way.

I think that it is no coincidence that it is the characters who apparently lack any strong religious faith--the members of the Argan family--whom Werfel presents most successfully. In the single crucial episode in their lives reported in Chapters Three and Four, they emerge as clearly defined individuals, whose inner lives involve a convincing ambiguity. Werfel also succeeds in suggesting that they reflect on religious issues in a way very like Dostoyevsky's characters do. After Part One, the Argans drop out of the novel entirely apart from a few minor references the narrator makes.

First and foremost, Werfel presents the Argans as wholly admirable people. They are not only kindly and unpretentious, but have a great deal of independence and integrity. They are all musically very gifted, and yet lack artistic snobbishness. The father, Leopold, an Austrian diplomat, has taken a public stand against Naziism for which he has already begun to suffer as the novel begins. A year later, with the invasion of Austria, Leopold is arrested, tortured, and thrown into a concentration camp. The Argans represent a pocket of civilization and integrity that is about to be swallowed up by the obscene course of world politics. Werfel wants to emphasize that the Argans' civilized outlook cannot really deal with the problems of tragedy and death--and yet he is very far indeed from mocking or condemning or dismissing them. The narrator reports that Leopold bears his fate with dignity, and we see in their reaction to their son's death that grief does not rob them of their humanity. Werfel does not take the easy way out and allow the Argans to become deeply demoralized by their suffering. He does not try to demonstrate that their lack of religious faith makes their lives fall apart. And yet Werfel does suggest that something very important is missing in their lives.

Werfel's characterization of the Argans is striking because it manages to evoke an ambiguous sense of their inner unease along with their openness and strength. It is not an unease that questions or threatens their love for one another, but rather an unease that simply does not know what to do with itself. It is an unease of unspecifiable origin, that seems to grow out of their very fullness of life and of the strength of their loyalty to one another.

The episode from the Argan's life Werfel presents centers on a party held in honor of Livia's birthday. Numerous people from the surrounding area attend: Leopold has an extraordinary capacity for making friends. Philipp is the central figure in the episode. He acts as master of ceremonies for what amounts to a variety show in which most of the main characters, including Teta, perform. Theo notes that there had always been something exuberant and wild in Philipp that he had kept hidden, and expressed mainly through a puzzling and piquant irony. But in his performance at the party, his almost desperate wildness is unmistakably apparent. He appears as a one-man band, playing a drum set, saxaphone, trumpet, and accordion, and accompanied by his father on the piano. The vitality and effectiveness of his performance also contains something disturbing and almost annoying. A small exchange that occurs between him and his parents just before dawn brings out the very ambiguous and strained quality of his inner life, along with his parents' somewhat troubled reaction. Through a few small hints, Werfel suggests a great deal about the characters involved:

> "Herr Leopold Argan, Frau Livia Argan, I wish to pay you a compliment. It is said that nobody can choose his own parents. That is a blatant lie. I chose you otherwise I would not . . ."
> He paused and went fiery red. Then he burst out: "I'm awfully happy to be alive!"
> "That is the greatest compliment anyone can pay his revered begetters," said the expert laugher, beaming. Leopold carefully inspected the battery of bottles on the table in front of him.
> "We must drink to that in something extra potent, old sobersides," he said.
> Philipp, however, had already vanished. The gramaphone, which

> had stopped a couple of minutes for breath, began to wail again.
> I noticed as we clinked glasses to toast to her son's joy in
> life, that Livia did not join us. (pp. 94-95)[2]

Here, the contrasting elements that Werfel brings together really create an effective tension. Philipp's confession is clearly sincere, and yet his exaggerated formality suggests a note of irony, and his sudden arrival and departure, and subsequent noise making suggest the impatience and unease involved in his exuberance. His parents' unease is also evident: Leopold's response is somehow distracted, and Livia does not join the toast. It is not that she dislikes or is irritated by her son's behavior. Her silence rather suggests a brooding anxiety that is somehow holding its breath.

In the morning, Philipp, racing down a slight incline on a mountain path with his friends, slips and fractures his skull. By evening, he is dead.

The story of the Argans is in many ways a self-contained narrative, and the moment of Philipp's death is the climax of that narrative. The presentation of his character has emphasized the sheer vitality of his personality--a vitality that was not aimless, but that included real meaning and hope, despite the unease it harbored. The climax draws attention to the sheer fact of the cessation of life. In his presentation of Joe's death in *Light in August*, by contrast, Faulkner emphasizes not so much the contrast between death and life itself, as the tragedy of a life that could end as Joe's does--in utter humiliation and personal isolation. The experience of death Werfel evokes is closer to that we find in Myshkin's execution stories. Unlike the two men condemned to death whose experience Myshkin tries to grasp, Philipp is only semi-conscious till the very end, and is not aware that he is dying. But his family and Theo do directly confront his death. Their experience is really even more intense than Myshkin's, since they must confront the death of their closest loved one, with whom they have lived every day for years. Werfel describes Philipp's last moments with a series of vivid metaphors. The family, along with Theo, are present. Philipp's death appears as an abrupt, meaningless, and incomprehensible breach in experience. The event appears not so much as something sad or tragic, as alien and even grotesque. Philipp dies, in effect, by asphyxiation, since the breathing centers of his brain have been damaged by the fracture. Theo describes his last desperate, almost reflexive, gasps for breath:

> His convulsive struggles, as if he were hanging desperately over a rocky cliff, grew less frequent. His body stretched itself out in agony, in the birth-pangs of death. The moment of the end appeared with tremendous clarity. The razor-sharp borderline between Something and Nothing stood out before our eyes in an indescribable way. (p. 110)[3]

In the remainder of the chapter, Werfel describes the reaction of each of the other main characters, including Teta, to Philipp's death. Werfel closely relates their inability to come to terms with his death to the depth of their attachment to him. At one point Leopold complains that Theo is incapable of understanding what Philipp's death means to him since Theo has never had a child. Theo, in spite of himself, feels thankful that at least Philipp was not his own son. Werfel's presentation of the reactions of the Argans and Theo to Philipp's death is full of details that seem slightly odd, and yet exactly right. In the first few days, there are very few tears. Livia, especially, is silent, and seems somehow frozen. Her face was "like that of a young girl" and was very red. Her skin seemed taut. When Theo, following a sudden impulse, tries to embrace her, she coldly rejects him. She sits silently staring at her dead son until she collapses from exhaustion. Livia seems to know that there is no help and no possible consolation for the meaningless and outrageous fact before her.

Both Doris and Leopold seek out Theo for consolation, and Theo senses uneasily the utter inadequacy of the consolation he has to offer. Werfel suggests that Livia's astounded brooding silence is the truest reaction to death--and that Leopold's desperate need to express himself represents a sort of attempt to evade the reality. In Leopold's distracted and desperate conversation with Theo, the family's experience of the utter nonsense not only of Philipp's death, but of death itself, receives its most direct and striking expression.

> "It is contemptible of me, Theo, but I cannot stand it up there. . . I cannot look at him . . . Not because he is my child, but because he is <u>not</u> my child, do you understand, Theo? . . . That is not my child up there, but a stranger. . . . So strange, so strange, so horribly strange and it breaks my heart that my own son is so strange, so utterly strange. A couple of hours were enough, and he can no longer recognize me and I can no longer recognize him. . . And that is death, a meaningless, degrading, despicable alienation. (p. 116)[4]
> [. . .]
> He raised his fists and cried out, in a voice that was painfully loud, into the night that embraced his dead son: "Do you know what is wrong with us god-damned modern men? We get along so well with life, disgustingly well. . . But we can't get along with the opposite lying in the room upstairs. None of us can, Theo, none of us, no one . . ." (p. 117)[5]

Once Leopold and Doris have collapsed, Theo goes to keep watch over Philipp's body, and discovers Teta there. Her reaction to Philipp's death contrasts strikingly with that of the other characters. Although she has known Philipp his whole life, she shows none of the restless desperation or paralyzed shock the other characters do. Teta is quietly and carefully reading prayers over Philipp. Werfel wants to suggest that while "modern man" cannot come to terms with death, Teta has in fact done so. The narrator explicitly makes just such a statement and holds Teta up as an example. When Teta says "I wouldn't like to die like the poor young gentleman here," the narrator asserts, "Now I understood her."(p. 121)[6] Theo senses her implied criticism of the Argan family, who had not prepared their son for the afterlife. Werfel clearly wants to contrast Teta's composure with the desperation of the other characters and to directly associate her composure with her religious faith. But of all the scenes in the novel, this one illustrates the weakness of Teta's characterization most strikingly. Teta simply cannot play the role Werfel wants her to play. Her religious response seems trivial and almost empty in the context of the powerful scenes immediately preceding.

The first reason for the trivial impression she makes is that there is no hint that she is at all taken aback by Philipp's death. Her faith seems to come not as a response to the problem of death, so much as to represent a state of mind that simply sees no problem. Werfel provides a striking image of her calm complacency in her reaction to a sudden noise outside:

> During an interval when the moon was veiled in clouds a nightjar close by, probably from the great copper beech, uttered its repellent, foreboding croak. Teta cast a glance at the dead boy as if checking to make sure that everything was still in order, and then continued reading in her prayer-book, slowly picking out line after line. (p. 119)[7]

Ought not Teta's calm to suggest the possibility that she is simply so narrow and insensitive that the death of another, and the problem of death itself, simply fail to move her? When her dominant feeling is that _she_ would not like to die like Philipp has, ought not the possibility to open up that her faith is rooted simply in self-centeredness, a possibility that would radically call into question the validity of her faith? The second reason for the triviality of her characterization is that Werfel fails to follow up on ironic possibilities, such as these, that he really does suggest. In this case, Werfel has passed up an opportunity to suggest a real sense of dialogue in the narrator's mind about Teta. The narrator just begins to be irritated by Teta's statement that Wolf's howling is an expression of grief for Philipp. But he soon finds himself agreeing with Teta's implied criticism of the Argans, even though, like all "modern men," he cannot bring himself to share Teta's faith. Theo's irritation with Teta is quickly suppressed.

The scene ends with a discursive passage in which Theo expresses a number of judgments about Teta. The passage begins with the assertion, "Now I understood her." Here, as throughout the novel, the narrator does not identify himself with Teta's faith, but expresses the judgment that his own lack of faith is wrong. The passage ends with a clear judgment that Teta's primitive faith is really far preferable to his own hesitant religious speculations. The problem is that the novel offers us little more about Teta than this indirect judgment. One wishes that Werfel had let Teta appear to the narrator in a more ambivalent way--that he had let the narrator's irritation with Teta appear stronger or more justified; that he had let Theo <u>wonder</u> about Teta more, in both a negative and a positive way. The inclusion of a few incidents in which Teta's self-centeredness and narrowness might have had some serious consequences, or in which it might have appeared in a more obviously offensive way, along with some suggestion of sensitivity to religious problems and of a more emotional experience of faith, might have helped.

The most curious thing about the novel is that Werfel seems to want the ironic alternatives function non-ironically. Teta's narrowness is all we really have of her, and Werfel tries to elevate that narrowness to a role it cannot fulfill. Teta, as a literary character, is not strong enough to bear the thematic weight Werfel attempts to load her with. The extreme practicality of Teta's outlook smothers the possibility of the kind of positive interpretation possible for a character like Myshkin. Rather than developing a positive alternative in tension with his ironic suggestions, Werfel simply attempts to deny the irony in those suggestions themselves.

In general, it is important that personal characteristics in tension with a character's convictions be brought forth. A conviction suggests inner consistency and definiteness, but the concrete reality we experience through empathy is essentially indefinite, elusive, many-sided, and incomplete. The many-sidedness of concrete reality means that there must be some aspects of any human being that at least appear to be in tension with his statements of commitment. A presentation of a fictional character's commitment will lack something essential if aspects of that character that cast doubt upon, or are at least hard to reconcile with, that commitment, are not selected for emphasis. If a character is to appear in a plausible way, he must appear, through the perception of the implied author, as a problem, and not simply through direct assertions. Werfel begins to present characters in this way, but he does not carry the project through.

While Part One, which contains the story of the Argans, comprises one third of the novel, it is only a prologue, and is labeled as one. One of the central weaknesses of the novel is in fact Werfel's failure to integrate the story of the Argans with Teta's—particularly in light of the extensive treatment the Argans receive. The final two parts of the novel are Theo's reconstruction of Teta's life after she leaves the Argans, which he bases on the information he gained from his friend Johannes Seydel. In Parts Two and Three, Werfel attempts to somehow get behind the barrier Teta begins to represent in Part One, and to resolve the doubts and questions about her he originally suggests. Werfel wants to demonstrate through the narrative that Teta actually is capable of seeing through Mojmir and of preserving her faith; and that she is not really self-centered, but has in fact always been attached to Mojmir as a human being and not merely as a means to get into heaven.

Mojmir exposes himself by carrying his con-game just a step too far. He writes her that he is to become priest of Hustopec, Teta's native town, and promises her she will be able to live there with him. When she travels to Hustopec and finds things are quite different, she sets off in search of Mojmir, finally discovering him in Prague. Her encounter with Mojmir is the climax of her story and her decisive rejection of him effectively removes him from the rest of the novel as an ironic element. It is not that her rejection of Mojmir is in itself implausible: rather, by placing that rejection, presented in a one-sided way, at the climax of the plot, Werfel betrays his rhetorical intention. One senses that Werfel wants to communicate through his novel the judgment "Teta is right." Since Teta is presented in a one-sided way, that judgment does not appear as a real possibility. And we cannot relive the validity of that judgment in the way we relive the panoramic feeling a novel's climax normally evokes. The judgment appears neither as a possibility nor as the truth.

The Mojmir Teta discovers is far worse than she feared. She finds him in a shabby disorderly apartment which doubles as his place of business. He specializes in crossword puzzles, party tricks, and obscene photographs. Despite his squalid living conditions, his personal appearance is refined: he carries a perfumed hankerchief, for example. His suaveness and impeccable grooming in the midst of squalor suggest that he somehow thrives on squalor. Mojmir is clearly a devil figure. Teta also meets his wife, an abused-looking, viciously resentful woman, who tells of Mojmir's active extramarital sex-life. After he recognizes Teta, he tries to explain--and Werfel's portrayal of his initial embarrassment and gradual return to his suave art of gulling, is really funny. She learns that his education, which she had paid for, had turned him into an intellectual. He says he cannot believe in Catholicism because he is more honest than the priests-- his critical understanding has made him incapable of sharing in their hypocrisy.

Up to this point Mojmir had represented the ironic possibility that Teta's faith was groundless foolishness; her faith had at least to some extent depended on Mojmir's elaborate fabrications. Now she faces him directly, and the effect of their confrontation is to smother the ironic alternative. Mojmir's art of deceit, even now, begins to take her in--she does not want to believe what she sees. But Werfel has Teta emerge from the struggle victorious. Werfel seems to want to make us root for Teta-- and we may be quite embarrassed if we discover he has taken us in. One may find oneself rooting for Byron as he returns to Lena in the last chapter of Light in August, or for Lena as she interrogates Lucas; but at the same time, Faulkner wants us to wonder about those characters. He lets the possibility arise that they are merely foolish. Teta might indeed be compared to Lena in the extreme naivete and steadfastness of her faith.

But the two authors present that naive faith in strikingly different ways. Consider the two scenes in which Lena and Teta face the two con-artists—Lucas and Mojmir—in whom they have so naively trusted. Both seem to have a strange power over their deceivers; they both hold them fast with their gaze, calm and intent. But Faulkner tells us something about Lena that Werfel could not bring himself to tell us about Teta: "Then he [Lucas] looked at her, at her grave face which had either nothing in it, or everything, all knowledge." But the very language in which Werfel presents Teta's rejection of Mojmir is one-sided. When, for example, Mojmir tells her that his education taught him that Catholicism was an antiquated superstition, Werfel presents her response as follows:

> Her voice was hard as she uttered the following words, in which it cannot be denied that there was a certain element of greatness:
> "You have not learned that which was right, Nephew, but that which was false." (p. 226)[8]

The narrator's one-sided comment upon Teta's statement is typical of the way Werfel presents Teta in the novel, and could not contrast more strikingly with the paradoxical and ambiguous remark the narrator makes about Lena in *Light in August*. Werfel eliminates Mojmir as an ironic force in the novel, and this elimination begins through this one-sided presentation of Teta's rejection of him. The very function of the climax is the elimination of irony. But Faulkner maintains the ironic alternative to the end: we last see Lena dragging Byron along supposedly in search of Lucas.

Once disabused of Mojmir's lies, Teta does fall into despair, but she is not vanquished by it. She retains the conviction that there must be something she can do. When she notices an announcement of a pilgrimage to

Rome, her hope is reborn. On the pilgrimage, she meets Johannes Seydel, Mojmir's opposite, who comes to replace Mojmir unequivocally in her life. Teta had needed a human being as an intermediary between her and God, and Werfel tries to indicate that she had some real feeling for Mojmir. Seydel is a person both whom she can love, and also who can pray for her and absolve her. But as Teta transfers her trust and latent desire to serve others to Seydel, there is a question Werfel neglects. What reason do we have to suppose that anything more than human love is involved? Teta's almost adolescent love for Seydel involves an ironic possibility Werfel seems to simply ignore.

Seydel is not an implausible character, and his openness and willingness to help Teta, and to befriend her, put him in a positive light. The fact that he is not impressed by the other participants in the pilgrimage, which is really more like a pretentious travel tour, also leads us to legitimately trust him. But the way Werfel presents Seydel's experience of Teta is unsatisfying. No character, including Seydel, really wonders about Teta, in the way everyone wonders about Myshkin in The Idiot. Seydel's one-sided response to Teta indicates Werfel's rhetorical intention more clearly than anything else in the novel.

Teta, after an intense inner struggle, confesses to Seydel the whole story of Mojmir, and even gives him the letters to read. She lays her whole life before him, and through him the Catholic religion comes to life for her again: her inability to confess had kept her from communion. Werfel uses Seydel as a tool to help eliminate ironic possibilities. In their interview in the catacombs, Seydel had begun to confirm the impression that there was something very selfish in Teta's attitude toward Mojmir. But after reading the letters, he takes it all back:

> "Listen to me, Fräulein Linek. I take everything back. In the catacombs I was almost convinced that you had been lacking in love and sympathy for the fellow. But now I thank God that you were guilty of only one thing with respect to this pickpocket of the soul, namely, fear of the truth. It would have been a very great misfortune if you had really been fond of him. . . ."
> Teta interrupted him by raising her hand like a schoolgirl in the classroom.
> "Begging your pardon, is that a very serious sin, fear of the truth?"
> Seydel, with his boyish face, gave her a friendly smile.
> "It is not a sin, Fräulein Linek, but only a weakness. A very human weakness, moreover."(p. 352)[9]

Thereupon Teta asks him to absolve her; when he does, she falls to her knees and kisses his hands.

In my analysis of <u>Embezzled Heaven</u>, I have been trying to indicate the outstanding signs of Werfel's rhetorical intention, and to show how he has failed to fulfill that intention—how his novel has failed to mean what he wanted it to mean. Up to a certain point, the characters, and many of the incidents in the novel, are believable, interesting, and even intriguing. But in the course of the novel, Werfel selects and isolates certain aspects of those characters, and certain possible responses to those characters, and favors them over others. Werfel wants his novel to have not merely an aesthetic conclusion, but almost a logical one. Trying for a triumphant conclusion, he obtains cloying sentimentality. The final aim of the plot is the elimination of ironic alternatives. But we remember the ironic alternatives originally suggested—they have not dissolved as Werfel may have wished them to. The fact that these alternatives linger, but are unacknowledged, creates a sense of numbness in the reader's mind. Perhaps this sense of numbness can be identified with the feeling of implausibility. It is also an essential aspect of sentimentality.

I feel that the concluding scene from <u>Embezzled Heaven</u> that I have described above is implausible not because I believe the incidents in that scene to be impossible, but because I sense that competing possibilities have been suppressed, and a single possibility brought to the fore. And because the entire plot aims at this implausible scene, the novel lacks unity. I cannot identify with the implied author in the way Werfel wants me to--through empathy I am not convinced that Teta's faith is genuine, and I am not convinced that the possibilities that have dropped out are to be rejected. The scene is unconvincing because it would have us experience the character in terms of a consistent set of judgments and beliefs, but empathy cannot convince us of the validity of such beliefs. Empathy cannot reach the conclusion that one possibility is to be preferred over others--such a conclusion can be reached only through a person's own actual self-commitment. And may not the essence of sentimentality be just such blurring of the distinction between feeling and decision? Sentimental novels such as <u>Embezzled Heaven</u> may tempt the careless reader to feel he has actually made a decision simply because he feels certain possibilities more strongly than others.

NOTES TO CHAPTER EIGHT

[1] The quotations from Embezzled Heaven are from the Firth translation, although I have made a number of changes, mostly in the direction of greater literalness. Page references to the translation are hereafter given in the text, and the original quotations are given in the notes. Franz Werfel, Embezzled Heaven, tr. Moray Firth (New York: Viking, 1940); Der veruntreute Himmel (Stockholm: Bermann-Fischer, 1939), p. 18. "Er versteht alles was man sagt . . . mehr als mancher Mensch" (p. 28).

[2] "'Herr Leopold Argan, Frau Livia Argan, ich hab euch ein Kompliment zu machen. Es heisst, dass sich niemand seine Eltern aussuchen darf. Schwindel! Ich hab euch mir ausgesucht, sonst würd ich nicht . . '
Er machte eine kleine Pause und wurde feuerrot, weil er sich vor uns schämte. Dann aber brach mit voller Kraft das Geständnis aus ihm:
'Ich bin nämlich so furchtbar gern auf der Welt!'
'Das ist wirklich das grösste Kompliment, das einer seinen Herren Erzeugern machen kann', strahlte der Lacher. Leopold aber prüfte eingehend die Flaschenbatterie, die auf dem Tisch stand:
'Darauf müssen wir etwas ganz Starkes miteinander trinken, nüchterner alter dummer Bursche . . .'
Philipp jedoch war schon wieder verschwunden. Das Grammophon, das ein paar Minuten lang Atem geschöpft hatte, heulte von neuem los. Es fiel mir auf, dass Livia nicht mit uns angestossen hatte, als wir auf die Lebensfreude ihres Sohnes tranken." (p. 101)

[3] "Das sich Aufbäumen und die Zuckungen des Bergsteigers, der rettungslos zwischen den Felsen hängt, wurden immer seltener. Der Körper streckte sich in der Agonie, in den Geburtswehen des Todes. Mit ungeheurer Schärfe trat der Augenblick des Endes in Erscheinung. Sinnfällig ohnegleichen war die messerscharfe Grenze zwischen Etwas und Nichts." (p. 117)

[4] "'Es ist eine Gemeinheit, Theo, aber ich halts oben nich aus . . . Ich kann ihn nicht ansehen . . . Nicht, weil er mein Kind ist, sondern weil er n i c h t mein Kind ist, begreifst du das Theo? . . . Der dort oben ist nicht mein Kind, er ist ein Fremder . . . So fremd, so fremd, so todfremd, und das drückt mir das Herz ab, dass mein eigner Junge so fremd ist, so todfremd . . . Ein paar Stunden haben genügt, dass er mich nicht mehr erkennt und dass ich ihn nicht mehr erkenn . . . Und das ist der sinnlose Tod, diese niederträchtige hundsföttische Entfremdung.'" (pp. 122-23).

[5] "Er hob die Fäuste hoch und schrie verletzend laut in diese Nacht, die seinen Toten umschlossen hielt:
'Weisst du warum wir modernen Menschen so gott-verdammt sind?! . . . Mit dem Leben kommen wir alle glänzend aus, ekelhaft glänzend . . . Mit dem Gegenteil dort oben im Zimmer aber kommen wir nicht aus, lieber Theo, keiner von uns, keiner . . .'" (p. 124)

[6] "'Ich möchte nicht sterben wie der arme junge Herr da hier . . .'[. . .] Jetzt verstand ich sie." (p. 127)

[7] "In dieser Lichtpause liess eine Wiesenschnarre in nächster Nähe,

wahrscheinlich aus der grossen Blutbuche, ihren widerwärtigen, leidweissagenden Ratschenlaut ertönen. Teta warf einen Blick auf den Toten, als prüfe sie, ob alles in Ordnung sei, dann las sie weiter in ihrem Gebetbuch, langsam mit den Blicken jede einzelne Zeile einerntend." (pp. 125-26)

[8]"Sie sagt mit eckigem Ton folgende Worte, denen eine gewisse Grösse nicht abzusprechen ist:
'Du hast nicht das Richtige gelernt, Neffe, sondern das Falsche.'" (p. 227)

[9]"'Nein, hören Sie Fräulein Linek, ich nehm alles zurück. In den Katakomben war ich fast überzeugt, dass sie es dem Burschen gegenüber an Liebe und Teilnahme haben fehlen lassen. Jetzt aber dank ich Gott, dass Sie diesem Beutelschneider der Seele gegenüber nur eine einzige Schuld gehabt haben, die Furcht vor der Wahrheit . . . Ein ganz grosses Unglück wärs gewesen, wenn Sie ihn wirklich gern gehabt hätten . . .'
Teta unterbrach ihn und hob die Hand wie eine Schülerin:
'Wenn ich bittlich sein darf, ist das eine sehr schwere Sünde, die Furcht vor der Wahrheit?'
Seydels knabenhaftes Gesicht lächelte sie voll an:
'Das ist keine Sünde, Fräulein Linek, sondern nur eine Schwäche. Eine sehr menschliche Schwäche übrigens.'" (p. 343)

CHAPTER IX

The Conflict between Rhetorical Aim and Fictional Form

in Bernanos' The Diary of a Country Priest

Embezzled Heaven reflects all sorts of indecision. Werfel introduces elements that seem to be very ironic, but then almost immediately attempts to deny the irony. The narrator is very close to the implied author, yet neither seems to have decided whether to present Teta's faith as only a possibility, or as the truth. But insofar as it does appear as a possibility, it appears in isolation from alternatives. Such one-sidedness, I have argued, may be considered the very essence of sentimentality. Three additional factors contribute to the weakness of her characterization: Teta's religious commitments do not appear as responses to real religious problems honestly faced; the terms in which she expresses her faith lack emotional suggestiveness and seriousness; and her actions fail to evoke the sense of a conviction as a possible motivation just beyond the reader's grasp.

Bernanos has a much clearer idea of what he is up to than Werfel, and in many ways he succeeds where Werfel fails. Werfel does not seem to know what to do with ironic alternatives and challenges to Teta's faith. He seems reluctant to have Teta confront reality. One of the most striking aspects of Embezzled Heaven is the absence of dialogue: Teta's curt discussions with characters such as Herr Bichler, Mojmir, and even Johannes Seydel fail to reflect the kind of mutual awareness of the possible validity of the opposing viewpoint that we find in Dostoyevsky's characters. Bernanos allows little doubt as to the firmness of the religious commitment of his central character, the curé d'Ambricourt. Yet, he clearly suggests that the curé experiences the force of competing possibilities. The Christian life, in fact, appears as a constant struggle against evil, despair, and unbelief. Nothing could be further from Bernanos' vision than Teta's bland confidence. In his ability to suggest the possible validity of a spectrum of competing commitments, and to portray the conflicts among them in concrete situations, Bernanos can be compared favorably with Dostoyevsky. Both Dostoyevsky and Bernanos present commitments as responses to religious problems honestly confronted. And the way in which Myshkin and the curé express their commitments has real emotional force. But Bernanos, unlike Dostoyevsky, consistently favors one commitment over others. The novel concludes not with a spectrum of competing voices, but with one voice.

As we read the novel we are drawn into the curé's situation as he faces his work, his own limitations, and the disheartening ubiquity of evil. We are drawn into an experience of the overall situation of the world that includes competing possibilities for religious commitment. And I think that Bernanos' portrayal of the curé; his mentor the curé de Torcy (who is a very different kind of priest); the atheists Dr. Delbende and Dr. Laville; and the Comtesse and her daughter Chantal in their desperate struggle with sin and despair are all strikingly effective. But our empathy is frustrated by a certain heavy-handedness. It is not merely that the plot structure is somehow forced; a certain tone creeps into Bernanos' writing again and again that suggests the intrusive presence of the real author. Bernanos seems to want to point out too clearly what we are supposed to think of each episode. He drops hints that are too obvious. His hints suggest not something vague and indefinable, as Faulkner's and Dostoyevsky's do, but rather a definite conviction. Instead of saying that

Bernanos hints, we might rather say he prods.

The effect of prodding results largely from the way Bernanos uses the diary form. The curé d'Ambricourt narrates the entire novel, except, of course, the last few pages describing his death. He includes not only his personal and spiritual reflections, and wild jottings made in moments of great distress, but long accounts of theological discussions, and a number of striking scenes in which he describes his work as a priest. The curé's reflections upon the experiences he recounts are not in themselves implausible or overly judgmental, though they certainly are judgmental to some extent. The problem is that Bernanos presents them in such a way that they are exempt from the dialogical interaction we begin to sense in the scenic passages. Bernanos emphasizes that though the curé shares a great deal with the other characters, he does not share his innermost thoughts and religious experiences, but reserves them for his diary. And these personal reflections are one of the places where Bernanos' heavy-handedness is most evident.

The diary form need not have given the curé's consciousness a privileged position. Goethe, for example, treats the author of the Bekenntnisse einer schönen Seele, which appears as part of Wilhelm Meisters Lehrjahre, very ironically. Her "Confession" is full of the most sincere religious reflections and statements of commitment, and while Goethe casts great doubt on her character, he does not exclude the possible validity of her faith. But Bernanos does not cast any real doubt on the curé. He makes it clear that the other characters really do not understand the curé, and he allows no ironic tension to develop between the curé's private account of himself and the way he appears in scenes.

Bernanos' presentation of the curé also contrasts with Dostoyevsky's presentation of Myshkin. We always have the impression that there is something about Myshkin Dostoyevsky cannot reveal--we experience a gap in our experience of Myshkin that suggests the possibility of something beyond that we cannot quite reach. Myshkin is "sphinxlike." The relative weakness of the curé's characterization may lie in Bernanos' attempt to somehow fill the same kind of gap through the way he uses the diary form. Bernanos wants to get inside of the curé in a way Dostoyevsky realized he could not get inside of Myshkin. The result is that, at many crucial points, we experience not a gap in our empathy, but the simple absence of empathy.

In this section, I shall analyze The Diary of a Country Priest in terms of the conflict between evocative elements and authorial prodding. First I will attempt to give an account of the role this conflict plays in the characterization of the curé and in the portrayal of his interaction with characters who represent alternative viewpoints, indicating how Bernanos gives the curé's viewpoint a predominant position. Then I will deal with the role this conflict plays in the dynamics of the plot. The central problem Bernanos faces is whether a religious conversion can be placed at the climax of a plot, and function as the central event around which the entire novel is organized. Here, the conflict between evocation and prodding is especially acute. The central problems of the novel are whether the curé can save the souls of any of those around him from hatred and despair and whether he himself can be at peace. The resolution of these two problems constitutes the climax and the conclusion of the novel. I will try to show that Bernanos presents this resolution as a real resolution, and that he wants to exclude the alternative that the resolution is not what it appears to be. The scenes that function as aesthetic climax and conclusion are supposed to make a point, but the point is a definite religious conclusion. The whole structure of the novel seems to prod us in a certain direction, and as a result, the implied author tends to dissolve.

The action of The Diary of a Country Priest covers the tenure of the protagonist as priest of his first parish, the village of Ambricourt. Bernanos nowhere mentions his name. He grew up under conditions of crushing poverty, and despite his sickliness, excelled academically, and was finally assigned a double parish whose responsibilities far exceed his capacity. As the novel begins, he is in fact already dying of cancer. Ignoring signs of his failing health, he engages in what becomes an almost superhuman struggle to fulfill his obligations despite his weakness and the growing realization that he is utterly unprepared to deal with practical affairs, and that the village is completely rejecting him. His inner life is dominated by a terrible feeling of loneliness that is broken only by his friendship with the curé de Torcy.

The aim of the first half of the novel is to make clear his seemingly complete failure as a priest--his projects fail in humiliating ways and his attempts to express his sincere religious convictions and longings in the pulpit and in catechism class meet with a contempt and mockery of which he is all too well aware. He seems to be denied every worldly success, every comforting bond to the world around him. But despite the clear consciousness of his own incompetence, and of the complacent tenacity of the village in its pettiness and evil, the curé has an inner will to endure. Though he thinks of himself as nothing, and though he feels acutely the pain of his rejection by the world, he does not accept the world's authority over him. He feels he has failed in his duty--but not because he has failed in the world's eyes. His judgments against the world and against the complacency and conniving he finds in the church are firm, and often bitter. The only authority he accepts is the authority of God, though he must constantly struggle with the temptation to despair over the world's failure to accept God, and, on a more natural level, over his own human isolation.

The curé lives in the continual consciousness of the power of evil, and the novel contains many vivid expressions of his experience of that evil, of his longing for release, and of his faith in God. As the novel begins, he is considering his village, which he feels is "devoured by ennui." He looks out over the village, under a "desolate, ugly November sky," and it appears to him like an "exhausted beast" sprawled out in the cold mist. Hearing some cattle, and seeing a boy coming home from school who will soon lead them to shelter, he thinks:

> And my parish, my village, seemed to be waiting too--without much hope--after so many nights in the mud, for a master to follow towards some improbable, unimaginable shelter.
> Oh, of course I know all this is fantastic. Such notions can scarcely be taken seriously. A daydream . . . Villages do not scramble to their feet like cattle at the call of a little boy. But no matter! Last night, I believe a saint might have roused it.(p. 8)[1]

Here, I think, Bernanos effectively evokes the curé's religious consciousness. Bernanos presents us not with blank assertions of belief, but with a vivid image that evokes a real sense of longing, a longing that might be compared with that we find in Myshkin. The image is effective in itself; it has poetic and even religious value apart from Bernanos' intention, which later becomes clear, to associate mud with hell and the boy with Christ. The village is bogged down in moral and religious lethargy which is like the thickness of mud; like a helpless animal, it lacks the will to lift itself up, despite the onset of darkness.[2] The incongruousness of the image suggests the radical desperation with which the curé responds to the human condition. But even in this early passage, the conflict between evocation and prodding begins to show itself. This passage exemplifies a pattern evident at every level in the novel. At first Bernanos suggests a sense of dialogue within the curé's consciousness. The curé begins with a very strong impression and then seems to question the validity of that impression. Bernanos does suggest alternative possibilities, but the passage ends in a way that seems to exclude alternatives: "N'importe!" he exclaims, "Hier soir, je crois qu'un saint l'eût appelé." The curé asserts his conviction that his perception was valid. He isolates and affirms one possible tendency within the feeling he evokes, and rejects other tendencies.

There is no reason why assertions of conviction cannot find a place in a novel--but Bernanos' presentation of the curé's assertion seems somehow unconvincing. I think the reason for this weakness is that these deeply personal statements of the curé are neither challenged by other voices in the novel nor placed in an ironic light by other aspects of the curé's personality. The problem with the passage in isolation is that the reader cannot verify through empathy whether the curé's perception reflects a longing that aims at something real, or that is only a vain and foolish dream. Statements have an inherent tendency to appear as direct assertions, and the function of literary technique is to counteract that tendency. A passage that sounds excessively assertive in isolation might have been made to evoke the sense of an alternative possibility, if placed in the right kind of context. But since Bernanos does not provide that context, the assertiveness within the language of the passage itself begins to jar.

An essential aspect of Bernanos' technique is to allow the assertive tendency to repeatedly seep back into his language at crucial junctures. Since Bernanos, in the context of the whole novel, does not challenge the curé's assertions with real alternatives, and does not work his assertions into real dialogue, the curé's statements begin to appear as direct assertions actually made by the real author

As I have pointed out, Bernanos allows the curé's inner consciousness to engage in real dialogue with the other characters, but he attempts to somehow circumscribe a region of the curé's consciousness that is exempt from dialogue. Dialogue, as it appears in Dostoyevsky, takes place not only between characters, but within the consciousness of the implied author. Not only explicit discussion, but also ironic contrasts between a characters's account of himself and the way he appears in scenes, may be involved. Bernanos includes a great deal of discussion, but neglects ironic contrast and keeps the curé's innermost spiritual state a secret from the other characters, though not from the reader. Real dialogue is introduced, but somehow subordinated.

The most extended discussions in the novel are those the curé d'Ambricourt has with the curé de Torcy, his only real friend. The curé de Torcy is a very vigorous and plain-speaking individual, who hides a deep sensitivity to injustice and suffering behind a brusk exterior. On their first meeting, he immediately senses the kind of person the curé d'Ambricourt is, and he responds both with deep sympathy, and with open criticism. He tells the younger priest the story of a vestry woman at one of his former churches who literally worked herself to death trying to keep the church absolutely spotless. He compares her to the younger, idealistic priests of today, such as the one before him. (The main difference, he says, is that his vestry woman had more fortitude.) "The mistake she made wasn't to fight dirt, sure enough, but to try to do away with it entirely. As if it were possible! A parish is <u>bound</u> to be dirty" (p. 15)[3] The curé de Torcy maintains that a priest can hope for little more than to achieve the limited goal of commanding his parish, of inspiring respect and maintaining order. One senses that Torcy is in fact very well able to deal with the world on its own terms, that he is not, like his younger colleague, thrown into confusion by the pettiness and guile so common among the souls entrusted to his care. But Bernanos effectively suggests a real conflict in the curé de Torcy between his practicality and his sympathy for his younger friend. In his conversations, we sense that he is really weighing alternatives in his mind.

The most powerful conflict the curé de Torcy faces grows out of his inner rebellion against the injustice of poverty. This inner rebellion contrasts strikingly with his vigorous insistence that one must accept the fact that a parish, and a Christian society, are "bound to be dirty." He is a man who finds pity to be a "powerful and devouring" emotion. In himself, he finds the seeds even of a violent revolutionary: but he tells his friend that they must teach not revolution, but poverty, to the poor. Christ promises them a kingdom not of this world: they must honor and be faithful to the poverty of the present. He does not make this statement with the kind of arrogant or prissy insensitivity one might be tempted to expect. He knows how hard it is to accept; he is well aware of his own inward rebellion against it; and he points out that priests have no business telling the rich that the poor should be content with their lot.

I dwell on the curé de Torcy because it seems to me that he is in many ways the most successful character in the novel. In him, Bernanos has created an individual of true complexity, whose life contains central conflicts and contradictions that we do not find resolved in any obvious or definite way. And the curé d'Ambricourt gives him as much trouble as anything. Bernanos effectively suggests the deep friendship that unites the older and the younger man, but the curé de Torcy's opinion of his younger friend is uncertain and paradoxical. In each of their meetings, we sense that he is constantly trying to size up his younger colleague, and that he senses something attractive, yet disturbing, that he cannot be quite done with.

On their last meeting before the death of Dr. Delbende, Torcy finally comes out with his judgment. He points out his friend's lack of common sense, his utter lack of knowledge of people, and his general incompetence--and yet he insists that his friend not become a monk, but should continue as a parish priest. For all his blunt and cutting criticism, there is something he admires in his colleague. "You risk yourself," he says. Torcy recognizes very well that prudence is always a good idea, but that "prudence is the final imprudence when by slow degrees it prepares the mind to do without God." (p. 83)4 There is something really paradoxical and compelling about Torcy's estimation of his friend. One senses the workings of a mind trying to come to terms with something just beyond its grasp. Torcy's definite judgment is expressed in somewhat paradoxical terms. And despite his support of his friend, Torcy remains an intensely practical man who cannot help but sense something very foolish in the curé d'Ambricourt.

The curé de Torcy experiences his friend in a way very like many of the characters in The Idiot experience Myshkin: with a mixture of wondering, admiration, perplexity, and disapproval. And in The Idiot, the implied author experiences Myshkin with the same sort of wondering and perplexity. But the overall impression of the curé d'Ambricourt we gain from The Diary of a Country Priest is strikingly different from Torcy's experience of him. Through our empathy with Torcy's experience of the curé d'Ambricourt, the legitimacy and genuineness of the latter's spiritual state appear uncertain and questionable. Bernanos' presentation of Torcy's perception is true to the way we perceive commitments through empathy. But the overall structure of the novel has the effect of dismissing such doubts and uncertainties. It is not merely that the first person form of the diary lets us in on certain thoughts and feelings of the curé the other characters do not know; rather, Bernanos wants to replace a perspective of perplexity with a perspective of certainty. This contrast between kinds of perspectives is already evident in the abrupt difference in tone Bernanos allows to arise between Torcy's actual conversation and the diarist's interspersed comments. But the difference between the dialogical perspective and the perspective of certainty that supercedes it is even more clearly evident in the treatment of their mutual friend, the atheist Dr. Delbende.

Dr. Delbende is a rather eccentric old physician with a declining practice; it may be that he really is not a very good doctor. But the curé and he instantly take a special liking to one another. The curé senses a sincerely felt religious pain in the man, and writes that he "communes with" it. Bernanos presents Dr. Delbende's atheism effectively and fairly. He is an atheist for reasons that both his clerical friends understand and sympathize with. His atheism stems from the same thirst for justice that is so powerful in the curé de Torcy. But he could never convince himself, as Torcy had done, that his struggle for justice should put him on the side of God and the church. He has some very cutting things to say about established religion, with which, one senses, Bernanos sympathizes: "Why, damn it all, after twenty centuries of Christianity, to be poor ought not still to be a disgrace." And he asks: "Why the devil must they [i.e. priests] show such respect to the powerful of the earth, who revel in it." (p. 74-75)5 But one senses that his rebellion goes deeper: he cannot understand how God can create and permit a world so intolerably unjust. But he can find no cause in the world to espouse. He feels human society is ruled by a kind of enemy, and resorts to individual and very eccentric and questionable blows against particular injustices he encounters. And his attempts to set things right often gets him into trouble.

Dr. Delbende feels there is something that unites him with the two priests. He tells the curé d'Ambricourt that the three of them are "the sort that isn't got down. Nobody understands exactly why. By the grace of God, you'll say. But you see, my dear fellow, I don't believe in Him." (p. 72)6 Delbende raises the alternative that the inner strength the three men share is not based upon some kind of higher reality, or at least that no one can know what it is based on. But in the course of the novel, Bernanos seeks to eliminate this alternative from consideration. Dr. Delbende commits suicide--and apparently in reaction to a rather unimportant setback. Apparently he can be "gotten down" more easily than he thought. His suicide is but one example of the consistent pattern Bernanos follows--he begins to evoke a sense of alternative perspectives, only to dismiss them in one way or another. Signs of Bernanos' attempt to eliminate alternative perspectives are already evident within the scene itself. Bernanos resorts to a very clumsy device to make his point. When Delbende says, "I wonder if it's not just pride at the root of us all," laughing raucously, his dog suddenly cowers, shivering and growling as it looks up at its master. (p. 72)7 When Delbende has finished speaking, and the curé sits silently "communing with" his pain, the dog comes up and lays his head on the curé's knees.

The curé is silent when Delbende has ceased speaking, and we learn that Delbende was "a little uneasy at my silence." He then describes his experience of Delbende's pain, but in a way that is really more assertive than evocative. This passage represents an outstanding example of the pattern evident everywhere in the novel: the curé begins by seeming to consider possibilities, but ends by making assertions that annul alternatives. I have underlined the phrases that make the shift in tone from evocation to assertion apparent.

>   Then he stopped speaking, a little uneasy at my silence. Of course, I have very little experience but <u>I thought that</u> I recognized instantly a certain inflection betraying some profound spiritual hurt. Would others <u>perhaps</u> be able to find the right words to appease and persuade? <u>I don't know such words</u>. True pain coming out of a man belongs primarily to God, <u>it seems to me</u>. I try to take it humbly to my heart, just as it is. I endeavor it make it mine, to love it. <u>And I understand all the meaning</u> hidden in the expression that has now become trite: "to commune with," <u>for it is true that</u> I commune with his pain. (p. 76)
>
>   Il s'est tu, un peu gêné par mon silence. Certes, je n'ai pas beaucoup d'expérience mais <u>je crois reconnaître</u> du premier coup un certain accent, celui qui trahit une blessure profonde de l'âme. <u>Peute-être</u> d'autres que moi sauraient alors trouver le mot qu'il faut pour convaincre, apaiser? <u>J'ignore ces mots-là</u>. Une douleur vraie qui sort de l'homme appartient d'abord à Dieu, <u>il me semble</u>. J'essaie de la recevoir humblement dans mon coeur, telle quelle, je m'efforce de l'y faire meinne, de l'aimer. <u>Et je comprends tout le sens caché</u> de l'expression devenue banale "communier avec", <u>car il est vrai que</u> cette douleur, je la communie. (p. 95)

The reflections upon his conversation the curé records in his diary, like all of his reflections upon the opposing viewpoints of others, disproportionately suggest that he has understood Dr. Delbende, but that Dr. Delbende has not really understood him. Bernanos creates the impression that the curé has really seen into Dr. Delbende, and does not include any suggestion that there is something the curé has failed to see. He suggests that Delbende is perplexed and disturbed by the curé, and is very uneasy in his unbelief. Dialogue takes place at a certain level, but the curé's most private reflections seem somehow exempt from dialogue. The reason for this apparent exemption is that Bernanos juxtaposes nothing with the curé's reflections that can really challenge them ironically, and the curé's own mode of expression is itself completely free of irony. His personal reflections are lifted up out of the dialogue and represent something of which Delbende has no inkling. They are consistently so direct and sincere that they no longer appear as mere alternatives, but as the point of view decisively favored by the author above all others. The curé's reflections often create the effect of authorial prodding.

Assertions are aesthetically dangerous in a novel because they tend to attract attention to themselves as assertions and to recall the reader to the situation of being addressed by the real author. It is precisely this tendency in assertions that needs to be frustrated if they are to function evocatively. It would be possible for statements as direct and confident and sincere as the curé's to function effectively in a novel, but only if they were countered by other, conflicting statements or voices that were equally confident, direct, and rhetorically striking. The tentative, uncertain, and even tortured tone of the conflicting viewpoints cannot compete with the vibrant and utterly convinced tone of the curé's reflections. The curé may well seem much less powerful as a character, in artistic terms, than Torcy or Delbende, and some of his statements may seem contrived or even mushy. But the fact that Bernanos consistently presents even that mushiness without irony, and allows the curé's voice to supercede all the others betrays the novel's rhetorical intention.

The first half of the novel depicts the curé's inexorable decline. At the beginning, he had felt inadequate and he often became caught in very humiliating situations. But by the end of the first half of the novel, he is close to utter despair. He faces an increasingly tortuous struggle with pain and exhaustion; he gradually realizes that he can expect nothing but mockery, spite, and at best grudging tolerance from his parishioners. His receipt of an unsigned note forms a kind of climax. The note concludes: "Sorry for you but we say again: Get out!" (p. 93)[8] Dr. Delbende's death is the final blow.

These outward failures are accompanied by a crushing inner spiritual crisis. Day by day, he feels more and more empty, more and more alone, more and more dead. Many of his expressions of spiritual exhaustion and creeping despair do not seem to me to be at all mushy, but are among the most effective elements in his characterization. There is no sentimentality at all in the evocation of his complete isolation from the world, and inexplicable and inescapable separation from God:

> What lay behind me was no longer our familiar everyday life, from which we are willing to slip away through the spirit of prayer, all the while certain in the back of our minds that we can return as soon as we wish. Behind me there was nothing. And before me, a wall, a black wall. (p. 93)[9]

Yet Bernanos does not let the curé be overcome by despair. The power of his despair itself arises largely from his conviction that he must struggle against it; his exhaustion from the fact that he will not cease to confront and resist such a powerful adversary.

Everything in the first half of the plot works to bring the curé to this position of spiritual emptiness. But the climax of the plot is his conversion of the Comtesse. Bernanos seems to be asserting that it is his very emptiness that allows him to become a conduit for divine grace. The conversion also represents the turning point in his own life. He finds that it is with his encounter with the Comtesse that he is finally able to pray again. The conversion represents the beginning of his own spiritual regeneration. The last half of the novel portrays his consistent progress. His spiritual life moves forward to a definite victory despite the recurrent necessity for painful struggle.

Bernanos wants the central conversion scene to unite the novel, and it does fit into a clear pattern. As Bernanos presents him, the curé's central aim in life is to save souls, and it seems he is incapable of that. But, as I will try to show, Bernanos presents his conversion of the Comtesse unambiguously, as the real fulfillment of that aim. The absence of irony is nowhere more clear than in his dramatic encounter with her. As I pointed out earlier, Bernanos tries to exempt the central part of the curé's inner life from dialogue. The way Bernanos exempts the meaning of actions and spiritual positions from dialogue is nowhere clearer than in the case of the conversion scene. Bernanos makes it clear that no one but the curé and the Comtesse know the true nature of what passes between them the evening of her conversion, and, as it happens, she dies before morning.

As it also happens, her daughter has imperfectly heard the whole scene through a window and the story spreads to the Comte, the village, the church hierarchy, and finally to the curé de Torcy. This chain of events does create the condition for a limited kind of dialogue. Bernanos presents a whole range of possible reactions to the conversion. No one knows quite what to make of what happened. Everyone is perplexed and disturbed, and some are frightened and appalled. Even the curé de Torcy does not quite know what to make of it. Partly because the Comtesse's daughter had somewhat misinterpreted the event, Torcy initially criticizes his friend's behavior in the harshest terms. But the sense of dialogue is limited because Bernanos again makes it clear that while the curé understands their reactions, none of his critics really know what happened between him and the Comtesse, and he believes it to be his duty to keep silence. None of their responses is really adequate to the dramatic forcefulness of the conversion scene itself, and his critics' tentativeness and confusion cannot challenge the unambiguous sincerity of the curé's account of the event.

Through a detailed analysis of the conversion scene and its role in the novel The Diary of a Country Priest, I would like to show how Bernanos betrays his intention to present the conversion without irony, as a real conversion; how he attempts to force the meaning of his novel to be a particular commitment; and why his attempt to fulfill these intentions compromises the plausibility and aesthetic unity of the novel. Throughout, I want to emphasize that the peculiar impression the novel makes results from the fact that it is in so many respects believable and significant, but that its effectiveness finally gives way under the pressure of Bernanos' rhetorical intention. The novel contains many effective parts, but those parts do not work together to create an effective whole. I will attempt to trace the conflict between evocation and prodding, and to specify the points at which the one gives way to the other.

In the first half of the novel, as Bernanos introduces the three obviously religious characters I have discussed, he also introduces to us the village, and the story of the Comtesse's family. Until the conversion scene we learn very little of the situation at the Comtesse's household, but the curé's brief meetings with the governess, Louise, and the daughter, Chantal, create a sense of foreboding. The conversion scene is occasioned by a meeting with Chantal two or three days before. Chantal had come to him of her own will, and she begins to reveal to him the tangle of jealousy and spite that exists beneath her family's polished upper-class exterior. She is a violently rebellious teenager who hates her parents with a vicious and unrelenting passion. The curé takes a surprising tone--suddenly no longer hesitant and uncertain, he speaks in terms of commanding authority. The climax of his lecture is almost shocking. He tells her:

> "There is not only a communion of saints; there is also a communion of sinners. In their hatred of one another, their contempt, sinners unite, embrace, intermingle, become as one; one day in the eyes of Eternal God they will be no more than a mass of perpetual slime [ce lac de boue toujours gluant] over which the vast tide of divine love, that sea of living roaring flame which gave birth to all things, passes vainly." (p. 122)[10]

After a few days have passed, he goes to visit the Comtesse, and although it was the farthest thing from his mind, he suddenly finds himself announcing: "I've come to talk about your daughter, madame." (p. 130)[11] While he hardly knows what he is going to say from moment to moment, he again launches into an exploration of conscience. His tone is like the one he assumed before Chantal, only a little less harsh and a good deal more respectful. The scene moves toward her conversion step by step: Initially she shows a kind of sceptical resistance, seeming not to take him seriously; but she hides an unacknowledged need to discover what he is up to. Then suddenly, she confesses the entire ugly story of a family ruled and bound together by simmering hatred. Once her confession is complete, a sudden shift in the narrative presentation again occurs: whereas before the Comtesse appeared as a participant in a vicious family conflict, now she appears as a rebellious soul struggling against God, and struggling, at the same time, for salvation. The next shift takes place when she herself realizes the nature of her struggle; and the final shift, as she wins the struggle for salvation.

Bernanos tries to present religious beliefs as truths rather than as possibilities, and his presentation is implausible for that reason. But Bernanos' presentation differs from Werfel's (and is like Dostoyevsky's) in one essential respect: In The Diary of a Country Priest, religious beliefs are effectively presented as responses to religious problems. The desperation Chantal and her mother feel in the face of the chains of hatred they have locked about themselves suggests a longing for a way out. They consciously face their human situation, and that situation perplexes and torments them in a way they cannot understand or be done with. The turmoil within the Comtesse and her daughter contrasts sharply with the callous complacency of the Comte. Unlike him, they have a real sense of injustice. They have both been wronged in many ways, and as a result harbor a very basic kind of grudge, which we might call a grudge against the nature of things itself. Bernanos calls this grudge hatred of God. Because of their grudge, they have become unable to love and unable to forgive. Their obsession with the evil they have suffered and their obstinacy in hatred suggest reflectiveness in a way very like Nastasya's obsessiveness and wild rebellion do.

Prior to the conversion scene, we have learned that Chantal has been tormenting her governess Louise and trying to get her fired; that her mother wants to send her to England against her will; and that Chantal hates all three of them with a passion, but has only recently become disenchanted with her father. Though the Comtesse seems at first to want to dismiss the curé, at the same time she feels somehow drawn out by him. She confesses the entire story, not penitently, but almost defiantly. Her family situation might be described as a rigid set of interlocking triangles. We learn that her husband has been unfaithful to her from the start, "grossly, stupidly, like a schoolboy," and that the present crisis was precipitated by Chantal's discovery of her father's carryings on with Louise. But a deeper bond of hatred united mother and daughter. The Comtesse has been grieving eleven years for her son who died in infancy. She feels that Chantal had hated him from the beginning, and the Comtesse tells us that Chantal and her father had become inseparable from the day of her son's death. Now, she is trying to send Chantal away, in the knowledge that she will never return to the family she hates.

These people have clutched their grief and injured pride in their hearts for years, taking revenge on the world and on those around them by refusing to hope. The Comtesse feels that she has maintained her dignity. She has endured; she has not made an issue of her husband's infidelity, or protested against her daughter's manipulation of her husband. But her dignity is of a very cold and heartless sort. The Comtesse lacks sympathy for her daughter's disillusionment with the Comte. Her confession reaches its climax as she cries out: "Is my daughter's pride of more consequence than mine? Can't she go through what I've had to go through?" (p. 139)[12]

The characterization of the members of the Comtesse's family includes complexity and conflict of motive within the characters and convincingly drawn contrasts between the characters. And the suggestion of the beginning of a wavering attitude in the Comtesse toward the curé is also effective. In the course of the Comtesse's confession, Bernanos begins to suggest a doubleness in her not unlike the doubleness Dostoyevsky suggests in Nastasya's attitude toward Myshkin. Bernanos suggests that there is something about the curé that attracts her, but he does not, until a certain point, specify what it is. It is somehow believable that she might suddenly feel the impulse to unburden or explain herself to the curé, with his strangely convinced and yet utterly self-effacing demeanor, particularly at this point of crisis in her life. She wants to get rid of him, yet every time she takes a look at him, she feels drawn back into the conversation.

The series of shifts it seems to me the reader cannot follow begin as the curé prepares to leave, at the end of the Comtesse's confession. She detains him. It is as if she felt there was something in him she had to prevail against, and yet at the same time secretly desired to submit to. As the scene progresses, the violence of the conflict between these motives increases, but at the same time she becomes increasingly open to the curé, and assumes at moments a tone that is almost pleading. In a sudden burst of openness, she asks, "How have I sinned?" and almost involuntarily lets the confession slip out that she does not expect her daughter to return. Then suddenly, the terms of their encounter shift. She is no longer just a distraught and resentful mother, but a rebel against God.

> My patience suddenly gave out. "God will break you!" I shouted. She uttered a kind of moaning cry. But not a cry of defeat imploring mercy--a sigh rather, the deep sigh of a creature gathering up strength for defiance.
> "Break me! God's broken me already. What more can he do? He's taken my son. I no longer fear Him." (p. 142)[13]

The curé then begins a kind of sermon in which he states that her refusal to love will separate her from her son for all eternity—because "hell is not to love anymore." Her son will not even be able to share her suffering, since to be utterly unable to love, he says, means that one has nothing left to be shared. The curé then tells us simply that "She watched me with extraordinary attention." (p. 144)[14] Her resistance is obviously wearing down: she is unable to complete her objection to his statements about hell, and she becomes somehow captivated by the tear that suddenly begins to fall down his cheek. Again the curé tells us "Her eyes never left mine." A dialogue ensues, apparently in a much quieter tone, since—as the curé writes—"She rested both her hands on my arm, her face almost touching mine." (p. 145)[15] She asks how she can be separated from her son for all eternity if she loves him, and he replies that if she wants to love she must not reject God's love. More and more, she sounds as if she really wants an answer from him, and is not simply trying to get him out of the way. At the conclusion of this stage, another shift occurs:

> She answered after a long pause: "Would you deign to show me my hidden sin? The worm in the fruit?"
> "You must resign yourself to . . . to God. Open your heart to Him."
> I dared not speak more plainly of her dead child, and the word "resign" seemed to astonish her.
> "Resign myself? To what?" Then suddenly she understood. (p. 146)[16]

The first shift implied that she was already facing God, and the second shift that she has realized she is. But there is nothing in the scenic presentation that challenges these clear implications. The progression of incidents moves forward, each step aiming at some unambiguous implication or definite assertion. The scene presentation fails to acknowledge that the reader does not know that "she understood."

The Comtesse's rebellion flares up again in response to the curé's command that she resign herself:

> She reared like a viper: "I've ceased to bother about God. When you've forced me to admit that I hate Him, will you be any better off, you idiot [imbecile]?"
> "You no longer hate Him. Hate is indifference and contempt. Now at least you're face to face with Him." (p. 147)[17]

These are the last words we hear from her as an unbeliever.

Before the moment of conversion occurs, Bernanos inserts some of the curé's reflections. His reflections follow the same pattern as before: at first it appears that the curé considers alternatives, but by the end of the passage, he has conclusively denied them. First, he records his sudden fear that he may have misinterpreted the situation, that he had simply been tricked by Chantal, and had confronted the Comtesse recklessly and irresponsibly. "I had tried to liven this frozen heart in an instant, to bring light into the innermost recess of a conscience that God's mercy intended to leave in the pitiful dark." (p. 147)[18] But the curé, and Bernanos, soon dismiss this alternative. We learn that "It was then that--there are no words for it!--that while I struggled against doubt and terror, a spirit of prayer came back to my heart." (p. 147)[19] At the very moment of her conversion, Bernanos re-introduces the privileged perspective of the curé's inner life, which throughout the novel had been exempt from dialogue, and that consistently overcomes the doubts it entertains.

The final shift is her actual conversion. She sinks into a chair, and opens a medallion containing a lock of her boy's hair, and begins to ask "will you swear to me--." But she "instantly read in my eyes that I understood and would swear to nothing." (p. 148)[20] Again the curé's inner voice returns: "I felt as though a mysterious hand had struck a breach in who knows what invisible rampart, so that peace flowed in from every side, majestically finding its level, peace unknown to the earth, the soft peace of the dead, like deep water." (p. 149)[21] The force of the curé's rhetoric at this point represents the clearest evidence of Bernanos' rhetorical intention. At the very center of the plot, the one voice that dominates the novel and is not effectively challenged, even rhetorically, by any other, presents an unambiguous account of the nature of the situation before us. Now she believes:

> "It seems quite plain to me," she said in a voice miraculously different [prodigieusement altérée] yet very calm. "Do you know what I was thinking just now, a moment ago?"

She tells us what she was thinking, but now no longer thinks: she wanted to take her boy to a place where God did not exist, and cry to him "Now stamp us out, do your worst!" (p. 149)[22] Her statement represents the unambiguous conclusion of a series of events that have led in an unmistakable direction. In a few moments, she surrenders to him, and then throws the medallion into the fire, in a gesture of resignation. The curé pulls it out, burning his arm, and she humbly apologizes. The next day, he receives a letter from her. The medallion is in the envelope with the letter. She expresses her gratitude to him in the sincerest terms. "I'm not resigned, I'm <u>happy</u>. I don't want anything." And later: "Don't lets mention it ever again. Never again. How peaceful that sounds! Never." (p. 153)[23]

The above statements and events are not hollow and lifeless, but strikingly suggestive. Their implausibility arises from the fact that their suggestiveness points in a single definite direction, and that they are not effectively challenged by conflicting suggestions. The predominance given to a single definite commitment suggests that the author intends to equate this commitment with the meaning of the novel. At the point in the structure of the novel at which we would expect the evocation of the elusive feeling of 'world' or 'the nature of things' we find the assertion of a definite commitment. The unambiguous suggestion of the resolution of the novel's central conflict is at the center of our attention.

The conversion scene begins to be implausible at the end of the Comtesse's confession of her miserable family situation. The series of shifts that begin at that point, and the directness and rapidity with which her resistance to the curé dissolves, somehow, it seems to me, leave the reader behind. I experience this feeling of being left behind more as a lingering discomfort than as a complete loss of interest: despite the implausibility of the change in the Comtesse, Bernanos includes much to hold the reader's attention. The curé describes his Christian faith in vividly rhetorical terms; their dialogue does get to the heart of some of the central issues in Christianity; and, for me at least, the feeling persists that the characters are confronting genuine religious problems. But throughout this very interesting scene, the hand of the author is evident, prodding the incidents forward to an unambiguous conclusion.

The final part of the novel begins with the Comtesse's sudden death the night of her conversion. Here again, Bernanos introduces the sense of alternative possibilities, only to dismiss them. The events of the conversion become public knowledge because of Chantal's eavesdropping. But of course, she heard imperfectly, and cannot really comprehend what happened. The curé must undergo another terrible trial. He must endure almost universal misunderstanding, including the misunderstanding of his closest friend. Torcy's response, I think, represents the sort of reaction that would have been very close to the implied author's, had Bernanos written a truly dialogical novel. But Bernanos wants to make it very clear that he is not writing that kind of novel. It may at first appear that Bernanos is suggesting a real alternative interpretation with Torcy's criticisms: "You did behave like an ass with the poor dear Comtesse--you were showing off!" (p. 177)[24] Apparently Chantal had claimed the curé left her mother in turmoil. "Is that true?" Torcy asks,

> "No."
> "Well how did you leave her then?"
> "I left her with God--in peace."
> "Ah" (he gave a deep sigh) "But suppose she died confronting your pitiless demands?"
> "She died in peace"
> "How do you know?"

At this point, Torcy asks the question the reader too probably wants to ask. The curé keeps silence. His answer comes in the same authoritative voice exempt from dialogue in which he has recorded his innermost feelings throughout the novel.

> I wasn't even tempted to speak of the letter. If the words didn't sound ridiculous, I would say that now I was silence itself. Silence and Night. "Anyway, she's dead. What are people to think? Scenes like that don't help anyone with a bad heart."
> I held my tongue, and on this we parted. (p. 179)[25]

After this conversation, Bernanos proceeds to further weaken Torcy as a challenge to the curé. Torcy returns, strangely troubled, and yet conciliatory and compassionate. He feels that the curé's problem is alcoholism, and he gently warns him of its dangers. It becomes clear he does not really understand his friend anymore. The curé writes that "As across a wide, invisible road, we seemed to be saying goodbye." (p. 181)[26] The curé asks Torcy to bless him, but Torcy says "You are in trouble, you must bless me." (p. 184)[27] The curé notices that for the first time his friend, as he leaves, is walking bowed. Torcy does not appear again in the novel, apart from a few references in summary. These details, it seems to me, all function to lift the curé's perspective out of the dialogue with Torcy's in which it had begun to be involved.

After his final encounter with Torcy, the curé advances, step by step, out of the doubt and turmoil that has assailed him throughout the novel. His unmistakable forward progress is like that of the Comtesse in the conversion scene. His descriptions of his spiritual state are in themselves striking and rhetorically effective, and he seems to be facing, at least to some extent, authentic religious problems. But the one-sided presentation tends, again, to leave the reader behind.

The conclusion of the novel represents the final confirmation of Bernanos' rhetorical intention. The curé must now face his own death. He finally travels to Lille to see the specialist Dr. Delbende had recommended to him. His first response to the news that he will soon die of cancer is one of the most effective and honest scenes in the novel. Before his visit, a sense of peace and joy had descended upon him, unlike any he had ever known. "What morning can be breaking in me?" he asks. (p. 215)[28] But the moment Dr. Laville, after a long hesitation, breaks the news to him, the curé tells us that "I was no more than a dead man among the living." (p. 234)[29] A very striking detail is at the center of the scene: "May God forgive me!" the curé writes, "I never thought of Him." (p. 235)[30] The curé's final struggle begins with a strikingly realistic and unsentimental encounter with death. But the conclusion of that encounter is somewhat less effective. When he dies, only a day and a half later, he has emerged victorious from the struggle:

> The thought that this conflict is over--there is no more reason for it--had already occurred to me this morning, but I was still dazed by Dr. Laville's revelation. It seeped into me only very slowly, like tiny drops from a stream at first. But now there are rising waters freshening to my spirit, overflowing. Quiet and Peace. (p. 251)[31]

The curé's final victory over doubt and despair is plausible for two reasons--he honestly confronts the doubt and despair, and his victory is expressed in a genuinely eloquent way. But the eloquence does not suffice to make the change within him entirely plausible. The directness and unmistakability of his forward progress, again, it seems to me, leave the reader behind.

The guiding principle of the plot of The Diary of a Country Priest is that conflicting voices are introduced, but that a single voice is then lifted above them. At the conclusion of the novel, only the curé's voice is left. He dies in the house of his friend Dufréty, a fellow seminarian who went back on his vows. Bernanos presents Dufréty as a very pitiful creature indeed. His attempts to justify himself are transparently vain. He is presented almost as a caricature of a lapsed priest. It is Dufréty who reports, in a letter to Torcy, that the curé's last words are "Grace is everywhere [Tout est grâce]." (p. 255/319) Dufréty represents, not a competing voice, but Bernanos' vision of the misery into which humanity is thrown by its attempt to do without God.

Bernanos' presentation of conversion and commitment, in the case of both the Comtesse and the curé, is implausible because it excludes details that might suggest alternative interpretations. Why are such details needed? Why can a conversion not be presented in straightforward, unambiguous terms? While a reader cannot identify with a character's decisions and commitments, he can identify with a character's feelings. On the level of concrete feeling, we somehow know what it means for certain characters to face what they face. Through empathy, we can really make contact with a kind of universality, even though we cannot specify or define that universality, or bring it into the clear foreground of our experience. It is out of this basic level of concrete human experience, with which we can empathize, that decisions and commitments arise. But in facing a character's decision or commitment, we face a different kind of elusiveness--we do not identify with a universal theme we cannot specify, but face a specific response with which we cannot directly identify.

The most telling question that may be raised about Bernanos' conversion scene is, how do we know the Comtesse has changed in the way she and the curé believe she has? The novel's mode of presentation does not seem to acknowledge the fact that we do not know. It fails to evoke the unique kind of elusiveness in our experience of the commitments of others. We face not the appearance of a decision which allows of differing interpretations, but the appearance of a decision that points to a single interpretation. In facing her decision, we face not a choice, but an answer. The presentation of decisions and commitments in <u>Light in August</u> and <u>The Idiot</u> is effective because the authors have evoked the sense of a gap between the appearance of a definite decision and alternative possible realities that account for that appearance. We identify with the experience of the implied author, who faces compelling and conflicting alternatives. But because of the absence of alternatives in The Diary of a Country Priest, we experience not a gap in our empathy, but the simple absence of empathy both for the characters and the implied author.[32]

The motive power of a plot has to do with the fulfillment or frustration of human aims. The fulfillment of such aims may involve the making of decisions; to even have an aim involves a decision; and as the example of The Idiot shows, the central human aim that impels a plot forward may well involve the need to make a decision about religious belief. Light in August begins and ends with a decision--Byron's sudden falling in love with Lena is not merely a matter of passion, but involves a commitment to her welfare and her future; his commitment changes his life; and his decision to return to Lena more or less coincides with the conclusion of the novel.

Plots move forward because human lives move forward. Human lives involve tendencies that drive them into the future and head for definite turning points: desires and wishes are frustrated or fulfilled; decisions have to be made; and at certain points a convergence of coincidences and a character's desire to know reveal a previously hidden reality to that character. But while a movement toward an aim--whether it be toward the fulfillment of a desire, or the making of a commitment, or the gaining of knowledge--may be the motive power of a plot, the climax or conclusion of a really successful plot does not seem to quite coincide with the achievement of that aim.

Faulkner and Dostoyevsky employ all sorts of devices to restrain the reader's temptation to carry the plot forward to a definite and firm conclusion. Consider the conclusion of Light in August. Faulkner does not attempt to portray Byron's inner life as he actually decides to return to

Lena. Rather, Faulkner deliberately pulls away--we simply learn that Byron storms off into the woods when Lena rejects his advances, and suddenly appears again around the bend the next morning, his mind already made up. We do not know exactly why Byron acts as he does, and the significance of the situation is uncertain. Lena says she is still looking for Lucas; she is probably just sightseeing, and may well marry Byron before long. But the conclusion is an effective turning point because it retains a sense of contingency and alternative possibilities. Its very status as a turning point is only a possibility. The novel does not conclude with the assertion that Byron has acted wisely, that his wishes will be fulfilled, that his fortunes will now change, and that he will be a different kind of man from now on. Rather, the aesthetic conclusion of the novel evokes a vivid feeling that all of these things <u>may</u> be true. This feeling of possibility is inseparable from the suggestion that the turning point may not be quite the turning point it seems to be.

A tragic plot, such as that of <u>The Idiot</u>, functions similarly. Myshkin's struggle to change Nastasya's and Rogozhin's inner convictions is an essential part of what moves the plot forward. Yet the climax of the plot--the scene in which Rogozhin and Myshkin both lose their minds at the dead Nastasya's bedside--cannot be simply identified with Myshkin's defeat. The inner tendency of the plot moves toward his defeat, and yet it never quite arrives at the assertion that 'Myshkin is defeated.' The point of climax does not coincide with any definite rejection of Myshkin by Rogozhin: Myshkin has apparently failed, but Rogozhin is still strangely attracted to him. Dostoyevsky allows all sorts of alternative possibilities to remain open: the possibility that Myshkin will continue to have a positive effect on others despite his failure, and the possibility that his desperate longing is really meaningful despite the role it seems to have played in destroying his sanity.

Whether they belong to a character or the implied author, decisions and commitments may be aspects of a dramatic climax or conclusion, but only as possibilities. Both characterization and plot dynamics contain tendencies to go beyond feeling and arrive at definite decisions, but an actual decision cannot be a part of the aesthetic experience. An effective plot somehow stops just short of the definite conclusion it seems to aim at. The plot may come tantalizingly close to a definite conclusion, but it then somehow turns back on itself. Conclusions and climaxes seem not so much to resolve problems as to recall the background of character and incident that has lead to a turning point, bringing together all of the central issues and conflicts in the work.

The Diary of a Country Priest has a structure that is generally comparable to that of Light in August and The Idiot. Bernanos' novel betrays an essential difference, not so much in plot structure, as in plot function. The structure of the conversion scene, and its place in the novel as a whole, suggest that the novel's theme is the validity of a definite conviction. The decision that the incidents seem to tend toward lies not just beyond the climax, but is identified with the climax. The conversion is implausible not so much because it is a conversion, as because of the role it is given in the plot. Bernanos wants his aesthetic climax to also be a rhetorical conclusion. In Light in August and The Idiot, possible convictions and decisions are elements included in the panoramic feeling of the world that the climactic scenes evoke. But in The Diary of a Country Priest, it seems as if Bernanos wants to present a definite conviction as the supreme factor that includes and subordinates every alternative conviction as well as feeling.

The novel The Diary of a Country Priest has a clearly defined dramatic structure. In the first half of the novel, we gain a sense of the curé's basic motives, and of the dynamics of the situations he confronts: the village's resistance, the church's complacency, his closest friend's qualified approval, and the dramatic situation of the Comtesse's family. The central conversion scene presents itself as the fulfillment of the curé's basic aims, as the resolution of the central problem of the Comtesse's inner life, and as the beginning of the resolution of the basic problem in the curé's own life. The scene is clearly meant to function as the dramatic climax of the entire novel. The second half of the novel deals with the way the curé must endure the judgments of the world upon the action of conversion it does not comprehend, and with the curé's steady progress toward spiritual salvation in spite of the new challenge those judgments represent. The same viewpoints he confronted in the first part are brought to bear upon him again in response to the conversion. As a result, he undergoes another intensely painful spiritual struggle. But he emerges victorious and dies in peace.

Though the conversion scene is clearly meant to be the novel's climax, it seems to me that the feeling of catharsis that a climax should evoke is missing. The moment of conversion does not aesthetically unite and sum up the novel in the way that its position in the novel's structure would lead us to expect. The climax points in Light in August and The Idiot evoke a powerful sense of a mysterious background through our empathy with the implied author's overall perspective. I think that what is lacking in our experience of the climax of The Diary of a Country Priest is precisely empathy with the implied author. We are led to a climax--but we then find we have little more than a few direct statements on our hands. At the point we expect should unite the whole novel, evocation is simply missing. A climax evokes a certain kind of realization: not the realization of the truth of a commitment, but the realization involved in our implicit and elusive sense of 'world' or 'the nature of things.' I think that the lack of evocation at the climax point of <u>The Diary of a Country Priest</u> can be explained by Bernanos' attempt to replace the aesthetic realization proper to the novel form he employs, with the realization of the truth of a commitment. Through empathy we can only experience a particular commitment as one possible response to our experience of the nature of things. But Bernanos wants to present a particular commitment as the one to be preferred above all others. Through empathy we can experience commitments as possibilities contained within feeling--but Bernanos wants to present a certain commitment as the final context that encompasses both feeling and alternative commitments.

NOTES TO CHAPTER NINE

[1]The quotations from The Diary of a Country Priest are from the Morris translation, although I have made a number of changes, mostly in the direction of greater literalness. Page references to the translation are hereafter given in the text, and the original quotations are given in the notes. Georges Bernanos, The Diary of a Country Priest, tr. Pamela Morris (New York: Macmillan, 1962); Journal d'un curé de campagne (Paris: Plon, 1936), p. 18. "Et lui, le village, il semblait attendre aussi--sans grand espoir--après tant d'autres nuits passées dans la boue, un maître à suivre vers quelque improbable, quelque inimaginable asile.
Oh! je sais bien que ce sont des idées folles, que je ne puis même pas prendre tout à fait au sérieux, des rêves... Les villages ne se lèvent pas à la voix d'un petit écolier, comme des bêtes. N'importe! Hier soir, je crois qu'un saint l'eût appelé." (p. 6)

[2]Georges Poulet, in "Le Temps d'un èclair," La Nouvelle Revue française, 12, no. 139 (July, 1964), 45-63; and 13, no. 140 (August, 1964), 250-66, analyzes the patterns of experience evident in The Diary of a Country Priest, emphasizing Bernanos' experience of the nature of evil. Bernanos suggests the inner reality of evil again and again through the image of a certain kind of mud: "Ce n'est donc pas inexactement que Bernanos emploie pour représenter l'inactivité finale des êtres pris dans le mal, l'image de la pâte, ou, plus souvent encore, celle de la boue. C'est que gelées, pâtes, boue, sont des fluides épais. Ils s'affaissent plutôt qu'ils coulent. Arrivés à l'extremité de leur pente, ils s'étalent, constituant une sorte de lac" (July, p. 51). This image is suggested in the curé's vision near the novel's beginning quoted above, and recurs in his conversation with Chantal, in which he describes sinners as ultimately forming a "lac de boue toujours gluant"--his image of hell (p. 122 [trans.]/152). Poulet has described the way Bernanos effectively uses poetic symbols to evoke the experience of the curé. But Poulet neglects the rhetorical context into which these symbols are placed. Such symbols do not 'evoke the supernatural.' Rather, they evoke a feeling which Bernanos then in effect asserts has something to do with the supernatural reality of hell.

[3]"'Son tort, ça n'a pas été de combattre la saleté, bien sûr, mais d'avoir voulu l'anéantir, comme si c'était possible. Une paroisse, c'est sale, forcément.'" (p. 15)

[4]"'La dernière des imprudences est la prudence, lorsqu'elle nous prépare tout doucement à nous passer de Dieu.'" (pp. 103-104)

[5]"'Après vingt siècles de christianisme, tonnere de Dieu, il ne devrait plus y avoir de honte à être pauvre. [...] Mais pourquoi diable prodiguent-ils de tels hommages aux Puissants de la Terre, qui s'en régalent?'" (pp. 93-94)

[6]"'Celle qui tient debout. Et pourquoi tient-elle debout? Personne ne le sait, au juste. Vous allez me dire: la grâce de Dieu? Seulement, moi, mon ami, je ne crois pas en Dieu.'" (p. 90)

[7]"'[J]e me demande si nous ne sommes pas simplement des orgueilleux.'"

(p. 90)

⁸"'On vous plaint mais on vous répète: Filez!'" (p. 115)

⁹"Derrière moi, ce n'était plus la vie quotidienne, familière, à laquelle on vient d'échapper d'un élan, tout en gardant au fond de soi-même la certitude d'y rentrer dès qu'on le voudra. Derrière moi il n'y avait rien. Et devant moi un mur, un mur noir." (pp. 115-16)

¹⁰"'Il y a une communion des saints, il y a aussi une communion des pécheurs. Dans la haine que les pécheurs se portent les uns aux autres, dans le mépris, ils s'unissent, ils s'embrassent, ils s'agrègent, ils se confondent, ils ne seront plus un jour, aux yeux de l'Eternel, que ce lac de boue toujours gluant sur quoi passe et repasse vainement l'immense marée de l'amour divin, la mer de flammes vivantes et rugissantes qui a fécondé le chaos.'" (pp. 152-53)

¹¹"'Je viens vous parler de mademoiselle votre fille.'" (p. 162)

¹²"'Faut-il faire plus de cas de l'orgueil de ma fille que du mien? Ce que j'ai enduré, ne peut-elle donc l'endurer à son tour?'" (p. 172)

¹³"La patience m'échappait.--'Dieu vous brisera!' m'écriai-je. Elle a poussé une sorte de gémissement, oh! non pas un gémissement de vaincu qui demande grâce, c'était plutôt le soupir, le profond soupir d'un être qui recueille ses forces avant de porter un défi.--'Me briser? Il m'a déjà brisée. Que peut-il désormais contre moi? Il m'a pris mon fils. Je ne le crains plus.'" (p. 177)

¹⁴"Elle m'observait avec une attention extraordinaire." (p. 179)

¹⁵"Elle ne me quittait pas des yeux [. . .] Elle a posé ses deux mains sur mon bras, sa figure touchait presque la mienne." (pp. 179-80)

¹⁶"--'Daignerez-vous me dire quelle est cette faute cachée, fit-elle après un long silence, le ver dans le fruit?...'--'Il faut vous résigner à... à la volonté de Dieu, ouvrir votre coeur.' Je n'osais pas lui parler plus clairement du petit mort, et le mot de résignation a paru la surprendre.--'Me resigner? à quoi?...' Puis elle a compris tout à coup." (p. 181)

¹⁷"Elle s'est redressée comme une vipère.--'Dieu m'était devenu indifferent. Lorsque vous m'aurez forcé à convenir que je le hais, en serez-vous plus avancé, imbecile?'--'Vous ne le haïssez plus, lui dis-je. La haine est indifférence et mépris. Et maintenant, vous voilà enfin face à face, Lui et vous.'" (p. 182)

¹⁸"J'avais voulu réchauffer d'un coup ce coeur glacé, porter la lumière au dernier recès d'une conscience que la pitié de Dieu voulait peut-être laisser encore dans de miséricordes ténèbres." (p. 183)

¹⁹"C'est alors--non! cela ne peut s'exprimer--tandis que je luttais de toutes mes forces contre le doute, la peur, que l'esprit de prière rentra en moi." (p. 183)

20"'Vous me jurez...' a-t-elle commencé. Mais elle a vu tout de suite dans mon regard que j'avais compris, que je ne jurerais rien." (p. 184)

21"Il me semblait qu'une main mystérieuse venait d'ouvrir une brèche dans on ne sait quelle muraille invisible, et la paix rentrait de toutes parts, prenait majestueusement son niveau, une paix inconnue de la terre, la douce paix des morts, ainsi qu'une eau profonde." (p. 185)

22"'Cela me paraît clair, fit-elle d'une voix prodigieusement alterée, mais calme. Savez-vous ce que je me demandais tout à l'heure?' [. . .] 'Satisfais toi! écrase-nous!'" (p. 185)

23"'Je ne suis pas résignée, je suis heureuse. Je ne désire rien. [. . .] Et puis, nous n'en parlerons plus, n'est ce pas? plus jamais! Ce mot est doux. Jamais.'" (pp. 189-90)

24"'Mais c'est vrai que tu n'as fait que des bêtises avec la pauvre comtesse, c'est du théâtre!'" (p. 220)

25"'Est-ce vrai?'--'Non!'--'Tu l'as laissée...'--'Je l'ai laissé avec Dieu, en paix.'--'Ah! (Il a poussé un profond soupir.) Songe qu'elle a pu garder en mourant le souvenir de tes exigences, de ta dureté'...'Elle est morte en paix.'--'Qu'en sais-tu?' Je n'ai même pas été tenté de parler de la lettre. Si l'expression ne devait paraître ridicule, je dirais que de la tête aux pieds, je n'étais plus que silence. Silence et nuit.--'Bref, elle est morte. Qu'est-ce que tu veux qu'on pense! Des scènes pareilles ne valent rien pour une cardiaque.' Je me suis tu. Nous nous sommes quittés sur ces mots." (pp. 221-22)

26"Nous avions l'air de nous dire adieu de loin, d'un bord à l'autre d'une route invisible." (p. 225)

27"'Tu es dans la peine, m'a-t-il répondu. C'est a toi de me bénir.'" (p. 229)

28"Quel jour va se lever en moi?" (p. 268)

29"[J]e n'étais déjà plus qu'un mort parmi les vivants." (p. 291)

30"Que Dieu me pardonne! Je ne songeais pas à Lui." (p. 292)

31"La pensée que cette lutte va finir, n'ayant plus d'objet, m'etait déjà venue ce matin, mais j'étais alors au plein de la stupeur où m'avait mis la révélation de M. le docteur Laville. Elle n'est entrée en moi que peu à peu. C'etait un mince filet d'eau limpide, et maintenant cela déborde de l'âme, me remplit de fraîcheur. Silence et paix." (pp. 312-13)

32Poulet recognizes that changes in Bernanos' characters are often abrupt and seemingly unmotivated. He makes this observation about Dostoyevsky also. According to Poulet, "Tel qu'il nous apparaît chez Bernanos, l'acte libre n'est motivé par aucun antédédent psychologique. . . . Au contraire il est l'acte même par lequel le moment se désolidarise d'avec le temps, pour affirmer son autonomie. Car si, pour le romancier traditionel, le devoir est de rendre aussi distinct que possible le lien causal qui unit tous les moments de la durée, le devoir pour Bernanos (et pour Dostoievsky aussi sans doute) est exactement inverse: c'est celui de rompre le lien entre les instants, afin de faire apparaître le pouvoir qu'a l'être de se fonder a nouveau en chaque instant" (August, p. 251). In Bernanos, these interruptions in time are supposed to represent incursions of the supernatural. I argue that Bernanos' representation of such gaps is not effective because he attempts to fill them in with a one-sided interpretation. The gaps we face in Bernanos are not merely gaps in temporality, it seems to me, but also gaps in empathy--gaps in the reader's experience of the character. Dostoyevsky's presentation, for example, of Nastasya's sudden decisions, is strikingly different from Bernanos' presentation of the Comtesse's sudden conversion--though both seem to be in a way unmotivated. We never know exactly what attitude Nastasya has toward Myshkin, or whether he really represents some sort of possible salvation for her. But it may be that Poulet recognizes the aesthetic problem Bernanos faces in trying to portray the intervention of divine grace: "Succession sans répétition, le roman de la sainteté ne peut-être qu'un roman explosé, pulverisé" (August, p. 266).

CONCLUSION

The conclusions I have drawn about the inherent weakness of the committed novel are based on certain assumptions about the nature of human consciousness. The aim of the novel form, I have argued, is to communicate the experience of the truth of a perception. Such communication is possible because a perception of an imagined world can be verified through empathy alone. Through a successful novel, such as <u>Light</u> <u>in</u> <u>August</u> or <u>The</u> <u>Idiot</u>, the author does not directly confront the reader with judgments and commitments. The experience the novel communicates arises from the structure of plot and character itself, that is to say, arises out of the concrete experience of an imagined world. The author does not separate himself from this structure in order to confront the reader directly. Rather, the actual situation of author confronting reader is suspended.

In <u>Embezzled</u> <u>Heaven</u> and <u>The</u> <u>Diary</u> <u>of</u> <u>a</u> <u>Country</u> <u>Priest</u>, it is likewise true that the author does not explicitly separate himself from the fictional structure. The novels are written as if their entire meaning were to appear through our experience of the imagined world itself. The narrator is unmistakably a character in both novels, however closely he may reflect the author's viewpoint in each. In neither novel does the author blatantly and explicitly step in to tell us what to think of the events the narrator presents.

Bernanos communicates his rhetorical intention not so much through explicit authorial intrusion as through the fictional context in which he places his characters' beliefs. By failing to include ironic perspectives on his favored characters, by failing to challenge their beliefs with convincing alternatives, and by placing an unambiguous conversion at the climax of the novel, Bernanos implicitly intrudes his own actual position taking into the reader's experience of the imagined world. This intrusion weakens, but does not completely destroy, the unity and plausibility of that world. The intrusion is evident through the distortion of perception arising from the author's neglect of ironic perspectives. By trying to make the world appear as he thinks it should appear from the perspective of his commitment, Bernanos in fact prevents the world from appearing through his novel in its true depth and ambiguity.

The aim of the novel form is to communicate the truth of a perception of an imagined world. By trying to do more than this with their novels, Bernanos and Werfel in a way accomplish less. But the novel is not the only literary, or even narrative, form that there is. Other forms may not depend exclusively upon evocation of feeling in the way that the novel does.

There are two kinds of expressive language--evocative and rhetorical. Rhetorical language employs the evocation of feeling, but its guiding aim is the expression of commitment. A successful rhetorical statement does not invite the reader to relive an experience, but directly confronts the reader with a judgment. The meaning of a sermon, for example, is a commitment, but an effective and honest sermon does not intend for that meaning to be verified simply through the process of listening or reading, the way the truth of an artwork is verified through listening or reading. The listener can verify the truth of the commitments avowed in a sermon only through his own action, decision, living, believing. The meaning of a sermon is not the truth of a commitment in the way the meaning of a novel is the truth of a perception.

An important objection to the viewpoint I have developed is that there are many highly successful literary works whose meaning does seem to be a definite religious commitment. Works such as the narrative books of the Old Testament, the Gospels, the <u>Divine Comedy</u>, <u>Pilgrim's Progress</u>, and <u>Rasselas</u> come to mind. At this point, I can do no more than sketch a possible answer to this objection, and in doing so, suggest in a general way how the concepts I have developed may be applied to narrative genres different from the novel.

I would propose that a literary work need not be either purely evocative or purely rhetorical. Works such as <u>The Diary of a Country Priest</u> fail not because they have a rhetorical aim, but because they attempt to force an evocative structure to function rhetorically. But if a work employs both evocative and rhetorical elements, and respects the integrity of each, it is possible for that work to succeed. In such a work, the author directly confronts the reader, but places himself alongside the imagined world he evokes, rather than trying to appear through the imagined world itself. He allows the imagined world to show forth its own mystery and ambiguity, and does not conceal the tension between that ambiguity and the commitments he espouses. Essentially rhetorical works, such as sacred texts which happen to be narratives, do involve a kind of authorial intrusion. But that intrusion is of an essentially different kind from that in <u>Embezzled Heaven</u> or <u>The Diary of a Country Priest</u>. The aesthetically debilitating effects of intrusion arise when direct judgments, either explicit or implied, take the place of evocation. Modern religious novels of the kind I have examined are weak because they fail to respect the tension that always exists between feeling and commitment.

WORKS CITED

Bakhtin, Mikhail. *Problems of Dostoyevsky's Poetics*. Tr. R. W. Rotsel. Ann Arbor, Mich.: Ardis, 1961.

Battenhouse, Roy. "The Relation of Theology to Literature." In *Religion and Modern Literature: Essays in Theory and Criticism*. Ed. G. B. Tennyson and Edward E. Ericson, Jr. Grand Rapids, Mich.: Eerdmans, 1975.

Benson, Carl. "Thematic Design in *Light in August*." *William Faulkner: Four Decades of Criticism*. Ed. Linda Wagner. East Lansing: Michigan State Univ. Press, 1973.

Berdyaev, Nicholas. *Dostoyevsky*. Tr. Donald Attwater. London: Sheed, 1934.

Bernanos, Georges. *Journal d'un curé de campagne*. Paris: Plon, 1936; *The Diary of a Country Priest*. Tr. Pamela Morris. New York: Macmillan, 1962.

Booth, Wayne. *The Rhetoric of Fiction*. Chicago: Univ. of Chicago Press, 1961.

Bowling, Lawrence E. "William Faulkner: The Importance of Love." In *William Faulkner: Four Decades of Criticism*. Ed. Linda Wagner. East Lansing: Michigan State Univ. Press, 1973, pp. 109-17.

Brooks, Cleanth. "Implications of an Organic Theory of Poetry." In *Literature and Belief*. Ed. M. H. Abrahms. New York: Columbia Univ. Press, 1958, pp. 53-79.

--------. *The Well Wrought Urn*. Cornwall, New York: Cornwall Press, 1947.

Burkhard, Willy. *La genèse de l'idée du mal dans l'oeuvre romanesque de Georges Bernanos*. Zurich: Juris Druck, 1967.

Bush, William. "Bernanos: Un 'Dostoievsky Francais'?" *Mosaic*, 5, no. 3 (Spring 1972), pp. 145-50.

Conrad, Joseph. "Preface to *The Nigger of the Narcissus*." In *Discussions of the Novel*. Ed. Roger Sale. Boston: Heath, 1960, pp. 91-93.

Dalton, Elizabeth. *Unconscious Structure in The Idiot*. Princeton: Princeton Univ. Press, 1979.

Derrida, Jacques. *Of Grammatology*. Tr. Gayatri Chakravorty Spivak. Baltimore: Johns Hopkins Univ. Press, 1977.

Dostoyevsky, Fyodor. *The Idiot*. Tr. Constance Garnett. New York: Random House, 1935.

--------. *The Notebooks for The Idiot*. Ed. Edward Wasiolek. Chicago:

Univ. of Chicago Press, 1967.

Eliot, T. S. "Hamlet and his Problems." In *Critical Theory Since Plato*. Ed. Hazard Adams. New York: Harcourt, 1971, pp. 788-90.

Faulkner, William. *Light in August*. New York: Random House, 1959.

Forster, E. M. *Aspects of the Novel*. New York: Harcourt, 1954.

Frye, Northrop. *Anatomy of Criticism: Four Essays*. Princeton: Princeton Univ. Press, 1957.

Goethe, Johann Wolfgang. *Werke*. Vol 3. Ed. Erich Trunz. Hamburg: Wegner, 1959.

Heidegger, Martin. *Sein und Zeit*. Tübingen: Niemeyer, 1963; *Being and Time*. Tr. John Macquarrie and Edward Robinson. New York: Harper, 1966.

--------. "Der Ursprung des Kunstwerkes." In *Holzwege*. Frankfurt: Klostermann, 1950; "The Origin of the Work of Art." Tr. Albert Hofstadter. In *Poetry, Language, Thought*. New York: Harper, 1971.

Husserl, Edmund. *Cartesian Meditations: An Introduction to Phenomenology*. Tr. Dorion Cairns. The Hague: Nijhoff, 1973.

Hirsch, E. D. *Validity in Interpretation*. New Haven: Yale Univ. Press, 1967.

Iser, Wolfgang. *The Act of Reading*. Baltimore: Johns Hopkins Univ. Press, 1974.

James, William. *The Principles of Psychology*. New York: Dover, 1950.

--------. *The Varieties of Religious Experience*. New York: Random House, 1929.

Kierkegaard, Søren. *Fear and Trembling*. Tr. Walter Lowrie. Princeton: Princeton Univ. Press, 1968.

Krieger, Murray. "Dostoyevsky's 'Idiot': The Curse of Saintliness." In *Dostoyevsky: A Collection of Critical Essays*. Ed. Rene Wellek. Englewood Cliffs, N.J.: Prentice-Hall, 1962.

Lesser, Simon O. "Saint and Sinner: Dostoyevsky's *The Idiot*." *Modern Fiction Studies*, 4 (Autumn 1958), pp. 221-24.

Linnér, Sven. *Starets Zosima in The Brothers Karamazov: A Study in the Mimesis of Virtue*. Stockholm: Almqvist, 1975.

Lipps, Theodor. *Ästhetik: Psychologie des Schönen und der Kunst*. Hamburg: Voss, 1906.

Magliola, Robert. "The Phenomenological Approach to Literature." *Language and Style*, 5 (Spring 1972), pp. 79-99.

May, William. "Code and Covenant or Philanthropy and Contract?" In Ethics in Medicine: Historical Perspectives and Contemporary Concerns. Ed. Reiser, Dyck, and Curran. Cambridge, Mass.: MIT Press, 1977.

Miller, Robin Feuer. Dostoyevsky and The Idiot: Author, Narrator, and Reader. Cambridge, Mass.: Harvard Univ. Press, 1981.

Niebuhr, H. Richard. Radical Monotheism and Western Culture. New York: Harper, 1970.

--------. The Responsible Self. San Francisco: Harper, 1978.

Onasch, Konrad. Dostojewski als Verführer: Christentum und Kunst in der Dichtung Dostojewskis. Zürich: EVZ-Verlag, 1961.

Pachmuss, Temira. "Dostoevskij und Franz Werfel." German Quarterly, 36, no. 4 (November 1963), 445-58.

Panichas, George A. The Burden of Vision: Dostoyevsky's Spiritual Art. Grand Rapids, Mich.: Eerdmans, 1977.

Pitavy, Francois. Faulkner's Light in August. Tr. Gillian E. Cook. Bloomington: Indiana Univ. Press, 1973.

Poulet, Georges. "Phenomenology of Reading." In Critical Theory Since Plato. Ed. Hazard Adams. New York: Harcourt, 1971, pp. 1212-22.

--------. "Le temps d'un eclair." La nouvelle revue francaise, 12, no. 139 (July 1964, 45-63); and 13, no. 140 (August, 1964, 250-66).

Ricoeur, Paul. "Metaphor and the Main Problem of Hermeneutics." In The Philosophy of Paul Ricoeur: An Anthology of his Work. Ed. Charles Reagan and David Stewart. Boston: Beacon, 1978, pp. 134-48.

Scott, Nathan, Jr. "The Collaboration of Vision in the Poetic Act: The Religious Dimension." In Literature and Belief. Ed. M. H. Abrahms. New York: Columbia Univ. Press, 1958.

Shestov, Lev. "Dostoyevsky and Nietzsche, the Philosophy of Tragedy." In Dostoyevksy, Tolstoy, and Nietzsche. Ed. Bernard Martin. Athens: Ohio Univ. Press, 1969.

Slabey, Robert. "Myth and Ritual in Light in August." In Studies in Light in August. Ed. M. Thomas Inge. Columbus, Ohio: Merrill, 1971, pp. 75-97.

Slatoff, Walter. Quest for Failure: A Study of William Faulkner. Ithaca, N.Y.: Cornell Univ. Press, 1960.

TeSelle, Sallie McFague. Literature and the Christian Life. New Haven: Yale Univ. Press, 1966.

Tillich, Paul. *Theology of Culture*. Ed. Robert C. Kimball. New York: Oxford Univ. Press, 1959.

Turnan, Marysia. "Dostojewskij und Franz Werfel: Von östlichen zum westlichen Denken". *Sprache und Dichtung*, 73. Bern: Haupt, 1950.

Ushenko, Andrew Paul. *Dynamics of Art*. Bloomington: Indiana Univ. Press, 1953.

Vickery, Olga. *The Novels of William Faulkner*. Baton Rouge: Louisiana State Univ. Press, 1964.

Werfel, Franz. *Der veruntreute Himmel*. Stockholm: Bermann-Fischer, 1939; *Embezzled Heaven*. Tr. Moray Firth. New York: Viking, 1940.

Wheelwright, Philip. *The Burning Fountain*. Rev. ed. Bloomington: Indiana Univ. Press, 1968.

Whitehead, Alfred North. *Adventures of Ideas*. New York: Macmillan, 1967.

---------. *Modes of Thought*. New York: Macmillan, 1958.

Wimsatt, W. K., and Monroe Beardsley. "The Intentional Fallacy." In *Critical Theory Since Plato*. Ed. Hazard Adams. New York: Harcourt, 1971, pp. 1015-21.

Wimsatt, W. K. "The Structure of the Concrete Universal in Literature." In *The Verbal Icon*. London: Methuen, 1970.

For Product Safety Concerns and Information please contact our EU
representative GPSR@taylorandfrancis.com
Taylor & Francis Verlag GmbH, Kaufingerstraße 24, 80331 München, Germany